STUDIES IN MUGHAL HISTORY

STUDIES IN MUGHAL HISTORY

ASHVINI AGRAWAL

MOTILAL BANARSIDASS
Delhi ☐ Varanasi ☐ Patna

First Published in 1983

Head Office : Bungalow Road, Delhi-110 007
Branches : 1. Chowk, Varanasi-1 (U.P.)
2. Ashok Rajpath, Patna-4 (Bihar)

Printed in India
By Shantilal Jain, at Shri Jainendra Press,
A-45, Phase-I, Naraina, New Delhi-110 028.
Published by Narendra Prakash Jain, for Motilal Banarsidass,
Delhi-110 007.

CONTENTS

PREFACE

The Mughals who ruled over India for two and a half centuries, have been accepted at all hands, as the most significant rulers of the Medieval times. Descendants of two great soldiers of Central Asia—Taimur and Chingiz Khan, the Mughals have become a legend in themselves, in history. The expansion of their power after the first battle of Panipat ushered in a new era, not only in political arena but also in the fields of enlightenment and scholarship. Their zeal for war and conquest has not overshadowed the aesthetic side of their life. It resulted in the blending of two alien cultures—Hindu and Muslim, and in the emergence of what is known as the Mughal Culture. The long span of Mughal period in the annals of Indian history, inspired a host of writers, contemporary and posterior, native and foreign, court historians and independent biographers to pen down one or the other aspect of the story of the Mughals. As a result we have today, innumerable works on the Mughals. A cursory glance at them almost convinces a person that there is not a straw left unturned and not an iota to be added to the existing literature on the subject. But a deep study shows that there is always a scope for a fresh interpretation of the existing material and to view it from an entirely different angle. The present work is the result of such a point of view.

The present monograph—'Studies in the Mughal History', mainly deals with the relations of the great Mughals with the contemporary powers in India and outside the country, with the exception of a chapter on the Genesis of Din-i-Ilahi. The book is divided into seven chapters with an elaborate introduction on the general history of the period. The Introduction is divided into two parts. It has been tried to acquaint the readers with a sketchy account of the Mughal history from the establishment of the Mughal rule to the time of Maratha supremacy, before plunging into deep discussions.

In the first chapter entitled 'The Nature of the Mughal Conquest', the factors which were responsible for the establishment, expansion and ultimate downfall of the Mughal empire in India have been analysed in detail. It has been shown that Babar shared the glory with Akbar of establishing a powerful empire in India. Babar applied his strength to set his foot firmly in the country while it was the genius of Akbar, who strengthened the roots of the empire with his able statesmanship, utilising the energies of both the Rajputs and the Afghans. Similarly the responsibility for the downfall of the empire was equally shared by Shahjahan and Aurangzeb who squandered the wealth of the country on their wasteful policies and alienated the people with their religious bigotry. It has been shown that the lack of political sagacity amongst the later Mughals resulted in their failure and brought about their ultimate dowenfall.

The next two chapters have been denoted to the relations of the Mughals with the two important and powerful ruling classes of India of that period—the Afghans and the Rajputs respectively. In the second chapter dealing with the Mughal-Afghan relations, the position of the latter has been discussed in details. It has been shown that in the three phases of their relationship, the first (1526-1540) was characterized by the Mughal dominance, in which the Mughals established their power in Hindustan after striking a severe blow on the crumbling Afghan power. But Humayun's lack of the genius for leadership as also his generosity to a fault soon led to his expulsion from India by Shershah and the eclipse of Mughal power from 1540 to 1556. This marks the second phase of the Mughal-Afghan relationship. The qualities of Shershah, as a statesman and military leader have also been assessed in detail. In the third phase from 1556 to 1630 the Afghans were consigned to oblivion as a ruling power. However, the Afghans of Kararani clan continued to shoot trouble for the Mughals in Bengal. Their account has been duly taken care of. The narrative ends with an account of the rebellion of Khan Jahan Lodi and its ultimate suppression by Shahjahan in 1630. An endeavour has been made to give reference of almost all the Afghan nobles of any note.

The Rajputs played a very important role in the drama of Mughal-India and any study of the political history of the

Mughals remains incomplete without a discussion of Mughal-Rajput relationship. The third chapter is devoted to this topic. It covers all the ruling houses of Rajputana, who were of any note. The history of all the Rajput ruling families which had relations with the Mughals has been traced in minute detail. It has been shown that the Mughal dominance over these heroes of the sandy deserts of India was due to the fact that the Mughals knew how to respect their susceptibilities, and also because they had become exhausted by centuries of warfare and internal discord and the Mughals were mighty soldiers.

The Genesis of the Din-i-Ilahi, the new religion started by Akbar has been dealt with in the fourth chapter, making a shift from the main theme of the book. It has been noted that the ancestors of Akbar from the time of Taimur and Chingiz Khan had been great patrons of learning, art and sciences and this had softened the edge of orthodoxy in the house. The liberal and sublime creed of the Sufis also had a great impact on the religious leanings of the Mughals, specially Akbar, and this ultimately led to the birth of Din-i-Ilahi in 1582. The formulation of Akbar's religious policy has been given the due attention and discussed in details.

Chapter five deals with the Mughal policy towards the powers in the Deccan. It has been divided into two parts: The first dealing with the Mughal conquest of the Muslim kingdoms of the Deccan and the second with that of the Marathas under Shivaji and his successors. A detailed account of the Mughal policy towards Deccan from the time of Akbar to that of Aurangzeb has been presented together with a critical analysis of the causes and consequences of their policy. The readers have been provided with ample material to obtain a complete insight of the roots of Mughal behaviour in Deccan. In this context, the opportunity to introduce the history of the Marathas, who proved to be a great factor in the ultimate downfall of the Mughals, has been utilized.

The frontiers of the Mughals in the north-west always remained a problem for them. Every change in the transfrontier provinces, which had once been their homeland forced the Mughals to pay a serious attention in this direction. As has been said in the book itself, "the love of motherland, the Pride of possessing ancestral dominions, and the military needs of the empire had combined to make the frontier problem extremely consequential for the Mughals." All these points have been discussed in the sixth chapter entitled 'The Frontier Problem of the Mughals.'

The last chapter deals with the foundation of Maratha power in India and the decline of the Mughal empire after the death of Aurangzeb. The first quarter of the 18th century saw the establishment of the Maratha power in India, but even they could not remain united after the death of their great leader and the country broke up into numerous fiefs under different Sardars. But it was the Maratha leaders who very soon established their supremacy over the greater part of India and the Mughals lost their prestige and got entangled in the court intrigues. The foreign invasions proved to be the last straw in this mishap.

An earnest effort has been made to draw a clear picture of the Mughal period in the field of politics and diplomacy. A brief bibliography at the end and an Index shall provide a ready reference to the readers. We are fully aware of the fact that the footnotes have not been arranged in scientific manner and some printing mistakes have crept in. Though we have added an errata at the end, but still we crave the indulgence of generous readers for any shortcomings in this book.

INTRODUCTION

I

RISE OF THE MUGHAL EMPIRE

Babar's invasion of Northern India was the end of a series of invasions continuing off and on for the past three centuries. Under their invincible leader Chingiz Khan the Mongols had swept through the regions along the Indian frontiers destroying kings and massacring their peoples but had spared India. After Chingiz Khan the Mongols who had settled down in these regions and inter-married with the Turks continued to harass the Delhi Sultans ever since the days of Alauddin Khilji. In 1398 under Taimur they had invaded India and shattered the Delhi Sultanate.

BABAR

Babar was the lineal descendant of both Chingiz Khan and Amir Taimur—of Chingiz Khan on the mother's side and of Taimur on the father's side. After the death of his father Umar Shaikh Mirza he succeeded to the small Central Asian principality of Farghana near Samarkand, at the young age of twelve. Since then he had had a tempestuous career of war and conquest, of great triumphs and crushing defeats, of royal splendour and terrible sufferings. He thus grew up steeled by his experiences of war, and wise by the reverses of fortune. He was very brave and therefore he was called Babar or Tiger though his real name was Zahiruddin Muhammad. He became king of Farghana at the age of twelve, after the death of his father and at the age of sixteen he became the king of Samarkand in addition to Farghana. When he conquered Samarkand he was very happy; for it was at Samarkand that his great ancestor Taimur ruled. But he lost it, and after much difficulty conquered Kabul in 1504. He ruled over Kabul for twenty years and was planning to invade India when Daulat Khan, the Governor of the Punjab invited him against Ibrahim Lodi. After a few preliminary attacks, in 1525 he conquered the Punjab and returned early next year at the head of an army of 12,000 picked cavalry supported by an artillery. Ibrahim Lodi encountered him on the field of Panipat on the 26th April 1526. He was defeated and killed, inspite of his huge army eight times as big as Babar's. This splendid victory was due to Babar's scientific combination of the artillery and cavalry with superior military tactics and weapons. Delhi and Agra were immediately occupied and with this was laid the foundation of the empire of the Mughals who had a glorious rule of more than a century and a half to their credit.

After the victory at Panipat the task of founding an empire had only begun for Babar. Except Delhi and Agra no part of Ibrahim's dominions had submitted. The Afghans were still hostile and strong in the eastern provinces. Rana Sanga or Sangram Singh the mighty leader of the Rajputs did no like Babar to stay to be an obstacle to his ascendancy in Northern India. Apart from the attitude of the Afghans and Rajputs, Babar's own chiefs and soldiers were eager to return from the hot and parched plains of Northern India to their cool mountain-homes beyond the frontier. Babar however, succeeded in persuading them to stay on by appealing to their cupidity, and led them against the Afghans who were gathering strength around Jaunpur. Hardly had the Afghans been defeated and dispersed when came the alarming news that Rana Sanga was coming towards Agra with a vast army. That was the supreme trial for Babar, and he exerted his utmost to inspire his tired and dispirited soldiers to face the trial for the sake of their honour and religion. The two armies came face to face at a place called Sikri, a few miles from Agra. The Rajput army nearly 80,000 strong was led by a man who was as brave a warrior as Babar himself. But Babar's army nearly ten thousand strong was better disciplined, composed mainly of the cavalry and equipped with a powerful park of mobile artillery. In the battle that was joined on the 16th March 1527, the Rajputs fought with wreckless valour, and at the outset it appreared as if they would win. But superior tactics and weapons prevailed. Sword and shield whatever be the strength and heroism of the men who wielded them were no match for bullets and canon-balls. After a desperate fight that reged from morning till evening the Rajputs were overwhelmed and Rana Sangram Singh fled away from the stricken field. That broke the power of the Rajputs, and simplified the task of Babar.

Babar followed up his victory by storming the Rajput fortress of Chanderi in Malwa and by a campaign against the Afghans in Bihar. The latter were defeated on the banks of the Gogra, and Babar felt that he had practically subdued all those who were obstacles to his rule in India. He now retired to Agra for a brief rest after feverish activities extending over the period of three years. He utilized his leisure in ordering the affairs of government and building himself a palace surrounded by gardens, running streams and fountains on the pattern of Samarkand. Since Babar came from the beautiful cities of Samarkand and Bokhara and the cool climate of Central Asia, he did not like the people of Hindustan, who according to him lacked refinement and artistic sense, and the climate of Hindustan that was unbearably hot. In his famous autobiography he wrote about Hindustan that there were "no good houses, no good fresh meat, no grapes or melons, no good fruits, no ice or cold water, no good food or bread, no baths or colleges." The Mughals till the end disliked the hot weather of India and built palaces surrounded by gardens and fountains and equipped with marble baths and pavillions in order to mitigate the rigour of the hot weather. But in spite of all that when the heat was unbearable they shifted to Kashmere.

Babar died at Agra on the 26th Dec. 1530, and there is a touching story connected with his death. His beloved son Humayun was dangerously ill, and Babar in his anxiety to save his life performed the well-known ceremony of walking three times round his bed, repeating as he walked "let all your suffering come on me." Soon after this, it is said, the son recovered and the father fell ill and died. Though he was only forty eight at the time of his death Babar had been a king for 36 years, and at death left an empire that stretched from Patna to the Pamir and from Kashmere to Malwa. He was a brave warrior and born leader of men. He had a fine temper and a keen appreciation of beauty in nature and art.

He was a poet, musician, and reputed writer of Turki prose. His memoirs are regarded as one of the finest in the world.

HUMAYUN

His Rule & Flight From India

Babar was succeeded by Humayun his eldest son. Humayun had three brothers Kamran, Hindal and Askari, who were always disloyal to him and gave him much trouble. Humayun was a man of affectionate and kindly disposition, brave and generous, but lacked resolution. Since Babar had not lived long enough to consolidate his conquests, Humayun found himslef in an insecure position. The Afghans rose against him in the east and Bahadur Shah in Gujrat. He defeated Bahadur Shah and annexed his kingdom but before he could complete the work, he was called away to face the Afghans under Sher Khan. Sher Khan was a very shrewd man and able general. He had strengthened his position in Bihar, and rallied the Afghans round his banner. He defeated Humayun at the battle of Chaunsa in 1539 and again near Kanauj in 1540. The defeats were due chiefly to the disloyalty and lack of co-operation on the part of Humayun's brothers. After that Humayun fled away from Delhi and in the course of his wanderings through Sind and Rajputana, his son Akbar was born at Amarkot on 23rd November 1542. Then he thought of going to Persia and while on his way his wicked brother Kamran, who was the governor of Kabul intended to capture him with an evil motive. Fortunately Humayun escaped and reached Persia with safety. The Shah of Persia generously helped him with troops, and with his help he recovered Kandahar and Kabul from Kamran. He ruled over Kabul for ten years (1545-55)before he could turn to Hindustan for the reconquest of his lost kingdom from the descendants of Sher Shah.

SHER SHAH SUR

The Revival Of Afghan Power.

After the flight of Humayun, Sher Khan ascended the throne of Delhi under the style of Sher Shah, and founded what is known as the Sur dynasty. He was one of the greatest kings of India. He ruled only for five years, 1540-45, but during this brief period he did more for the welfare of his subjects and for the establishment of good government in the country than any other king before him. He conquered the Punjab, Malwa, parts of Rajputana, Sind, and Bengal, and set up an efficient system of administration. He built a network of highways to connect the different parts of the empire that made the work of governement easy and helped the growth of trade and communication. The roads had trees planted on two sides for shade and rest houses built at regular intervals for the benefit of the travellers. The empire was divided into small provinces and each province was composed of a number of parganas or groups of villages. Each pargana was placed in charge of five officers, viz. a military officer, a judicial officer, a teasurer and two writers one to write Hindi, the other Persian and they conducted the administration there. Land was surveyed and then assessed, the share of the state being fixed at one fourth of the produce to be paid in cash or kind. Tyrannical land owners and zamindars were severely punished, and the village officers were responsible for the maintenance of peace and the detection of crimes in their areas. Law and order were strictly enforced. A standard coinage was issued, and encouragement was given to trade and commerce by the abolition of a number of vexatious tolls and duties. He maintained a standing army, and paid his soldiers cash salaries regularly. Religious persecution was stopped and the people were happy. It was owing to these achievements that Sher Shah has been regarded as one of the greatest kings of India. He died in May 1545 and had paved the way for constructive work of Akbar.

Sher Shah's Successors and Humayun's reconquest of Northern India

He was succeeded by his son Islam Shah (1545-54). He was an energetic king, and autocratic ruler. He reduced the power of the Afghan nobles and chiefs. Though they did not like it, they could not resist the power of Islam Shah. After his death the pent-up energies of the Afghans broke out in revolts, and the empire under the rule of the vile wretch Muhammad Shah Adil, who had murdered the rightful heir and usurped the throne, was torn into shreds. Anarchy and confusion reigned in Northern India, and taking advantage of it Humayun, who was closely watching the affairs of the Sur dynasty attacked and recovered his lost throne of Delhi in July 1555. But hardly had he occupied the throne for six months when Humayun had a fall from the stairs of his Library and died of its effects.

AKBAR THE GREAT (1556-1603)

Akbar's accession and the Second Battle of Panipat.

At the time of Humayun's death Akbar his eldest son was in the Punjab pursuing a section of the Afghans with his guardian Bairam Khan. As soon as the news reached him Bairam Khan got him crowned in the garden of Kalanaur in the Gurdaspur Distict of the Punjab on February 14, 1556. Since the Mughal hold on the country was still insecure, the brave Hindu general of Muhammad Shah Adil called Himu marched on Delhi and wrested it from the Mughals who retreated and joined Akbar's camp near Panipat. Himu proclaimed himself king under the style of Vikramajit and as he pursued them a battle was joined at Panipat, known as the second battle of Panipat, on the 5th November 1556. Himu was defeated and captured and subsequently put to death. With this victory Akbar commenced his reign, which continued for half a century and was the most glorious period of medieval India. A vast empire was conquered and consolidated; government was conducted on the most liberal principles; and there was a degree of understanding and good-will between the Hindus and Muslims never known before.

During the first four years after his accession, Bairam Khan ruled the kingdom as the Regent. Akbar possessed a forceful and domineering personality. He overthrew his regent Bairam Khan in 1560 and in another four years (1564) he freed his government from the interferences of his male and female relations. About this time he initiated the policies on which he based his subsequent administration. Since the Afghans were the enemies of the Mughals who had supplanted them Akbar wanted to make Rajputs his friends. With this intention he married a Rajput princess of the house of Jaipur in 1562. The abolition of the practice of enslaving the prisoners of war and their families (1562), of the pilgrim tax (1563), and of the Jiziya (1564) made not merely the Rajputs, but the Hindus in general well-disposed towards Akbar. Their loyalty and co-operation made the task of empire building easy for him. The temporary unrest among the orthodox Uzbeg chiefs due to Akbar's conciliatory attitude was soon crushed, and then Akbar embarked on a scheme of conquest. In 1564 Gondwana was conquered; in 1567 Chitor was occupied inspite of the heroic resistance of the Rajputs; in 1572 Gujrat was annexed and in 1576 Bengal was wrested from its last Afghan king Daud. By 1576 Akbar's empire extended over the whole of Northern India except Kashmere, Sind and Orissa. In the pride of success everywhere, Akbar determined to crush Rana Pratap Singh of Mewar who had given him offence not merely by insulting Man Singh whose father's sister Akbar had married, but by refusing to submit to Akbar even though the rest of Rajput states had submitted. Therefore Akbar sent Man Singh at the head of a Mughal army to attack Mewar, and Rana Pratap opposed them at Haldighati. A deadly contested battle was fought in which the Mughal army was victorious owing to the use of firearms and artillery. Then the Mughals occupied Chitor the capital and the plain country of Mewar. Rana Pratap retreated into the wild fastnesses and from there kept up a guerilla warfare for nearly twenty years. Before his death in 1597 he had recovered all his lost territories except Chitor, Mandalgarh and Ajmer. In spite of the heavy odds the brave Rana had triumphed, and Akbar in spite of the resources of a vast empire had failed in his object.

As soon as the conquest of Bengal, Gujrat and Malwa had been accomplished Akbar set about organizing an efficient system of administration. He followed the example of Sher Shah and employed a very able Hindu administrator Raja Todar Mal to organize the department of revenue administration. Todar Mal attempted a regular survey of the land before the government share was ascertained on the basis of the area under crop, the kind of crop, and the fertility of the soil. The land revenue was fixed at one third of the produce which was to be paid in cash to the local officers appointed by the government. The peasants were given receipts for the payments they made. Many vaxatious dues were abolished, and illegal exactions and oppressions by government officials were severely punished. These regulations gave much relief to the people, and they were so sound that they formed the basis of the Indian revenue administration under the British.

Then Akbar organized a strong central government divided into several departments, each with a head and a staff of large number of assitants and clerks. They formed the imperial secretariat located at the capital. The government was carried on by a large number of carefully graded officials who formed the imperial service. All officers of the empire from the highest to the lowest, whether belonging to the civil or to the military, were classified into thirty-three grades, with fixed scales of pay, which they received in cash from the treasury. They were all called mansabdars, that is holders of mansabs or offices, in other words officers, and the system was called mansabdari system. The highest officers of the empire were the Vakil or the Prime Minister, the Vazir or the Finance Minister, the Bakshi or the War Minister and the Sadr or the Minister in charge of the Ecclesiastical Department. Their duty was to tender advice to the emperor when he needed it, and carry on the day-to-day administration.

Akbar maintained a standing army composed chiefly of the cavalry. The infantry played a subordinate part. He regarded artillery as a very important branch of his military organization. He had a liking for fire-arms and introduced many improvements himself. At the time of war his standing army was reinforced by the contingents supplied by the mansabdars. He also maintained a body of gentlemen troopers called Ahadis, who formed his body guard.

Akbar's attitude towards Religion.

In matters of religion Akbar was tolerant and had enlightened views. Though in the beginning of his career he was an orthodox sunni Muslim, he gave up orthodoxy as he came into contact with the learned men of other religions, viz Hinduism Jainism, Zoroastrianism (that is the religion of the Parsees) and Christianity. He built a house of worship called Ibādat Khānā, in which were held debates and discussions by the representatives of the various religions while Akbar presided. Christianity was represented by the Portuguese fathers Aquaviva and Manserrate. Akbar had a retentive memory and a keen intellect. He could easily grasp and remember the basic principles of all religions and after listening to the debates he discovered that all religions were alike in their essentials. He therefore respected all religions, and did not like that there should be any conflict between their followers. His intimate friend and secretary Abul Fazl who was one of the greatest philosophers and scholars of the age and wrote the famous works of Ain-i-Akbari and Akbarnāmā, held similar views The ideal of Sulh-i-Kul or peace with all, that he had learnt in his childhood from his tutor was dear to his heart. He therefore wanted that the people living in one empire, under one imperial rule could live in greater unity and peace if they had one religion to follow in the place of several. He therefore pieced together some of the essentials of all the religions he knew of, and formed a new ecclectic faith called Din-i-Ilahi or Divine Faith. He wanted the people of his empire to follow the new faith, of which he was the founder. The object underlying the attempt was praiseworthy no doubt, but it did not appeal to the people, and though some of his friends and others actuated by the motive of pleasing the Emperor adopted it, it died a natural death after Akbar.

Owing to these views and religious experiments of Akbar there was much discontent among the orthodox sections of his Muslim subjects. They started a rebellion in the eastern provinces of the Empire and invited Akbar's half brother, Mahmud Hakim Mirza who was ruling over Kabul in semi-independence to attack from the north-west. Akbar was in great danger, but with remarkable ability he suppressed the rebellion and pursued Hakim Mirza into Kabul, where he submitted and then was pardoned (1581).

After this Akbar undertook the conquest of Kashmere which was accomplished in 1586, of Sind, Beluchistan and Kandahar between 1591 and 1595, of Orissa in 1592 and of Ahmadnagar, Khandesh and Berar between 1598 and 1600. Thus his vast empire stretched over the whole of Northern India and a part of the Deccan, and was divided into fifteen subahs or provinces. His last days were rather unhappy due to the rebellion of his most beloved son Salim and the murder of his most intimate friend Abul Fazl brought about by Prince Salim. He died in 1605.

Akbar's Patronage and Greatness.

Akbar was a great builder, a lover of arts, music, and poetry. In 1570 he had started building at Fatehpur Sikri a city of his dreams and shifted his capital there. He believed that Agra was not lucky for him, because all his children born there had died while Prince Salim born by the blessings of Shaikh Salim Chisti, at Fatehpur Sikri lived. Akbar called the best artists of India and abroad to build his palaces and gardens and the city of Fatehpur Sikri. In his court lived the greatest musician of India Tansen and some of the greatest painters of that time. Akbar extended liberal patronage to poets, philosophers and scholars. He got many Sanskrit works and Babar's memoirs in Turki translated into Persian. There was a galaxy of talented men and generals in his court. The country was peaceful and prosperous under his rule. His genuine interest in the welfare of his subjects, his friendly attitude towadrs the Hindus, his liberal patronage to men of genius in all the walks of life and his exceptional ability in selecting right men for his work made his rule of fifty years one of the most glorious periods in Indian history. Alone among the muslim rulers he never forgot that the majority of his subjects were Hindus, and that the Hindus and muslims alike were entitled to equal treatment. There lay his greatness. Of him has been written that "he was a born king of men with a rightful claim to rank as one of the greatest monarchs of history. That claim rests solely on the basis of his extraordinary natural gifts and magnificant achievements."

JAHANGIR (1605-1628)

Akbar was succeeded by Prince Salim, who ascended the throne under the style of Jahangir. The early years of his reign were disturbed by the rebellion of his eldest son Khusrou. After it was suppressed Khusrou was handed over to Prince Khurram Jahangir's favourite son, who got him strangled to death a few years later. In 1611 Jahangir married

Mehr-un-nisa, whom he loved passionately from early youth, after getting her husband murdered. After he married her she was called Nur-jāhān, or light of the world. She was a very talented and beautiful lady. Owing to her remarkable ability Jahangir left the affairs of government under her control. For nearly fifteen years she practically ruled the empire in conjuction with her brother Asaf Khan and her father Itimād-ud-daula. Her brother Asaf Khan's daughter was subsequently married to Prince Khurram—later on Shah Jahan. The domination of a woman led to inefficiency and intrigue and one after another Mahabat Khan the greatest general of the empire and Prince Khurram the most capable of the royal princes, revolted to ovethrow her supremacy.

Submission of Mewar.

Since Akbar had left a well organized and peaceful empire Jahangir was not required to undertake any long and arduous campaigns or wars of conquest. The only wars that were waged were against Rana Amar Singh of Mewar in Rajputana and Malik Ambar of Ahmadnagar in the Deccan. Rana Amar Singh who had succeeded Rana Pratap was soon tired of the unending and fruitless warfare with the Mughals and made peace. Jahangir showed his appreciation of the greatness and bravery of the Rana by constructing two marble statues, one of the Rana and the other of his son, which were placed in the garden below the audience window. The Mughal attacks on Ahmadnagar were successfully resisted by a very capable leader Malik Ambar who had taken over the control of the government of that Sultanate. The imperial armies could not make any head-way till his death in 1626. One of the notable incidents of his reign was the arrival of Sir Thomas Roe who had come as the accredited ambassador of James I to seek trade privileges for the English Company in the Mughal Empire. There were court intrigues over the question of succession during the last days of Jahangir. When in November 1627 he died on his way to Kashmere, Asaf khan the partisan and father-in-law of Prince Shah Jahan proclaimed him emperor and secured the throne for him in his absence. Shahjahan came to Agra and formally ascended the throne in 1628 after having removed all possible rivals from his path. Asaf Khan was rewarded by being appointed as Prime Minister.

SHAHJAHAN (1628-59)

Shahjahan continued the aggressive schemes of his father in the Deccan. After the rebellion of Khan Jahan Lodi was suppressed, Shah Jahan himself directed the operations against Ahmadnagar. During the course of the war his favourrite wife Mumtaz Mahal for whom he had an ardent love died of child-birth at Burhanpur in June 1631. Her body was carried to Agra where her mourning husband raised later a splendid mausoleum in her memory, the like of which has never been built anywhere in the world. That is the famous Tajmahal standing on the north bank of the Jamuna in Agra. In the mean while the war against Ahmadnagar was continued by Shahjahan's generals and it ended in 1636 when Ahmadnagar was partitioned between the emperor and the Sultan of Bijapur. That year Prince Aurangzeb came as the Viceroy of the Mughal Deccan which comprised the four provinces of Khandesh, Telingana, Berar and Daulatabad and continued till 1644. He had succeeded in putting the affairs in tolerable order when he was transferred to Central Asia to direct the military operations in Balkh. It was a highly expensive campaign which Shahjahan had undertaken with the object of recovering his ancestral dominions in Central Asia. But in spite of the exertions of Prince Dara and Prince Aurangazeb who took over command alternately it ended in a disatrous failure. In 1648 Kandahar was also lost to the Persians. By 1653 the campaign in Central Asia was abandoned, and Prince Aurangzeb returned to the Deccan as its Viceroy. Back in the Deccan he, for the first time, heard of the activities of Shivaji who had seized some forts and territories belonging to Bijapur. Aurangzeb did not much mind it because he was himself bent upon annexing the territories of Bijapur and Golconda. He hated their sultans as they were Shiahs and he himself was an orthodox Sunni. In 1656 he invaded both Golconda and Bijapur and had gained some advantages, when he was directed to make peace by the order of Shahjahan. Shortly after this Aurangzeb had to leave the Deccan to take part in the War of Succession.

AURANGZEB

The War of Succession and Triumph of Aurangzeb.

The War of Succession between the sons of Shahjahan is one of the most painful and darkest episodes in the annals of the Mughal dynasty in India. As there was no law of succession among the Indian Mughals, all the sons of the Emperor aspired for and claimed the throne. Consequently there was often trouble over succession, and under Shahjahan, it assumed a bitter form. The four sons of Sahjahan, viz. Dara, Shuja, Aurangzeb and Murad who were in charge of the governments of Delhi, Bengal, Deccan and Gujrat respectively suspected each other of designs to seize the throne when Shahjahan was ill, and prepared to face each other on the battle field. Dara was a capable and amiable prince, but like Akbar eclectic in religious matters for which he was disliked by a large section of the Muslims. Shuja loved a life of pleasure and ease, and was incapable of sustained effort. Aurangzeb was orthodox, shrewd, resourceful and unscrupulous. Murad was exceptionally brave but passionate, dissolute and brainless. They proceeded to fight out their claims in defiance of Shahjahan's authority, and as the result of a bloody war that ensued Aurangzeb emerged triumphant. Shuja with all his family was driven to destruction. Dara was defeated, captured during his flight, and executed; and Murad was arrested, judicially tried, and punished with death. After defeating Dara at Shamugarh, Aurangzeb captured the fort of Agra where Shahjahan lived, and imprisoned Shahjahan there because he had favoured the claims of Dara, whom Aurangzeb hated as an apostate from Islam. Thus ended the War of Succession and Aurangzeb had waded through the blood of his relations to the throne which he formally ascended in 1659. His old father lived as a prisoner for seven long and bitter years till his death in 1666. That was the most heartless act of Aurangzeb and it gave a tragic touch to the reign of Shahjahan, whose court was one of unparalleled magnificence and whose reign dazzled the eyes of the world by its glory and splendour. Shahjahan had a passion for fine buildings. He built the Jumma mosque and the fort and the palace at Delhi. In this palace he constructed his famous audience halls, the Diwani Khas and the Diwani Aam, the latter of which bears the beautiful marble screen with scales of justice and the former the famous inscription : "If there is a paradise on earth, it is this, it is this, it is this."

In the Diwani Aam or Public audience Hall stood the world renowned peacock throne with its legs of gold and twelve pillars of emerald, each one of which bore two peacocks encrusted with gems, supporting a rich canopy, the whole throne blazing with jewels. The exquisitely beautiful Tajmahal and the lovely Pearl Mosque were built at Agra. The artists and painters executed works which are some of the finest in India. Numerous poets and calligraphists scholars and musicians flourished in his court. But with all this grandeur, the government seems to have been inefficient and corrupt. The people were poor and oppressed, and religious persecution had been started against the Hindus. The age of tolerance had disappeared with Akbar and Jahangir, and with them the days of prosperity and greatness of the empire.

II

FALL OF THE MUGHAL EMPIRE AND THE RISE OF THE MARATHAS

The reign of Aurangzeb extending over a period of nearly fifty years (1659-1707) is one of the most consequential in the history of Medieval India. It was during his reign that there occurred events which undermined the strength of the Mughal empire, and brought it to the verge of its fall. It was his reign that recorded the growth of the European settlements in India, and the rise of the Marathas who were destined to play an important role in the fortunes of India. He inherited one of richest and most prosperous empires of the world. In less than fifty years he had completely ruined it. Akbar had built up that empire by removing social and religious barriers which had divided the sovereign from his subjects and by a policy of tolerance and conciliation towards all. Aurangzeb ruined it by raising the barrier of religion between him and his subjects, and by seeking to stamp out every religion but his own. His hatred of the Shiah faith was only one degree less than that of Hindu religion. For the first ten years of his reign he experienced little trouble. His affairs in the north and south were fairly prosperous. But as he freely gave vent to his religious bigotry and indulged in a policy of religious persecution after 1669 people revolted in the different parts of his empire. The war with the Rajputs and the Marathas broke out simultaneously after 1679 and continued till the end of his reign. It crippled the military strength of the empire. The revolt of the frontier tribes about at the same time deprived the imperial army of fine recruits that came from those regions. After 1689 Aurangzeb came into deadly grips with the Marathas in the Deccan and by the time of his death in 1707, he had been overwhelmed by the disasters inflicted upon him by the Marathas. That is the outline picture of his reign of fifty years.

Early years of Aurangzeb's reign

Aurangzeb started his reign by abolishing a large number of taxes and cesses of various kinds, which created a good impression about the new emperor. In 1667 he ordered Mir Jumla the Governor of Bengal to invade Assam. After some initial success he died of the hardships of the campaign. He was succeeded by Shayista Khan, who continued his work, occupied Chittagong in 1665 and cleared the nests of pirates around the deltas of the Ganges and the Brahmaputra. In 1672 the tribesmen of the North-west Frontier gave much trouble and defeated an imperial army. It was only after 1675 when Aurangzeb himself visited the scene of operations that the trouble was over.

Rise of Shivaji

In the mean while the affairs in the Deccan were not very satisfactory owing to the activities of Shivaji. Shivaji the son of Shahji, a prominent nobleman in the service of Bijapur, traced his descent to the Ranas of Chitor. His mother was Jija Bai, a princess of the family of Jadhavs of Sindkhad, who traced their descent to the Jadhav dynasty of Devgiri. He was born at Shivneri in 1627 and his childhood was spent under the fostering care of his mother. From her he imbibed some of the finest virtues which distinguished Shivaji in later life. Due to his absence from home for a long time Shahji appointed Dadaji Konddev as the gauardian of his young son. Dadaji arranged to give Shivaji education befitting his status, but Shivaji was more inclined towards martial exercises, shooting and riding and feats of strength than towards book learning. He loved to listen to the stories of the heroes described in the Ramayana and the Mahabharata, and early aimed at becoming one like them.

As he began to grow he formed plans for looting the treasures and seizing the forts of Bijapur and induced his companions who were the sons of neighbouring zamindars to join him. He disliked to serve any Muslim king and desired a career of independence. At the young age of nineteen he seized the fort of Torna which belonged to Bijapur. With the treasures that he got there he equipped a small army of the hardy hill-men of the Western Ghats, called Mawlis, and captured some other forts and territories. After he annexed Kalyan and part of the Konkan the Bijapur Government sent Afzal Khan at the head of a powerful army to punish Shivaji in 1659. Shivaji however was more than a match for him; killed him by a clever device; completely defeated his army and seized all his treasures. Emboldened by these successes Shivaji annexed parts of the Bijapur kingdom and even raided Mughal territories. By now Aurangzeb was comparatively free to turn his attention to the Deccan. He sent his maternal uncle Shayista Khan as the Viceroy of the Deccan in 1660 with orders to stop the depredations of Shivaji. Shayista Khan miserably failed and barely escaped with life when Shivaji one night boldly attacked him in his camp in Poona. The Mughal army thus frightened became demoralized and Aurangzeb sent Jai Singh his greatest general to take charge of the operations from Shayista Khan who was disgraced and transferred to Bengal. Shivaji did not like to fight with Jai Singh who was a Hindu like him and Jai Singh also treated him with respect and consideration. A treaty known as the treaty of Purandar was concluded in 1665 between Shivaji and Jai Singh, and hostilities ceased. Then Jai Singh advised Aurangzeb to conciliate Shivaji by inviting him to the imperial court. On the invitation of Aurangzeb Shivaji went to Agra, but in his usual way Aurangzeb treacherously imprisoned him. Shivaji formed a clever plan, and with his young son escaped from the prison. After wandering in disguise for some time Shivaji reached his capital Raigarh in safety in December 1666, and became a sworn enemy of Aurangzeb. He devastated the Mughal territories of the Deccan by frequent raids and harassed the Mughal commanders by guerilla tactics. Aurangzeb was forced to confer upon him the title of Raja and let him alone. In 1674 he celebrated his coronation as an independent king at his capital, and invited numerous Hindu rajahs, noblemen, scholars and poets from all parts of India. Then he took the style of Chhatrapati. In 1676 he led his army into the Karnatic. On his way the Sultan of Golconda gave him a royal reception and agreed to send an army for his service and pay a tribute to him . The entire country from the Krishna to Mysore was conquered and annexed to his northern possessions between

Poona and Belgam, thus forming a rich compact state. The Mughals and all the Muslim states of the south feared him. In 1680 he died at Raigarh mourned by his subjects and remembered by all.

Achievement if Shivaji.

Shivaji was one of the greatest rulers of India who can be compared with Akbar. With very humble beginnings he rose to be the founder of an independent state in spite of powerful enemies like Aurangzeb and the Sultans of the Deccan. He showed by his action that the Mughals were not invincible, and inspired his countrymen, the hardy race of the Marathas, to make war on the Mughals and destroy their empire. There were few generals who knew the art of guerilla warfare better than Shivaji. There were few rulers who excelled him in organizing an efficient system of administration on original lines and in maintaining discipline. His administrative system is known as the Ashtapradhān system, because it consisted of eight pradhāns or ministers, who were in charge of the eight departments into which the entire government was divided. Shivaji was at their head and consulted them if and when necessary. He abolished the Jagir system and hereditary offices, paid his officers cash salaries, and never allowed anyone to oppress his subjects. In contrast to Aurangzeb he respected all religions, Hindu and Muslim alike, never destroyed any mosque, and treated women and children with the greatest care and consideration. He had built up a highly efficient and discplined army, consisting chiefly of the cavalary and match-lockmen. During military operations his soldiers were forbidden on pain of death to take women with them or plunder the people. When he overran enermy's territories he imposed Chauth and Sardeshmukhi i.e. one fourth and one tenth of the land revenue, on the people. He lived a chaste private life, honoured the saints of all religions, worshipped goddess Bhavani and regarded Ramdas as his Guru. He was great as a general, as a king, and as a man.

Religious Persecution of Aurangzeb.

Before Shivaji's death in 1680 the affairs of the Deccan and indeed of the whole empire of Aurangzeb were drifting.

to a crisis. That was due to the character and religious policy of Aurangzeb. By breaking faith with Shivaji (1666) whom he had invited to his court he made him his life-long enemy. Three years later, 1669, he initiated a policy of religious persecution. He ordered his provincial governors "to destroy with a willing hand the shrines and temples of the infidels, and put an entire stop to the teaching and practice of idolatrous forms of worship." Temples and shrines of the Hindus all over the country, including those in the sacred cities of Benares and Mathura were destroyed by thousands. Religious festivals and pilgrimages were stopped and to heighten the humilation of the Hindus, Jizia was reimposed. Consequently there broke out revolts in different parts of the country. The Jats rose in Mathura and killed its Muslim governor. They were put down with difficulty but rose again in 1681 and 1691. In 1691 they even desecrated the tomb of Akbar at Sikandra, and Aurangzeb could not do anything because he was then in the Deccan getting the beatings of the Marathas. In 1672 the Satnamis of Patiala state also revolted and hardly had they been crushed when the Sikhs were up in arms in the Punjab. In the mean while they had risen to be a power like the Marathas.

Rise of the Sikhs.

Since the days of Nanak the Sikhs had been steadily growing in number, unity and strength. Akbar was kindly disposed towards them, and had allowed them to build the Golden Temple at Amritsar. Jahangir put to death the fifth Guru Arjun because he had helped his rebel son Khusrou. But the Sikhs took a lesson from this and gradually organized themsleves into a military brotherhood. The sixth guru Hargovind kept on a constant warfare with the Mughals. Aurangzeb put to death their ninth Guru Tegh Bahadur (1675) since he refused to embrace Islam. The tenth guru, Govind Singh (1675-1708) was the real founder of the military power of the Sikhs, who now called themselves Khalsa or pure. The members of the Khalsa were required to abstain from wine, tobacco, and drugs, assume the title of Singh, and adopt as their badge five K's viz. kesh or hair, Kachh or drawer, Karra or bangle, kripan or dagger, and kangha or comb. It was the bitter religious persecution of Aurangzeb that lashed them into rebellion under their Guru Tegh Bahadur and after Tegh Bahadur was executed with torture, under Guru Govind Singh. Guru Govind Singh helped Bahadur Shah in his contest for the throne but was killed by an Afghan fanatic in 1708. With the growing weakness of the empire after the death of Aurangzeb the Sikhs could not be suppressed. Their community grew from strength to strength till at last in the 9th century they founded a powerful state of their own.

The Rajput War.

It was not merely the Marathas, the Jats, and the Sikhs whom Aurangzeb had made his enemies. Even the hereditary friends of the Mughal dynasty, the Rajputs were driven to revolt against him . After the imperial order of religious persecution was issued in 1669 over 250 temples were destroyed in the states of Jaipur and Udaipur in one single year. Even the Rajputs were not exempted from the Jizia. On the top of it all, in 1678 after the death of Raja Jaswant Singh of Marwar, Aurangzeb made mean attempts to annex his dominion and to seize his little son Ajit Singh and bring him up as a Muslim. That made the Rajputs furious. Mewar joined on the side of Marwar and they waged a war with the Mughals, which off and on continued throughout the rest of Aurangzeb's reign. The war weakened the military strength of the empire when Aurangzeb had to fight against the Marathas, and once for all removed the strongest pillar which supported the Mughal empire. In this war even his own son Prince Akbar turned against him and joihned the Rajputs. But Aurangzeb was too cunning for him. He contrived to separate the Rajputs from his son by a clever trick in 1681 so that Prince Akbar was forced to seek the shelter of Shambhaji the son of Shivaji and the king of the Marathas. Since Shambhaji took up the cause of Akbar, Aurangzeb patched up a hurried peace with the Rajputs and came to the Deccan to reckon with the Marathas.

Aurangzeb in the Deccan.

In order to frustrate the ambitious designs of Akbar Aurangzeb pursued him into Deccan. For the next twentyfive years that he was in the Deccan he made determined efforts to crush the Marathas but all went in vain. In anticipation of an alliance between the Marathas and the two Sultanates of Bijapur and Golconda, he turned his arms against latter in order to destroy them first and then came to grips with the Marathas. In 1686 he destroyed the independence of Bijapur and annexed it to the empire. A year later Golconda had the same fate. Then he employed his entire strength against the Marathas, seized and exucuted their king Shambhaji in 1689 and captured Raigarh, Shambhaji's capital, and his family by the end of 1689. A few years before, Prince Akbar had gone away to Persia. It appeared to Aurangzeb, as if the task that he had undertaken—the destriction of the Maratha power and the two Shiah states, had been accomplished. But he soon realized that he was up against a sea of odds. The entire Maratha people rose as one man against the invaders of their country. They resorted to guerilla warfare; harassed the imperial armies constantly; cut off their supplies; made sudden attacks and rapid retreats; and after thus tiring them out defeated some of the biggest armies and generals of Aurangzeb. Only one fort of the Marathas—Jinji defied the Mughals for seven years. Aurangzeb's efforts to subdue the Marathas and their country not only failed completely, but exhausted all the energies of his body and mind, and all the resources of his vast empire. Thus exhausted and heart-broken he died in the Deccan on the 21st February 1707, at the very old age of eightynine.

Failure of Aurangzeb.

His unusually long reign of almost fifty years had ended miserably for the empire. Owing to his long absence of twenty-five years in the Deccan the central authority had grown weak; the provincial governors had stopped sending their revenues regularly to the imperial treasury or to the Emperor in the Deccan; and the imperial administration was crumbling to pieces. The Rajputs, the Sikhs and the Marathas, the three martial races of India were up in arms against the empire, and the Hindus in general hated the rule of Aurangzeb because of his religious bigotry. Thus the empire so laboriously built up by Akbar and extended by Jahangir and Shahjahan was tottering to its fall when Aurangzeb closed his eyes. He had seen the gloomy picture of his miserable failure before his death and therefore he wrote thus in his last letter "My years have gone by profitless ......God has been in my heart yet my darkened eyes have not recognized his light. There is no hope for me in the future............The army is confounded and without hope even as I am......" Aurangzeb was a Sunni Muslim, highly orthodox and exceptionally industrious. He was of a puritanic bent of mind and thought it to be his duty as a Muslim king to stamp out idolatry. This conviction influenced all his acts and he staked an empire to act up to his conviction. In his religious bigotry he destroyed not merely the Hindu idols and temples, he put a stop to painting, music and the allied fine arts. He cared little for the popular sentiments and his acts definitely antagonized his non-Muslims subjects. It was the lack of their support and loss of their loyalty which ruined his empire.

Break-up of the Mughal Empire.

After the death of Aurangzeb there ensued a war of succession between his sons and ultimately the eldest succeeded in defeating the others and ascended the throne under the style of Bahadur Shah. He was a weak ruler though good and pious as a man. He wanted to curb the power of the Rajputs and the Sikhs but failed. After his death in 1712 there began endless troubles over the question of succession and between 1712 and 1719 as many as four emperors rose and fell. Power passed from their hands into those of their ministers and of these ministers, the Sayyid brothers.—Abdullah and Husain Ali were the most prominent. They were also called king makers. They deposed in 1719 Farrukhsiyar who was subsequently murdred by their orders. He was succeeded by two roi fenants who ruled for a few weeks each, and then by Muhammad Shah. Muhammad Shah contrived to kill the King-makers and ruled for nearly thirty years,1719-48. But he was so worthless that he could neither stop the foreign invaders from attacking his empire, nor his provincial governors from assuming independence. The Marathas became very powerful, spread into Malwa and Gujrat, and stamped out the imperial rule from those provinces. In 1739 Nadir Shah, the king of

Persia invaded the empire, and having overrun Afghanistan and the Punjab marched on Delhi. Delhi was occupied, its inhabitants were ruthlessly massacred, and then given up to plunder. As he returned home, he carried away a vast booty worth many crores of rupees besides the Kohinoor and the Peacock Throne. He also annexed the whole country west of the Indus.

Nadir Shah's attack gave the death-blow to the already sinking empire. Consequently many of the provincial governors asserted their independence. The Rohilla Afghans carved out a principality of their own in the north U.P.; the Marathas occupied Malwa and Gujrat; and the Nizam-ul-Mulk established himself in the Deccan with Haidarabad as his capital, The imperial authority remained in name and was effective only in a few districts round about Delhi. Hardly had the horrors of Nadir Shah's invasion been forgotten, when Ahmad Shah Durrani or Abdali who had made himself king of Kabul started his attacks on the Punjab. Fortunately he was defeated in 1748, but that did not deter him from continuing his attacks. After the death of Muhammad Shah his son Ahmad Shah succeeded to the Delhi throne and it was during his reign that Abdali's attacks became more frequent. In the mean while the Marathas had entered Delhi, the Gangetic Doab, and the Punjab, and thus came into conflict with Abdali. The Rohilla Afghans, tired of the depredations of the Marathas in Rohilkhand where they had settled down appealed to Ahmad Shah Abdali for help. The Marathas who had driven out Abdali's governor of Lahore and occupied the Punjab had thus offeneded Abdali. Owing to this conflict of interests the Abdali and the Marathas came into grips at the battle of Panipath fought on the 14th January 1761. The Marathas were disastrously defeated and it gave a set-back to their growing power for some years to come.

Rise of the Peshwas.

Since after the death of Aurangzeb the Marathas had been steadily growing in power. Shambhaji their king whom Aurangzeb had seized and excuted in 1689 had been succeeded by Rajaram. His direction of the war against Aurangzeb had brought success to the Marathas, and they had completely foiled the efforts of Aurangzeb to subdue their country. After his death his widow Tara Bai carried on the work of fighting the Mughals with great ability, so that by 1707 the Marathas realized that they had won the war against Aurangzeb. After the death of Aurangzeb, Shahu the son of Shambhaji who had been, since his capture in 1689, in the imperial camp was released and after some difficulty due to the hostility of Tara Bai, became king of the Marathas in 1708. He was a good-natured man peace-loving, but weak as a king. He had to overcome heavy odds to secure his position, and with his mild disposition and mediocre abilities he would have failed if a very shrewd and capable Chitpavan Brahmin, Balaji Vishwanath had not come to his assistance. Balaji Vishwanath was his Peshwa or Prime Minister, and by a clever policy of conciliation combined with force he brought all the turbulent Maratha chiefs under the allegiance of Shahu. Then he helped the Mughal Viceroy of the Deccan Husain Ali—one of the Sayyid brothers and king makers, overthrow Farrukhsiyar, Emperor of Delhi, and in return got the sovereignty of Shahu over Maharastra and the territories conquered by Shivaji, and his right to the Chauth and Sardeshmukhi over the Deccan, recognized by the emperor (1719). He reorganized the the administration of the state and after an eminently successful career died in 1720.

Peshwa Baji Rao 1720-40.

Shahu appointed Baji Rao, his son to succeed him as the Peshwa. Baji Rao was a born soldier and loved fighting and conquest. His policy was to extend the dominions of the Marathas by conquering the provinces of the Mughal empire that lay to the north of the Narmada. He led the Marathas to attack Hindustan, the heart of the empire. "Strike at the trunk" he said "and the branches will fall of themselves". His ambition was to plant the Maratha flag on the walls of Attock, and to replace the Mughal Empire by "Hindu-Pat-Padshahi." He conquered Malwa, Bundelkhand and Gujrat, and in 1737 appeared before the gates of Delhi which caused much panic in the imperial court. He defeated Nizam-uk-Mulk in many an encounter, and forced him to pay Chauth and Sardeshmukhi to the Marathas. His capable and loyal brother Chimnaji conquered for him Salsette and Bassein from the Patuguese in 1739. It was Baji Rao who placed the Holkar, Sindhia, and Gaikwar in charge of the different parts of his new conquests beyond the Narmada, and in course of time they became independent members of the Maratha confederacy.

Peshwa Balaji Baji Rao 1740-61.

In 1740 Baji Rao died at the early age of forty. His office was conferred upon his son Balaji Baji Rao, by king Shahu, During his time the office of Peshwa or Prime minister became hereditary in the family of Balaji Vishwnath. Since Shahu had left the management of his government to his Peshwas, their power grew rapidly, and after Shahu they became the real rulers of the state. Shahu died in 1749 and was succeeded by Ram Raja who was the son of Shivaji II and grandson of Tara Bai. Ram Raja was a weak and worthless young man. He had been deprived of the training which princes generally receive in their early life and was devoid of princely virtues Consequently he lost the confidence of his grandmother Tara Bai, and support of his officers. Tara Bai kept him as a prisoner and the Peshwa did not care to set him free. After his imprisonment in the fort of Satara he ceased to function as a king and the Peshwa became the ruler of Maharastra both in fact and in name. The Chhatrapati or the King cf the Marathas, henceforth existed only to send the robes of investiture to the Peshwa.

Expansion of the Maratha Dominion.

Balaji Baji Rao was extremely ambitious. He wanted the Marathas to conquer Northern India as far as Attock and Southern India as far as Mysore. Indeed the Maratha power reached its zenith during his regime. The whole country as far south as Tanjore and Mysore was conquered. Raghoji Bonsle established himself at Nagpur and extended his territories eastward as far as Orissa. Owing to the death of the old Nizam-ul-Mulk in 1748 there had broken out a civil war in Haidarabad and the Karnatic. The Nizam dreading the interference of the Marathas had invited the French under Bussy; and so long as Bussy was in Haidarabad the Marathas had not dared do any harm to the Nizam. But after the French withdrew from Haidarabad due to their own reverses in the Karnatic wars, the Marathas attacked the Nizam, and inflicted a crushing defeat upon him at the battle of Udgir in 1760. As the result of this victory the Marathas forced the Nizam to surrender Ahmadnagar, Bijapur, the fortress of Daultabad and a part of Bedar. In Northern India they overran Rajputana and the entire Gangetic Doab. In 1751 Safdar Jang the Nawab of Oudh invited them to help him against the Rohilla Afghans. The Marathas defeated them forced them to seek shelter in the hills and ransacked their country in such a manner that the Rohillas dreaded the Marathas and hated them ever afterwards.

Events Leading to the Battle of Panipat.

In 1757 Ahmad Shah Abdali had plundered Delhi and Agra, and annexed the Punjab where he left his son as governor. Immediately after his return Raghunath Rao the Peshwa's brother with his lieutenants Madhav Rao Holkar and Jayappa Sindhia marched on Lahore, drove out Abdali's governor and pursued him as far as Attock. This made Abdali furious. He collected a strong force, and after Raghunath Rao had returned to Poona swooped down upon the Punjab, dispersed the small Maratha army left there and marched upon Delhi. On his way he defeated at Thanewswar a strong Maratha force under Dattaji Sindhia who was subsequently killed at Barārighat. He then drove out the remnant of the Maratha armies from the neighbourhood of Delhi and invited by the Rohillas crossed over to the Doab to give rest to his troops. The news of these disasters reached the Peshwa just after the victory of Udgir. Immediately a strong army commanded by Sadashiv Rao and accompanied by Vishwa Rao the young son of the Peshwa was ordered to proceed against Abdali in March 1760. On the way Surajmal the king of Jats advised Sadashiv Rao to leave his heavy baggage and artillery behind but his advice was ridiculed. Then Delhi was occupied and the countryside was closed to the Afghans. But the Marathas who were hard pressed for money stripped the ceiling of the Diwan-i-Khas of its silver and looted the shrines dedicated to the Muslim saints. These proceedings enraged the Muslims, and the Nawab of Oudh who was so far a friend of the Marathas joined Abdali. The Rajput princes held aloof because of the depredations to which they had been subjected by the Marathas, and the Jats did not join. Thus without an ally either Hindu or Muslim, and without adequate supplies of money and foodgrains the Marathas pushed northward. As they proceeded towards Kurukshetra, Abdali crossed the Jamuna and came in their rear. The Marathas had to fall back and encountered Abdali at Panipat. For several weeks the two armies lay facing each other and trying to cut off each other's supplies. In this the Afghans were more successful than the Marathas, because of the assistance of the Rohillas and the Nawab of Oudh. The Marathas suffered terribly when their supplies were cut off and then in sheer desperation they attacked the Afghans. On the 14th January 1761 the battle was joined and the Marathas were disastrously defeated. Huge numbers of men were slain besides Sadashiv Rao, Vishwa Rao, and many notable commanders. This battle known as the third battle of Panipat checked the northward advance of the Marathas for several years. The news of this disaster broke the heart of the Peshwa and he died a few months later.

The third battle of Panipat marked not only a set-back of the Maratha power; if meant also the dissolution of the Mughal empire, which had been founded by Babar after the first battle of Panipat in 1526. Between these two battles the first and third battles of Panipat, some of the outstanding events of Indian history have taken place. They have been outlined above as a background for the study of specific features of the period, hereafter.

CHAPTER I

THE NATURE OF THE MUGHAL CONQUEST

The Mughal conquest of India is a unique episode in Indian history—unique in the sense that it was not merely a physical conquest, but also a conquest of the heart. While driving the people to a stubborn resistance, it eventually evoked the greatest loyalty from them. The power of the sword which characterized the first phases of the conquest gave place to the more enduring triumphs of diplomacy and winning of the heart. In fact these characteristics mark at once the weakness and strength of the Mughal conquest. Its weakness was due to the military character, and its strength to the winning of the heart and co-operation of the conquered. Nevertheless, it strikes a new note in the history of Muhammadan conquest of India. That such was the imperative need of the situation in which the Mughals found themselves in India, there is no doubt;for in history, as in other human sciences no phenomenon could be adequately explained without reference to its environment. The situation was not an easy one and for that matter was the most perplexing that ever confronted a conqueror of India.

To understand the situation it is not necessary to give a detailed survey of the political condition of India on the eve of Babar's invasion, for the simple reason that the conditions obtaining at that time did not determine the nature of the Mughal conquest of India. The Mughal conquest of India is a long process, and Babar's invasion was one of its many important events. He is certainly not "an empire-builder of the sixteenth century," if thereby we understand that he was the builder of the Mughal empire in India. He was one of the many, who "must be cosidered to have laid the foundations of the Mughal Empire,"[1] and that "as a conqueror and not as an administrator." Such conquerors have been

1. *An Empire-builder of the Sixteenth Century*, p. 163.

Amir Taimur in 1398, Humayun in 1555, and Akbar in 1556. Before these conquerors there was a host of invaders, belonging to the same race raiding Hindustan right from the middle of the 13th century, and paving the way for the more illustrious conquerors. Thus a survey of the situation would mean a descritption of the political condition of India obtaining from century to century, between 1398 and 1556, if we want to exclude the raiders from our account. But it has been customary to consider the Mughal conquest of India to have started with the conquest of Babar, and that is because he was the first of the Mughals to attempt the systematic conquest of Hindustan by remaining in Hindustan, which his predecessors did not. So did Humayun and Akbar, the latter being the most illustrious as he was the real conqueror of Hindustan and builder of the Mughal empire in India. A proper understanding of the situation would mean a scrutiny of the political conditions obtaining in Hindustan in the whole of the 16th century. But the scope of this essay forbids a detailed study of the situation and we have to remain content with scanning its chiefs features.

In the first place, the Hindus, that is, the Rajputs were not the only ruling power in Hindustan in the sixteenth century, as in previous centuries when Mahmud Ghaznavi, Muhammad Ghori and Qutbuddin Aibak started their conquests. Had it been so, the Mughal conquest and rule of Hindustan would have lost some of its most distinctive marks, and perhaps the conquest of the country would have been much easier. For, the superiority of the Mughals in military skill and organization would have received an impetus from their religious zeal, and it would have appealed to them as a holy war against the infidels. But as it was, the Mughals met not the infidels alone on the field, but the Muslims like themselves. In fact, they had to fight out issues with the Muslims first and Hindus later. This fact alone was calculated to affect adversely the vigour of the Mughal invasion, for the obvious reason that an unprovoked attack of a Muslim king upon another is against the injunctions of the *Quran* ,and Babar's was an unprovoked attack actuated purely by motives of conquest. Whether it did so affect or not, it certainly did not facilitate the task.

The second feature of the situation was that supremacy in

Hindustan had been divided between the Rajputs and the Afghans, and they were the two rival powers. They had built up power by great tact and steadiness, and their glory filled the whole of the 15th century. As a result of their long tenure of power, they were firmly rooted in the soil. To sway the sceptre of Hindustan, the Mughals had to wrest it from the Afghans and the Rajputs, one after another, and they were no mean enemies. The Afghans were as brave as they were wily and having won power, were not prepared to part with it easily, and many a field had to be won and lost before they submitted to the Mughals. Theirs was the most stubborn, and at the same time sustained resistance offered to the Mughals. But if the Afghan was brave and wily, the Rajput was bravest of the brave and generous to a fault. His generosity commended itself to the Mughal as his bravery inspired awe. A combination of the two powers—the Afghan and the Rajput would have been fatal to the Mughals; but that was never to be. The Afghans and the Rajputs could not unite against their common enemy. Neither could each, as a people, present a united front against the foreign foe. Their tribal organization, and their separatist tendencies gave a handle to the Mughals to conquer them piece-meal. Even so, they did not venture to join issues with the Afghans and Rajputs at once. They had enough of tact to take advantage of the Rajputs' generosity after they had impressed the Rajputs by their mettle, and to win them over to their side. They made Rajputs their friends and supporters in their task of conquering the Afghans. The credit is entirely theirs—of those who finding Hindustan under the sway of two poweful peoples, drew one of them to their side in order that they might subjugate the other, and it is here that the real greatness of the Mughals lies. Though meeting with a situation far more perplexing than any that had confronted Mahmud Ghaznavi Muhammad Ghori or Qutbuddin Aibak, they succeeded in handling it admirably, and left a name that is at once good and great; and it was perplexing because (i) the Mughals had not merely to justify their attack on the Afghans who happened to be Muslims like themselves, (ii) they had also to destroy the political power of the Afghans and Rajputs in order that they might rear their own.

These features, therefore, viz. the presence of a strong Rajput confederacy side by side with a disintegrating Muslim power, and the resistance offered by the one, and willing co-operation offered by the other after the first repercussions of their impact with the Mughals had died away —these characterise the century that made the Mughal conquest of Hindustan an accomplished fact as between Babar and Akbar. But if the Mughal conquest of Hindustan was completed in the 16th century, all the pioneering work had been accomplished in the 13th and 14th centuries that is, between the invasions of Hulaku Khan and Amir Taimur. The far-reaching effects that these invasions produced on the Sultanate of Delhi—on the home and foreign policy of a series of illustrious monarchs like Balban, Alauddin Khilji, Muhammad bin Tughlak etc. amply testify to the formidable nature of the Mughal menace constantly present beyond the north-western frontier. So long as the Delhi Sultans were strong enough to repel the attack of the Mughals, they remained the lords of Hindustan, but when Taimur attacked and carried everything before him, the Delhi empire ceased to exist. A large province of the Empire —the Punjab, was annexed by Taimur, and the rest fast disintegrated, giving rise to independent monarchies throughout the country. It was a piece of good-luck that no Mughal invasion occurred in the 15th century, and the independent monarchies found time to get strong and stable. In spite of the internecine wars that filled this century there was promise of a glorious future. But elements of life and art that were slowly taking shape received a rude shock when the country was thrown into a welter of anarchy as a result of Babar's invasions culminating in the battles of Panipat and Kunwa. The decisive nature of these two battles distinguished Babar's achievements from those of his predecessors and encouraged him to stay in Hindustan and lay the foundation of the Mughal Empire there. It is only in this sense that his invasion of Hindustan is more than an episode in the Mughal conquest of India. What he started was completed by Akbar but not before the kingdom had once been lost to and recovered from the Afghans. The revival of the Afghan power, therefore, points at once to the die-hard nature of the Afghans and the political sagacity of the Mughals.

Now confining our attention to the 16th century that witnessed the completion of the Mughal conquest of Hindustan, we are brought face to face with this striking fact that the political sagacity of the Mughals was as great a factor in the success of their conquest as their military ability. That is noticed at the very commencement of their conquests. Babar does not start abruptly like Muhammad Ghori, when he, like the latter sets his heart on the possession of the Punjab. Neither is he dictatorial like Amir Taimur. He shapes his conduct with the care of a gentleman and points out why he wanted to annex the Punjab. He says "as it was always in my heart to possess Hindustan, and as these several countries had once been held by the Turks, I pictured them as my own and was resolved to get them into my own hands whether peacefully or by force. For these reasons it being imperative to treat the hill-men well, this order was given : 'Do no hurt or harm to the flocks and herds of the people nor even to their cotton-ends and broken needles."[1] Then in his message to the people of Bhira he says : "The possession of this country by a Turk has come down from of old; beware not to bring ruin on its people by giving way to fear and anxiety; our eye is on this land and on this people; raid and rapine shall not be."[2] Then he sends a messenger by name Mulla Murshid to the court of Delhi to seek by peace the surrender of the districts of the Punjab he had overrun. That is the account of his first expedition into Hindustan undertaken in February 1519. He resorts to diplomacy rather than to force to achieve his object. Whether he had the scruples of conscience to satisfy when he was deliberately making an unprovoked attack on the kingdom of a Muslim king, it is very difficult to prove, but certain it is that he did try to impress on Ibrahim Lodi that he claimed the countries by the right of conquest by the Turks and by the right of descent from Amir Taimur. It was the only justification of his aggrandizing activities. He had a right to conquer the lost Indian provinces of his ancestor Taimur in the same way as he had a right to recover the lost Central Asian dominions. Therefore he felt no hasitation in

1. *Babar's Memoirs* translated by A. S. Beveridge, p. 380.

2. *Ibid.*, p. 381.

setting aside the claims of everyone except himslelf to the possession of the Punjab, and to that end in crossing swords with Ibrahim Lodi. This he did on the field of Panipat (1526), and Panipat secured his claim not only to the Punjab but to the throne of Delhi, which meant the sovereignty of Hindustan.

But the sovereignty of Hindustan as secured on the field of Panipat was of a precarious nature. It greatly enhanced the prestige of Babar no doubt, but he had yet to do much hard fighting and prove his mettle before that sovereignty was his in the real sense of the word. There were powerful enemies around viz. the tribal military aristocracy of the Afghans, and the powerful confederacy of the Rajputs under Rānā Saṅgrām Singh. For, the fall of Ibrahim Lodi on the field of Panipat did not bring about the downfall of the Afghan power; and however superficially or substantially it might have affected the tenure and strength of Afghan power, it did not touch the fringe of Rajput confederacy. And for aught we know of the power and prestige of the Rajputs under Rāṇa Saṅga—his vast territories, his exalted reputation as a warrior, his diplomatic triumphs in Malwa, and his aspiration for dividing the empire of Ibrahim between himself and Babar, it will be no travesty of truth to say that Panipat could not carry Babar far in the process of empire-building in Hindustan. That was what Babar realized just before the a battle of Kunwa. His dream of empire receded into the shadows of despair, and he was disillusioned about the reality of his achievements so far. Thus there was plenty of strenuous fighting and exertion to be gone through before the empire of Hindustan became his. The Afghan military chiefs had to be crushed singly as well collectively, and the Rajput menace had to be removed for good before he could hold a firm sway over Hindustan.

The magnitude of Babar's task could be properly realised when we say that it actually began with Panipat. Panipat set his foot on the path of empire-building, and in this path the first great obstacle was the opposition of the Afghan tribes. It has been said before that the fall of Ibrahim Lodi did not mean the collapse of Afghan power. That was due to the fundamental nature of Afghan polity. It was not a centralized government with authority concentrated in the hands of the king. There was no person or organisation exercising the supreme power. The state was a loosely knit confederacy of a number of military chieftains, representing the various sections or clans of the Afghans. Each one of them regarded himself supreme in his domains or *jāgirs*, and conducted himself as such throughout his tenure of power. Whomsoever they elected to obey became their king, and this obedience or allegiance was tendered during the period of good behaviour of the person chosen as king. Thus authority had been diffused amongst the local magnates, and they formed, more or less a powerful class, amongst whom the whole Empire had been distributed and who by virtue of their territorial possession controlled the allegiance of the community. This alienation of power and territory was due as much to the tribal traditions of the Afghans as to the peculiar nature of the Afghan conquest of Hindustan at the time of Buhlul Lodi. At any rate, the king was regarded by the Afghan nobles as the first among them, who was their equal for all practical purposes except that he received the voluntary allegiance of all the rest, and hence was their superior. He entirely depended upon his military aristocracy for power and prestige as much as for the defence of his kingdom, and could not have retained any, the moment he lost their sympathy. Hence, when Babar entered Hindustan as the destroyer of Ibrahim Lodi, the Afghan power had not been destroyed. Victory over the king was not victory over the kingdom. Since power and territory belonged to the Afghan nobles, the subjugation of the Afghan Empire involved the wresting of power and territory from them. Panipat had its own effects no doubt. It brought enormous gains to Babar; and his moral gains were even greater than the military and the material. Neverthless, Panipat inaugurated an era of conquest, which was begun by Babar and was closed by his grandson Akbar. The first phase of this era (1526-30) was spent in the subjugation of the Afghan nobles and the Rajput confederacy under Rānā Sanga. The second phase opended with the rule of Humayun, and the main interest centred round his abortive attempts at the subjugation of Malwa, Gujrat, and Bengal, and his expulsion from India by Sher Shah, whose rise meant the revival of

Afghan power. The third and last phase begins with Humayun's reconquest of the Punjab and Delhi, and ends with the brilliant achievements of Akbar in the domains of war and diplomacy by drawing in cordial co-operation the Rajputs on to his side, and thereby facilitating his task of counquest and consolidation. Thus the process of Mughal conquest extends nearly over the whole of the 16th century.

Now as to the first phase. The tribal organization of the Afghans and the divisions of power and territory amongst these chiefs made the task of empire-building doubly difficult for Babar. After killing Ibrahim, Babar could occupy only the whole of the Doab. North, south, and east of it, the whole country had been parcelled out between the Lohanis, Farmulis, and Sarwanis, and they had elected one of them, Darya Khan Lohani's son Bahar Khan as their king. The next task to which Babar set himslef was to crush Bahar Khan with all his following, and all those nobles, who did not join Bahar Khan. This he did by a clever device. He distributed the unconquered parts of the Afghan Empire amongst his nobles and commissioned them to go and establish themselves by driving out the Afghan nobles from those parts. With limited resources he could not afford to waste them in the subjugation of the nobles, specially when he had yet to meet Rāṇa Saṅgrām Singh. He never minimised the power of this great adversary; nor was he inclined to think that the Rāṇa would keep aloof and leave him undisturbed to pursue his own ambition. That is why he sent Humayun against Bahar Khan, and the nobles against other Afghan chiefs; and himself remained at Agra strengthening his position and organizing his resources. Hardly had the task of subduing the Afghan chiefs been completed, when he heard that the Rāṇā was on the move. Babar was going to meet his equal, and on the field of Kunwa, the first expriences of his adversary's strength were most depressing. Amid gloom and despair, however, he stuck on to his guns, and by that dash and resourcefulness which characterised Babar, he won a glorious victory over the Rajput leader. The Rajput confederacy was shattered and with it their reputation and self-confidence. For many years to come, they did not recover from this shock, and the Mughals were left free to pursue their schemes of conquest and consolidation. After the collapse of the Rajputs, the destruction of the petty Afghan chiefs was only a child's play for Babar. The strongest opposition that they could offer was in combination with the king of Bengal, at the battle of Gogra, and the utter rout that they had there took the sting out of them so long as Babar was living.

That, however, was not very long since Babar's death took place (Dec., 1530) only a year and a few months after. Babar, during the four years spent in Hindustan, had conquered the Punjab, the territories that we now call the United Provinces and North Bihar. Besides, Mewar as the leading Rajput State had formally submitted. That was all that he could do and what he had left undone was of even greater importance. He had not been able to set up a centralized form of government with himslef at the head, wielding absolute authority over all; he had no time to build up a sound financial system and machinery of administration; and lastly, he had not created any public and philanthropic institutions to attract the loyalty of the people over whom he was to rule. These short-comings of Babar were aggravated after his death by the irresolute character of Humayun, and the die-hard nature of the Afghan power. The scattered elements of the latter needed only a personality to galvanize them and that was supplied by Sher Shah. Humayun blundered from the beginning of his reign, and failed to comprehend the real magnitude of his task. He should have built up a sound system of government to suit the ideal of absolute monarchy and crushed ruthlessly all Afghan pretensions to power.

The second phase begins with Humayun's accession to the throne (Dec., 1530). He met enemies on all sides, disguised and therefore all the more dangerous. His own brothers were jealous of him. Bahadur Shah of Gujrat was no secret enemy of his, and lastly, from the very start of his career, Sher Shah's ambition was sure to clash with his best interests. Yet Humayun did not take timely measures against them and allowed them to grow to endanger his interests and, as for the last Sher Shah, to drive him out of India. His chief folly seems to have been his incapacity to comprehend the significance of the political factors obtaining at his time. His first great mistake was that he treated his brothers rather a bit too well, and they certainly did not deserve it. This he realized much later in life. The concealed intentions of Bahadur Shah behind his professions of good-will he did not understand, and foolishly allowed a vassal kingom of his, viz. Mewar to be despoiled by him. Bahadur's religious claim made him blind to the obligation that a sovreign owes to his subjects. Consequently he forfeited Rajput sympathy. He never tried to understand its worth, and therefore never attracted the loyalty of the Rajputs. What a great opportunity he neglected, when he was requested by Rāṇī Karṇāvatī to come to her assistance against Bahadur Shah, can be judged in the light of the attitude of Akbar towards the Rajputs. His mad rush through Malwa and Gujrat, only to realize that it availed him nothing in the end has a tragic touch. Then his conflict with the Afghans, led by Sher Shah, who while gradually building up his power had been neglected by Humayun; his defeat at Chausa and Kanauj; his flight into the Punjab and thence to Sind; his invitation to, and retreat from Jodhpur through a burning sea of sand—all these speak for themselves. He was expelled from India, not merely by the power of the Afghans, but because of his own folly, because of forfeiting the loyalty of the only race that would have been a match for them—the Rajputs. Humayun never suspected the potency of the Rajputs, and trying to fight the Afghans single-handed, he wrecked his empire, his dignity, and reputation. On these wrecks rose the Afghan Empire of Sher Shah. Such is the story of the second phase.

The interval between the second and third phases forms one of the greatest epoches of medieval Indian history. It is full of the brilliant achievements of Sher Shah. War, defence, diplomacy, government, public works, philanthropic institutions—all these inaugurate a new era in India. A highly centralized system of government crowned by a bureaucracy and characterized by full-blooded energy and efficiency marks a radical departure from the accepted methods of Afghan statecraft. New policies, pregnant with political wisdom, foreshadow far-reaching changes in the Muslim polity in India. All unwittingly he builds up a system, that was admirably suited to the political ideals of the Timurids, and this he bequeathed to Akbar who alone of all the Great Mughals could make the best use of it. But even the achievements of Sher Shah were not without defect. His administrative machinery was not an organism, not a living institution, that could dispense with personality, and therefore it could not survive the shocks of anarchy and disorder that followed Islam Shah's death. Such was the end of the Afghan glory.

That is where the third phase starts. Humayun recovered his lost throne of Delhi no doubt, but he did not live to recover his lost empire. Hardly had six months passed after his occupation of the throne when he was laid in the grave. He left behind a minor son surrounded by a swarm of enemies ready to dispute his claim to the throne; a kingdom in Hindustan on which the Mughal hold was highly precarious; an empire which lacked cohesion; a body of nobles who were more ready to promote their own interests rather than their master's; and a people whose loyalty he had done nothing to claim. Such was the heritage of Akbar. When he was enthroned in the garden of Kalanaur he actually possessed no kingdom. Kabul had been bestowed on Muhammad Hakim Mirza, then under regency; Punjab was the foot-hold of Sikandar Sur, who still disputed the claim of Akbar to the throne of Delhi; between Delhi and Chunar the country was claimed by Ibrahim Shah Sur and Muhammad Shah Adil, the latter of whom acted through his capable general Himu and was the de *jure* sovereign of the Afghans. All these had as good a claim as Akbar to the throne of Delhi. He could not turn to Kabul for assistance in his conquest of Hindustan. Fortunately the able guidance of Bairam Khan and his firm loyalty helped sweep off all these enemies, and Akbar was securely placed on the throne of Hindustan. The second battle of Panipat heralded the real foundation of the Mughal Empire in India. During the following four years of regency, he did much spade work, and when Akbar took up the reins of government a new era began in the history of Muslim rule in India. Gifted with a constructive genius of a very high order, an all-comprehensive intellect, a soaring ambition and personal magnetism, he was a born ruler of men. He could easily grasp the needs of the situation, in which the Mughals in India found themselves. If he had to establish an empire, he realized, he could not adhere to the beaten track of Muslim statecraft in India. There were powerful enemies who were to be exterminated, and diverse peoples whose love and loyalty won. In short, he had not only to impose his rule on the peoples of India, but also to enlist their support. That was a very difficult task indeed; for on the one side there were the disgruntled Afghans burning to take revenge; on the other there were the valiant Rajputs, proud of their past, and zealous of their independence. Sher Shah had, to a great extent, subdued their pride, and therefore left them sullen. They hated the Afghan, for he did not know how to deal best with them; he rubbed them on the wrong side. The unrelieved coercion that Sher Shah employed to curb them, had rendered the very name of the Afghan hateful to the Rajputs. There lay the key to the situation, and Akbar spotted it at once. With the eye of a statesman he saw that the uncertainty of the Mughal tenure of power was due to the basic fact that they were foreigners, as against the Afghans, who were the 'children of the soil', and so long as the Afghans remained to dispute the sovereignty of Hindustan, the Rajputs must be conciliated, and their co-operation must be ensured. Through them alone the Hindu populace could be best placated. Then only the Mughal rule could gain the moral support it lacked; then the Mughal Empire could be firmly established. A co-ordination of the Mughal diplomacy, the Rajput vigour, and Hindu loyalty, would successfully combat and crush the Afghans, and so long as the latter survived, that co-ordination was an imperative need for the Mughals, for the Mughal position in Hindustan either at the time of Akbar's accession or at the time of Babar and Humayun was essentially weak. The credit of Akbar lies in this fact that he of all the Timurids understood it best, and therefore could devise the best remedy.

Hence towards the Rajputs, he was more than conciliatory and their generous nature readily responded to his solicitations. His marriage with the Rajput princesses, his deferential treatment of the Rajputs, his concern to associate them in the administration, in short, his respect for their national susceptibilities opened out their heart to him, and they freely shed their blood for the cause of the Mughal Empire. Akbar's Rajput alliance was only a prelude to his attempts to secure

Hindu sympathy and support. That is why we notice a series of regulations issued in reversion of the usual anti-Hindu policy of the Indo-Muslim state. Religious toleration and unstinted recognition of the merit formed the key-note of Akbar's State, and here it is that Akbar's greatness is revealed to the best advantage. But all these were only a means to an end. The funadmental weakness of the Timurid position in Hindustan, the die-hard nature of Afghan opposition, the proud indifference of the Rajputs, and the timid distrust of the Hindus, all these were hard realities of a situation, which could be best countered by a free and full co-operation with the Rajputs and moral support of the bulk of the people, the Hindus. But the great utility of the means should not make us blind to the transcendental ability of the man, who devised the means. Akbar was the real moving spirit, and it was he who put the empire on a firm basis. His extensive conquests, his sound administrative measures, his methods of centralization of power, his institution of a Secretariat, his treatment of the diverse creeds and peoples of the empire—(though here he blundered into persecution of the Muslims) all these testify to the real greatness of the man. It was he who conquered Malwa from its Afghan ruler, and after depriving the Afghans of all their provinces in Hindustan drove out and killed the last powerful Afghan king of Bengal,—Daud. And was it not that Man Singh played an important part in the conquest of Bengal and Orissa ? It is indeed difficult to exaggerate the value of the Rajput alliance to the cause of Mughal Empire in India, and it was appreciated so long as there was the Afghan menace. Hence, Jahangir throughout his reign and Shah Jahan for some time followed the policy chalked out by Akbar. But by the time of Shah Jahan, the Afghans had been completely conquered. The last Afghan rebellion, that of Khan Jahan Lodi, was crushed in the second year of Shah Jahan's reign, and since the Mughals did not feel concerned about the Afghans any more, there came aobout impeceptibly a little stiffness in their relations with the Hindus. In reversion of the former policy, Shah Jahan prohibited in 1632 the construction of any new Hindu temple in his empire, and if this was the beginning, Aurangzeb's was the conssummation. The pendulum had swung back; there was no need of co-operation and cajolery. The Hindus must be coerced and persecuted and thus curbed. Aurangzeb's attitude towards the Hindus in general and the Rajputs in particular was an elaboration of this policy, which was entirely undeserved, and created so great a catastrophe that at last it ruined the Mughal Empire. Such was the sequel of Akbar's legacies to the Great Mughals.

As it has been hinted at the outset, the greatness of the Mughal rule was due to the winning of the heart of the subjects. That it was so till the first few years of Shah Jahan's reign, can be safely asserted. The Empire was fast expanding; peace and prosperity reigned in the kingdom; liberal patronage of the Emperors fostered the growth of art and liberature, trade and industry; religious toleration evoked a spirit of friendship and good-will between the two militant creeds in the empire; and as a cumulative effect of all these, the epoch was marked by the best forms of national self-expression in all the fields of human activities. The moment, however, the real leaven of all this many-sided development began to fail, the greatness and glory of the Mughals began to decline. Perhaps it was not felt during the reign of Shah Jahan, though the losses on the frontier i.e. of Qandahar and Balkh, ultimately proved to be harmful to the best interests of the empire. The real effect was felt during the reign of Aurangzeb, whose offensive anti-Hindu policy and deliberate insult to the Rajputs undermined the strength of the empire. How short-sighted he or his predecessor was in initiating an anti-Hindu policy could be best judged from this single fact that both of them thought that with the extermination of the Afghans and the establishment of the Mughal Empire, all the vexed problems of the Mughal statecraft could be set at rest. They could afford to neglect the Hindus and antagonise the Rajputs instead of placating the former and allying with the latter. They failed to see that at a time when the empire was rapidly extending, there might arise ever new problems, and they had to be successfully tackled. They forgot to realize that Akbar had introduced a new field for Mughal activities—the conquest of the Deccan, and it was likely to tax the empire and its resources. It was as arduous a task as the conquest of Hindustan. They had to come into conflict with new peoples and new states, and that called for plenty of political sagacity. But unfortunately, the Mughals were blundering in this direction; they were sacrificing the Rajput co-operation and Hindu loyalty to their religious bigotry. Hence in his attempts to conquer the Deccan, Aurangzeb failed. Hindustan was already ablaze when he wanted to conquer the Deccan, and in such a predicament, failure on all sides was only a foregone conclusion. The Mughal Empire was on the verge of disruption, because it failed to find a solution for the problems that were ever arising during the course of its rapid extension. It had outgrown its usefulness when it antagonised those, on whose co-operation and sympathy it had rested so far. Its fall was inevitable.

In conclusion, the Mughal conquest of Hindustan was possible because the Mughals enlisted the co-operation of the Rajputs against their adversaries, the Afghans. When the conquest of Hindustan was complete and they wanted to conquer Southern India, they did not realize that the co-operation of the Rajputs was also necessary. Indeed, it was necessary in a still greater degree. The Marathas and the Shiah states in the South presented an inasuperable barrier to the Mughal ambition because the brave and cunning Marathas inspired by a religious zeal and national spirit were more than a match for the Mughals, and the Muslim Shiah states though comparatively weak, were implacable in their enmity to the Mughals. Aurangzeb had already alienated the friends of the Empire, the Rajputs, and had goaded the Hindus, the Jats and the Sikhs to resist the Mughal authority by his impolitic measures. With Hindustan up in arms, he wanted to conquer the Deccan and thus determined to accomplish an impossible task. If the Rajput alliance and Hindu loyalty had helped the Mughals to conquer Hindustan these again should have helped them to conquer the Deccan. It would not have been impossible if the Mughals had possessed sufficient political sagacity. But since they did not, they failed to conquer the Deccan, and therefore to conquer India as a whole.

CHAPTER II

THE MUGHALS AND THE AFGHANS

The fifteenth century in India "is a time of unparalleled confusion, an irrational formless epoch lacking alike the elements of coherence and stability."[1] Such an estimate would lead us to believe that the century was characterized by wars and conquests, unmitigated anarchy, decay and destruction of the peaceful arts of life, and political dissipation. It is hardly a true picture of the times. The fifteenth century witnessed a regrouping of social elements, rise of new states, and revival of new traditions. It was a century of intense activities, rich in variety and content, and all contributing eventually to peace and progress. Before the first quarter of the century was over, a number of states had arisen in Hindustan and the Deccan. There was not a single central authority in India no doubt, but that was not a very unusual phenomenon. The geographical controls militated against such a possibility in the days when facilities for communication were very crude. Between the death of Alauddin Khilji and of Muhammad-bin-Tughlak only thirtyfive years intervene and when it is realised that exactly twenty years after the former event, started that series of rebellions which shattered the stability of the empire, one can understand the nature of the central authority that obtained in India under the Khiljis and the Tughlaks. Indeed the Muslims were at this time trying to understand the nature of geographical controls over their political supremacy in India. Muhammad-bin-Tughlak who understood it well, tried to act up to it, but failed. No wonder that India following her time-honoured traditions and physical configuration broke up into a congeries of states, when powerful personalities had vanished. These states continued throughout the century. and laid the foundations of progress for the Mughal empire

1. An Empire Builder of the 16th century.

Each one of them besides being the focus of political life, evolved, as the century advanced, multiple forms of national self-expression. Art, architecture, music, poetry, painting to name only the most important ones of the finer pursuits of life, flourished under the liberal patronage of the local kings. With the evolution of the Urdu language, an admirable medium for the exchange of thought, between the Hindus and Muslims, had been discovered. This had led to a better understanding of each other and the barrier of mutual distrust and suspicion was gradually disappearing. A spirit of compromise, of toleration was manifesting itself in every walk of life, and consequently principles of government and religious ideals were substantially affected. The century recorded the rise of Kashmere, Sind, Gujrat, Malwa, Rajputana, Jaunpur, Bengal, Vijayanagar and the Bahmani kingdoms as independent states, each one of them throbbing with political life. But alongside their political life they also delveloped new styles of art and architecture, as well as new forms of literature. If the Jahaz Mahal and Hindola Mahal of Mandu excelled in dignity and grandeur, the Tin Darwaza and the Jami Masjid of Ahmedabad embodied grace and symmetry as well as "poetry and creative inspiration"; if the Atala Masjid and the Lal Darwaza of Jaunpur displayed the vigour and simplicity, the Dakhil Darwaza and the Sat Gumbaj Masjid of Gour were distinguished by "a surprising boldness of design" and masterly finish. Indeed, if such were the splendid specimens of the North there were even more splendid ones in the South. The austere simplicity of the Jami Masjid of Gulbarga, "the elegance of outline, the unimpeachable proportions and refined details" of the Chand Minar of Daulatabad, and "the plastic form and mass, the values of contrasted light and shade" of the College of Mahmud Gawan of Bidar, exhibit a wonderful variety and skill. These local styles of architecture evolved because the rulers had severed connection with Delhi and they bore distinctive marks of an amalgam of the Hindu and Muhammedan style. So long as Delhi was the seat of power and source of inspiration, there could not be evolved these independent styles. And what happened in architecture, also happened in literature, religion and politics. In Kashmere Zainul Abidin's reign inaugurated a new era that was marked by royal benevolence, religious toleration and rise of Indo-Islamic literature. "He caused the Mahabharat and Rajatarangini to be translated from Sanskrit into Persian and several Arabic and Persian books to be translated into the Hindi language."[1] Equally glorious were the annals of Bengal under Hussain Shah and Nasrat Shah. Bengali literature got a great impetus from their liberal patronage. In Malwa the accession of the Khiljis to power synchronised with universal prosperity. Gujrat was raising to be a first rate power, while Mewar in Rajputana showed potentialities of a remarkable future both artistic and political. Apart from the political and cultural activities, there were signs of a great religious awakening. The impact of Islam on Hinduism had considerably affected the nature of the latter. After its first shock had died away, there arose thinkers, who wanted to ignore the rigidity of caste and creed, and tried to find a common platform for all. Brotherhood of man, and the attainment of God by means of single-hearted love and devotion were the basic principles of their thought, and thus in the 15th century the ground-work was ready for the Bhakti movement of the 16th century. It is therefore that the fifteenth century was pregnant with possibilities, of which the full magnitude was realized in the next century. And to the making of this century contributed the Afghan Lodis who rose to prominence in Northern India from humble beginnings in the Punjab.

The Lodis along with other Afghan tribes had settled in the Punjab for some time before they usurped the throne of Delhi. Many of them had taken service under the Sayyids, and under the last two rulers i.e., Muhammad Shah and Alam Shah, they became unduly powerful. Malik Buhlul Lodi was the governor of Sarhind under Muhammad Shah and "as the king's weakness and meanness of spirit became more apparent he gradually extended his influence over the whole of the Punjab and began to with-hold the revenue due to the royal treasury."[2] After the death of Muhammad Shah in 1444, Buhlul made secret preparations to seize the throne, on which sat Alam Shah, more feeble and vacillating than this father Muhammad Shah. In fact the kingdom was in

1. *C.H.I.*, Vol. III, page 282.
2. *Ibid.*, p. 282.

a distracted condition. The province of Multan never acknowledged the authority of Delhi; Darya Khan Lodi ruled over Sambhal, the western limit of which was the Jumna; Hasan Khan another Afghan held Rapri; and all these were the partisans of Buhlul. No wonder that after Alam Shah had retired to Budaun (1448) permanently abandoning the government to his brother-in-law, Buhlul found little difficulty in seizing the throne (April 1451), with the willing acquiescence of his nominal chief.

From the accession of Buhlul to the death of Ibrahim Lodi at the battle of Panipat is a span of exactly seventy-five years. It recorded the reigns of Buhlul, Sikandar and Ibrahim Lodi, and is a period of mingled light and shade, of bright beginnings spoiled by dismal failure. In fact the germs of decay and disintegration were inherent in the Afghan body politic. Apart from the tribal traditions which assigned the position of *primus inter pares* to the king, the distracted condition of the kingdom, to which Buhlul suceeded, put a premium on the personal ability and. tact of the king. It was not only that powerful states like Jaunpur, Malwa and Gwalior surrounded the Lodi empire; there were powerful chieftains within the empire itself, and they were loth to tender a willing allegance to the king. That was the legacy of the weak Sayyids. For, "in the time of Alam Shah the province of Multan had elected a ruler of its own, who never recognised, even formally, the royal authority and the rest of the Punjab as far south as Panipat and Hissar, was in the possession of Buhlul, whose relative Darya Khan Lodi held the district of Sambhal, the western limit of which he had pushed forward as far as the ford of Khvaja Khizu, on the Jumna near Delhi. Adjoining this petty state on the south was the state of Koil held by Isa Khan the Turk, and south of this state Hasan Khan, another Afghan, held Rapri. The lower Central Doab including Bhongaon, Patali and Kampil was held by the Rajput Raja Pratap, and to the west of the Jumna Daud Khan Auhadi, was independent in Bayana. Gwalior was an independent Hindu state, and such tracts of Mewar as did not acknowledge the rule of Daud Auhadi were held by native chieftains whose power extended almost to the gates of Delhi."[1] The Lodi tenure of power was, in

1. *C.H.I.*, Vol III, p. 225-226.

view of these divisions, highly precarious. They had not only to curb the pretensions of these, they had to successfully combat the aggressive designs of states like Jaunpur.

Indeed the whole reign of Buhlul was spent in incessant activities directed to the achievement of these two objects, and be it said to his credit that he succeeded admirably. Hardly had a year passed after his accession to the throne when the king of Jaunpur started trouble, and frequently invaded his kingdom. Inspite of the fact that Buhlul had to reckon with rebellious nobles, he not only successfully resisted his attacks, but actually annexed Jaunpur in 1486. Side by side he forced Darya Khan Lodi, Isa Khan, Mubarak Khan, Raja Pratap and Qutab Khan to submit to his authority. When he died he left to his son Sikandar Lodi (1489) an extensive and orderly kingdom. Sikandar's reign too was not devoid of troubles, but his ability and tact made him triumphant in the end. He attacked Bihar but did not gain much thereby. He reorganised the administration of Jaunpur and Sambhal, which had been brought under his direct control. When he demanded the daughter of Phaphamau King Salibahan, he was refused and an attack on the strong-hold of the Hindu king failed. His frequent invasions of the Gwalior state crippled its power, though he failed to annex it. He even formed designs of conquering Malwa. Though on the whole his reign was marked by vigour and promptitude he could not bridle the turbulence and violent temper of his tribesmen. He was apprehensive of his own nobles "who did not hesitate to belabour one another with sticks in his presence" and so far as possilbe kept them in good humour. But in this he did not succeed as well as his father Buhlul, of whom it is said that if at any time the nobles "were displeased with him, he tried so hard to pacify them, that he would himself go to their houses, ungird his sword from his waist, and place it before the offended party; nay, he would sometimes take off his turban from his head and solicit forgiveness saying 'if you think me unworthy of the station I occupy, choose some one else, and bestow on me some other office.' He maintained a friendly intercourse with all his chiefs and soldiers. If any one was ill, he would himself go and attend on him."[1] Instead

1. Tarikh-i-Daudi; Elliot and Dowson, IV, p. 436-437.

of conciliating Sikandar was of a domineering nature, and it was he who began the work of centralization, and of destroying the power of his nobles. He used to remove by underhand means nobles, on whom his suspicion fell and confiscated their property.This policy begun by him was carried to a logical conclusion by his son Ibrahim Lodi, whose inferior abilities proved his ruin. Ibrahim ascended the throne in 1517. His reign started with a civil war with his brother Jalal Khan and it showed in a lurid light the nature of loyalty of the Afghan nobles. Then he invaded Gwalior, which was annexed by him. But this success turned his head and he "now gave rein to those groundless and unreasonable suspicions of his nobles which prompted acts of capricious tyranny, and at length drove those who might have been the staunchest defenders of the throne into the arms of an invader."[1] He encompassed the destruction of Azami Humayun and his sons by treacherous devices and followed it up by that of Shaikh Hussain Qarmali governor of Chanderi. This incensed the nobles, and a wave of sullen resentment spread through the realm. Darya Khan Lohani governor of Bihar, Khan Jahan Lodi and others raised the standard of rebellion, but Ibrahim was inexorable. A stickler of etiquette he treated the nobles with very great harshness and humiliation that was entirely incompatible with the treatment of Buhlul. When Buhlul "in his social meetings—never sat on throne and would not allow his nobles to stand; and even during public audiences he did not occupy the throne, but seated himself upon a carpet"[2] Ibrahim made them all stand in the Durbar and quail before him. At this juncture Bahadur Khan, the son of Darya Khan Lohani proclaimed himself king in Bihar and he was joined by Nazir Khan Lohani, governor of Ghazipur. Daulat Khan Lodi, warned by his son, of the evil designs of the king on his life openly showed disaffection and invited Babar seeking his aid against the tyrant. But when all these ominous developments were taking place Babar was knocking at the gate of Hindustan.

Thus within five years of his assumption of royal office Ibrahim had undermined the prestige of his dynasty and the

1. *C.H.I.*. Vol. III. p. 249.

2. Tarikh-i-Daudi; Elliot and Dowson, IV, page 437.

stability of his empire. It was only a reaction to his efforts at centralization of power and at the establishment of absolute kingship. The nature of Afghan monarchy and the traditions of Afghan tribes contributed in a large measure to frustrate his attempts. The Afghan monarchy was essentially of a feudal type, and a spirit of excessive individualism characterized the Afghan tribes. He forgot that even in the time of Sikandar Lodi the Afghans enjoyed a considerable measure of independence. It is recorded that "one half of the whole country was assigned in jagir to the Farmulis, and the other half to the other Afghan tribes. At this time Lohanis and Farmulis predominated. The districts of Saran and Champaran were held by Mian Hussain, Oudh, Ambala and Hodhna by Mian Muhammad Kala Pahar; Kanauj by Mian Gadai; Shamsabad, Thanesar and Shahabad by Mian Imad; Marhara by Tartar Khan, brother of Mian Muhammad; and Hariana, Desua and other detached parganas by Khwajaji Shaikh Said. The chief of the Sarwanis was Azam Humayun and the principal chieftain of the Lodies were four; Mahmud Khan, who had Kalpi as jagir; Mian Alam to whom Etawah and Chandwa were assigned; Mubarak Khan whose jagir was Lucknow; and Daulat Khan who held Lahore".[1] Some kept great establishments "Azam Humayun, jagirdar of Karra, had 45,000 horse under his command and 700 elephants. Among those of lesser note were Daulat Khan, who had 4000 cavalry; Ali Khan Ushe who had 4000 also; Firoz Khan Sarwani who had 6000. Ahmad Khan also, the son of Jamal Khan Sarangkhani, when he was appointed to Jaunpur, had 20,000 cavalry under him."[2] Further so far as the Punjab was concerned the Lodis "never ventured to tax the loyalty of their officials"[3] and "were content with such acknowledgment of their supremacy as was indicated by occasional remittances of tribute or revenue." Ibrahim Lodi in the face of these facts committed a blunder when he deliberately determined to destroy the power of the military aristocracy. He had not the requisite resources for the task and perhaps the attempt was premature. At any rate he had detected the disease that was eating into the vitals of his empire no

1. Elliot and Dowson, Vol. IV, Wakiat-i-Mushtaki pp. 547-48.
2. Ibid pp. 545-46.
3. *C.H.I.*, Vol. III, page 241.

doubt but he had tried a remedy which was not well designed. Hence he failed, and his failure was the cause of the rise of the Mughal power in India.

"From the year 910" says Babar "when I obtained the principality of Kabul up to the date of events I now record (i.e. the defeat of Sultan Ibrahim Lodi), I had never ceased to think of the conquest of Hindustan." That was because he claimed it as his own by right of descent from Ameer Taimur. But it was not before full fifteen years had passed after the conquest of Kabul that he could give definite shape to his thought. The time chosen was also most favourable, for the purpose. Ibrahim Lodi had filled his home with troubles; his kingdom was seething with discontent. Punjab, on which Babar had set his heart was just the portion of his empire, which was ready to sever allegiance and welcome a foreign invader. Babar undertook his first two expeditions against the Yusufzais in 1519. These were of a pioneer nature meant to strike terror into the hearts of the frontier tribes, so that he might later have a clear line of communication between his base i.e. Kabul and his scene of operation i.e. the Punjab. But he advanced pretty far i.e. up to Bhira and sent from there Mulla Murshid as his ambassador to Ibrahim Lodi, asking for the surrender of the Punjab. This ambassador did not reach his destination, having been detained by Daulat Khan Lodi at Lahore. Encouraged by his success in the first two expeditions, he undertook a third in 1520 and advanced even farther than before. He reached Sialkot on the Chenab and it readily surrendered. There was only one more line of defence, i.e. the Ravi, which when forced, Lahore the capital of the Punjab would fall. But Babar could not effect it, for he had to meet the situation in Qandahar, and it was not before another four years had passed that he could undertake his fourth expedition.

In the meanwhile significant developments had taken place in the affairs of Ibrahim. Daulat Khan definitely alienated, had renounced his allegiance, and invited Babar to come to depose Ibrahim and set up Alam Khan on the throne instead. This was the finest opportunity for Babar and specially when there was no trouble at home to distract attention. But the pusillanimity of Daulat Khan during the first three expeditions of Babar is inexplicible, and equally so is the indifference of Ibrahim Lodi. It is a mystery why neither Ibrahim nor Daulat Khan stirred a finger to check the raids of Babar. They had thereby encouraged Babar and when Daulat Khan actually invited him, he became confident of his success. But his fourth expedition disillusioned Babar about the reality of Daulat Khan's intentions and of his prospective occupation of the Punjab. He realized that the deposition of Ibrahim Lodi was, for Daulat Khan, a preliminary to his establishment in the Punjab in entire independence, and Babar was to be for the purpose used as an instrument. The conflict of interests was inevitable.

Babar embarked on his fourth expedition in 1524, and occupied Lahore after defeating an imperial army in the vicinity of that city. This army had been despatched by Ibrahim Lodi to punish Daulat Khan for his treasonable designs, and Daulat Khan had been defeated and driven out. Here Babar realized that the occupation of the Punjab, necessarily involved a trial of strength with Ibrahim Lodi. Then at Dipalpur he met the fugitive Daulat Khan, and if at Lahore Babar was disillusioned about the reality of the occupation of the Punjab, at Dipalpur he was disillusioned about the reality of Daulat Khan's intentions. Daulat Khan resented the division of the districts of the Punjab by Babar, who retained Lahore to himself and assigned to him Jalandhar and Sultanpur, and meditated treachery. Fortunately for Babar, Dilawar Khan Daulat Khan's son divulged his father's designs and Daulat Khan was imprisoned with his other son Ghazi Khan. They were however released a little later, and then Babar returned to his country for reinforcements. After the departure of Babar, Daulat Khan gathered army, drove out Alam Khan from his jagir, made a futile attempt on Sialkot and even succeeded in dispersing an imperial detachment sent to punish him. In the meanwhile Alam Khan, who had gone to seek the aid of Babar at Kabul, after his expulsion from Dipalpur, returned with an order from Babar commanding his officers to help him against Daulat Khan, but as soon as he set his foot in the Punjab, he was won over by Daulat Khan. The allies now advanced upon Delhi but were defeated by Ibrahim Lodi in person near Delhi. Apprised of all these incidents Babar started on his fifth and last expedition and sweeping off all opposition before him he over-ran the whole of the Punjab, forced Daulat Khan and Alam Khan to submit, and then passed on to the banks of the Jumna, opposite Sirsawa enroute to Panipat. On the 21st April 1526 ensued that fateful encounter, on the field of Panipat, which resulted in the defeat and death of Ibrahim Lodi. One chapter of Babar's life closed and another opened and with this began also the groundwork of Mughal empire in India.

This was the first great clash between the Afghans and the Mughals. The Mughals did no doubt come out victorious by their superior organization and military skill, but this did not decide once for all that they should be supreme in Hindustan. Many a battle had yet to be fought, many a political problem solved and many a reverse of fortune patiently borne before the empire of Hindustan passed to them. It is a long drawn struggle--this struggle for power between the Afghans and Mughals and is full of human interest. Great sacrifices willingly made, innumerable difficulties bravely overcome, and some clever acts of diplomacy mark the Mughal side of the struggle. The first battle of Panipat did only the setting of the scene. Babar had only dethroned the Lodi dynasty; he had not conquered the Afghan empire; for the Afghan empire belonged virtually to the Afghan tribes and these had to be crushed before the sceptre of Hindustan passed into the hands of the Mughals. The Afghans, on the other hand, were no ordinary nemies. Their wily nature, wonderful bravery, dogged resistance and all these animated by an indomitable spirit of racial pride made the tenure of Mughal power highly precarious in Hindustan. Their long residence in the country as against the exotic origin of the Mughal, helped the former win the sympathy of the people. The Mughals had to get over this disability before they could firmly establish themselves in Hindustan. That is why the Mughals were once expelled from Hindustan, and the Afghans revived their lost power. And even then the Afghans could not long retain their sway. The Mughals wrested it from them and then crushed all the recrudescence of Afghan pretensions by a combination of military power and clever diplomacy. In fact it was more by means of diplomacy that they uprooted the Afghan power and destroyed the last vestiges of it; and their diplomacy had been mainly directed towards the winning of popular sympathy and Rajput support. The matrimonial alliance with the powerful Rajput houses, their respect for Hindu susceptibilities, made their rule extremely popular. All these were initiated by Akbar, and he it was who laid deeply and truly the foundation of the Mughal empire. A lesson had been learnt by the Mughals after their expulsion from India. So long as the Afghan power had not been destroyed root and branch, the Mughals could not found a stable empire in Hindustan, and for this popular sympathy and Rajput support were indispensable. This had been accomplished by 1630 about a century after the first battle of Panipat (1526). Thus the period between 1526 abd 1630 falls into three phases: the first from 1526 to 1540 characterised by Mughal domination; the second from 1540-1556, characterized by the expulsion of the Mughals and the revival of Afghan power under the Surs; and the third the revival of the Mughal empire and the destruction of Afghan power in India from 1556 to 1630. That is in brief the picture of the three periods of Mughal Afghan struggle for supremacy in India.

The battle of Panipat inaugurated an era of deadly contest and prepared the way for the battle of Khanwa. Babar's work of founding an empire had only begun and he now realised the magnitude of the task before him. "Every where the leaders of the Afghan tribes set themselves up as independent chiefs, and fortified themselves in convenient strong-holds. Kasim Sambali set himself up in Sambal; Nizam Khan in Biana;Hasan Khan Mewati in Mewat; Muhammad Zaitun in Dholpur; Tartar Khan Sarangkhani in Gwalior; Hussain Khan Lohani in Rabiri; Kutb Khan in Etawa; Alam Khan in Kalpi—Kanauj and the whole country beyond the Ganges, was still entirely in the power of formidable enemies like Nasir Khan Lohani and Maaruf Farmuli. The Afghans of this quarter set up a certain Bahadur Khan—under the name of Sultan Muhammad." Babar had to reduce the power of these chieftains. In the accomplishment of this task the immense military prestige,that he had gained on account of his victory at Panipat, and his determination to stay in Hindustan stood in good stead. Many of the petty chieftains dreaded his might and quietly submitted. So were Shaikh Guren. Shaikh Baizid,

Mustafa Farmuli, Firoz Khan, Mahmud Khan Lohani and others. They brought their armies also and joined Babar who thus had a fresh accession of strength. Then Babar thought of a brilliant device of reducing the country. "He made grants of towns and fortresses yet unconquered to prominent men and then sent them off with a small force to take possession." In this way Sambal fell to Humayun, Rabiri to Muhammad Ali Jang-Jang, Etawa to Mahdi Khwaja, Kanauj to Muhammad Duldai, Dholpur to Sultan Junaid Barlas. Thus a fair part of the Doab and a few districts outside it, were brought under the Mughal sway. In the meanwhile the Afghans in the east had viewed the proceedings of Babar with some alarm, and were massing their troops at Kanauj to force a battle. Humayun was despatched for the purpose, and he beat them steadily back and captured Jaunpur, Ghazipur and Kalpi. At this juncture he was ordered to give up further operation and returned to join Babar who had declared a holy war on Rana Sanga.

That was about the beginning of February 1527, and on the 16th of March 1527 was fought the battle of Khanwa, which shattered the strength of the Rajput confederacy under Rana Sanga and placed Babar in a position of unassailable power and military prestige. An empire had been definitely won, and it had now to be kept and continued. That was a task which involved firstly the destruction of the disgruntled Afghan military aristocracy and secondly the building up of an absolute monarchy on the ruins of Afghan political traditions consisting in the diffusion of power and feudal character of king-ship. The first was accomplished by Babar. He was a mighty warrior and he inflicted crushing blows on the Afghan nobility till at last it was prostrate. Between 1527 and 1529, whether the Afghan nobles were confronted individually or in league, they were invariably beaten. Husain Khan Lohani was defeated and drowned while crossing the Jumna, and Chandwa and Rabiri were occupied. Kutb Khan surrendered Etawa, and Biban, lord of Lucknow, also abandoned his possessions which fell into the hands of the invaders. But while Babar was busy besieging Chanderi, the Afghans in the east, headed by Biban and Baizid, had defeated a Mughal detachment and had occupied Lucknow. Babar, therefore, after the capture of Chanderi confronted the rebels in person, and defeated them at Kanuaj (12th-15th March 1528). The Afghans fled away pursued by a Mughal commander. They then took shelter in Bihar and Bengal and it was not till May 1529 that Babar was called upon to confront them again. Helped this time by the king of Bengal, who alone brought 24 divisions of the army into the field, they threatened the eastern possessions of Babar. At the battle of Gogra (6th May 1529) Babar met the confederates and routed them after fierce fighting. The rebels were dispersed and never after this disaster did they venture to trouble Babar, till his death in December 1530. Thus Babar successfully accomplished one of the two tasks; he had crushed the Afghan nobility and thus contributed to the work of Sher Shah. If Sher Shah built up a system of absolute kingship by centralizing power, it had been facilitated by the work of Babar. Had he not crushed the power of the Afghan nobility, the constructive work of Sher Shah might have been retarded by the revival of Afghan tribal traditions. Thus if Sher Shah contributed to the work of Akbar, Babar had contributed to that of Sher Shah, and it is on that account that Babar should have some credit also.

As for the other task, i.e,. the building up of an absolute monarchy he had no time for it. He had hardly succeeded in wresting power from his Afghan enemies when he was laid in the grave. Establishment of absolute monarchy in a country where there was none lately, involved centralization of power. Centralization of power again presupposes the maintenance of an efficient standing army, and a sound financial system that would help maintain a standing army. Babar had a standing army that was efficient but he had not a sound financial system. Indeed he had not been able to creat one. It is at this juncture that he died, and the difficulties under which he laboured and which did not adversely affect his tenure of power, recoiled with redoubled force on his son Humayun. And when that was combined with Humayun's lack of the genius for leadership as also with his generosity to a fault, we can understand why he was a failure, why he was expelled from India by Sher Shah who was strong in those very virtues which Humayun lacked.

Babar left to his son a fairly big kingdom in India comprising the whole of the Punjab, Sirhind, Hisar Firoza, Delhi and the Doab, Mewat, Biana, Agra, Gwalior, Kalpi, Kanauj, Sambhal, Lucknow, Khairabad, Oudh, Jaunpur, Karra-Manikpur, Bihar, Sirohi, Champaran, Gundega (?) and eight chiefships.[1] Besides these there were the transfrontier possessions of Kabul, Quandahar and Badakshan. But soon after his accession to the throne Humayun assigned the transfrontier possessions to Kamran, Sambhal to Askari and Mewat to Hindal in consonance with the traditions of his house. That the measure was beset with troubles, was realised a little later. Kamran whose ambition knew no limits, and who always considered himself better fitted to occupy the throne, now showed himself in true colours. On the pretext of visiting Lahore he occupied it and along with it all its dependencies (1532). Humayun was not in a position to chastise him, and hence he not only granted the Punjab to him, he also bestowed upon him Hisar Firoza in a fit of generosity. When Humayun's power was thus suffering diminution owing to the reckless ambition of his own brother ominous developments were taking place in the east, and the Afghans were fast rising under Sher Shah to menace the sway of the Mughals. The annals of the next few years centre round the personality of Sher Shah.

The rise of Sher Shah embodied the revival of Afghan power in India, and the chief point of interest in his life was that he displayed a constructive genius of the highest order, and founded and organized empire on sound bureaucratic lines—a thing that is rarely noticed amongst the Afghans. Farid, for that was the early name of Sher Shah, was the son of Hasan Khan, and the grandson of Ibrahim Khan Sur. Ibrahim had served several nobles of distinction under the Lodies and lived for a long time at Hisar Firoza where his son Hasan was born. In his youth Hasan served Raimal a Hindu officer of great note and probably picked up a working knowledge of revenue administration. Then he came to Bihar and served Nasir Khan Lohani, Daulat Khan Lohani and Biban Khan Jilwani one after another, and became so famous for his honesty that when Jamal Khan came as the governor of Jaunpur, he took him in his service.

1. Elliot and Dowson, Vol. IV, p. 262.

Hasan received three jagirs viz. Sahasaram, Khawaspur and Tanda from him on the condition of maintaining five hundred horse.

Farid was the eldest of the eight sons of Hasan. Born in 1486, he left his father's abode and went to Jaunpur at the age of fifteen owing to the partiality of his father towards the sons of his step-mother, a Hindu concubine raised to the status of wife, who had monopolised the love of old Farid. When Hasan came to know this, he requested Jamal Khan his chief, to persuade his son to return home. Jamal Khan tried his utmost to send Farid back but the latter protested and was allowed to remain in Jaunpur There Farid devoted himself to the study of languages, Quranic laws and commentaries and soon made his mark as a scholar. He was fond of the learned society and men of saintly character. About the year 1511 his father came to Jaunpur summoned by Jamal Khan to render military service and there heard of the reputation of his son which made him extremely happy. Hasan Khan was prevailed upon by his relatives to conciliate his son, and he did act accordingly. Farid was persuaded to go home and to manage the jagirs during his father's absence. Farid consented to the latter proposal on the condition that he was given absolute discretion in dealing with all the affairs and persons in the jagirs. Since Hasan agreed Farid came and took over the charge of the jagirs (1511) . For about eight years he managed them with great ability. He reduced to submission the unruly zamindars in the jagirs, drove to destruction all those who had persisted in disturbing the peace and prosperity of the people and protected the peasantry by a re-assessment of the land based on a system of survey and kabuliats in writing by which the peasants agreed to pay a certain rent. An exception was made where the local custom of only a divison of crops prevailed. These activities improved the condition of the jagirs and when Mian Hasan returned home (1519) he was overjoyed not only to find that his jagirs were prosperous, but also to hear that everyone spoke highly of the abilities and work of Farid. Farid would have continued in the management of jagirs had it not been for the intrigues of his step-mother who wanted her son Suleiman to take up the management. After a good deal of wavering Hasan consented and when Farid was apprised of it he left his paternal home and took service with Daulat Khan Lodi, one of the leading nobles at the court of Agra. Soon after died Mian Hasan and on the request of Farid Daulat Khan procured for him an imperial Farman conferring the jagirs on Farid and an imperial detachement to reinstate him in his possessions to the prejudice of his step-brother Suleiman. When Farid came back to his jagirs thus armed, Suleiman unable to offer resistance fled to Muhammad Khan Sur, Jagirdar of the pargana Chaund, a dependency of Baxar. Since the patron of Suleiman was more powerful and in those days of insecurity when Ibrahim Lodi's rule was disturbed by the rebellion of the Afghans, Ibrahim's farman was not likely to avail him much. Hence he attached himself to the service of Muhammad Shah who had set up his independence in Bihar. Farid served him faithfully and won his favour by unflinch-

the rebels had fled away Khan with his mother tendered submission to Babar and so did Sher Khan. Babar re-instated Jalal Khan and Sher Khan in their own position and returned to Agra. Jalal became the lord of Bihar acting through his mother Dudu, who became the Regent and Sher Khan became the Deputy of Dudu. When a little later Dudu died Sher Khan became nominally the Deputy of Jalal Khan, but virtually the master of the state. Sher Khan was an apostle of absolutism, and he proceeded to give effect to this principle by depriving the nobles of their jagirs, by insisting upon the regular payment of royal revenues and by safeguarding the popular interest against all aristocratic rapacity. In four years he had dealt a death-blow to the power of the nobility, promoted the welfare of the people, and had won the loyalty of the army "so much so that within the frontiers of Bihar no one dared disobey his orders." During this period he acquired the fort of Chunar. When Sher Khan was consolidating his power there came Mahmud Lodi again helped by the king of Bengal Nasrat Shah, to cross swords with Humayun who after his father's death had succeeded to the throne. The belligerants met at the battle of Doura (July 1531) and there Mahmud Lodi was not only beaten but was put to flight after the death of was actuated by this principle when he was the king of India would be seen later on. At any rate the reply incensed Muhammad Khan very much, and he sent an army against him and got him expelled. Then Suleiman and his brother got possession of the jagirs.

Expelled from his jagirs Farid went to the shelter of Junaid Barlas, the Mughal governor of Jaunpur, and serving him for two or three months at Jaunpur accompanied him to Agra where he was presented to Babar by the middle of 1527. He took part in the siege of Chanderi by Babar and accompanied the latter in his south Bihar campaign in the hot weather of 1528 and served him as a guide. In the meanwhile Muhammad Shah had died and his minor son Jalal Khan had succeeded to the throne. The change of succession had given rise to all sorts of troubles and Babar's invasion was therefore most opportune. His invasion scared away every body and Muhammad Khan Sur and Suleiman fled away from their jagirs. Sher Khan owing to his services to Babar was given his own jagirs as well as those of Muhammad Khan Sur. But he did not retain that of Muhammad Khan and after inviting him back he handed over his jagirs to him. Thus he won over an enemy and converted him into a staunch ally.

Now the Afghan leaders Maruf, Biban and Baizid set up Mahmud Lodi in the place of Muhammad Shah as the king of the Afghans (September 1528). Sher Khan in order to avoid suspicion that he was a creature of the Mughals took service with him and joined him when he marched against the Mughals about the end of 1528. The activities of Mahmud Lodi had frightened Jalal Khan, the minor son of Muhammad Shah who fled away towards Bengal and at the same time made Babar furious. The latter started immediately to drive out the Afghans. On the 5th March 1529 Mahmud Lodi was forced to retreat, but as Babar pursued him he was joined by the king of Bengal Nasrat Shah's Governor Makhdumi Alam, who was then campaigning in the Tirhut and other adjoining districts, and brought his twenty-four divisions of army to the battle of Gogra (6th May 1529). The defeat of the allies was followed by the flight of the Afghan nobles like Maruf and Baizid westward towards Lucknow and of Mahmud Lodi eastward into Bengal, where he found shelter with Nasrat Shah. After the rebels had fled away Khan with his mother tendered submission to Babar and so did Sher Khan. Babar re-instated Jalal Khan and Sher Khan in their own position and returned to Agra. Jalal became the lord of Bihar acting through his mother Dudu, who became the Regent and Sher Khan became the Deputy of Dudu. When a little later Dudu died Sher Khan became nominally the Deputy of Jalal Khan, but virtually the master of the state. Sher Khan was an apostle of absolutism, and he proceeded to give effect to this principle by depriving the nobles of their jagirs, by insisting upon the regular payment of royal revenues and by safeguarding the popular interest against all aristocratic rapacity. In four years he had dealt a death-blow to the power of the nobility, promoted the welfare of the people, and had won the loyalty of the army "so much so that within the frontiers of Bihar no one dared disobey his orders." During this period he acquired the fort of Chunar. When Sher Khan was consolidating his power there came Mahmud Lodi again helped by the king of Bengal Nasrat Shah, to cross swords with Humayun who after his father's death had succeeded to the throne. The belligerants met at the battle of Doura (July 1531) and there Mahmud Lodi was not only beaten but was put to flight after the death of his partisans Biban and Baizid. Doura cleared the way for Sher Khan to rise by removing the Afghan nobles and their leader from his path.

After the battle of Doura, Humayun set his heart on the conquest of Chunar and besieged it. When it came to the verge of surrender Sher Khan submitted and sent his son to serve the emperor with a contingent. This pleased Humayun and he, on the importunities of Sher Khan-left it under him. This was a mistake for which Humayun was to repent later on. But for the time being Sher Khan had outwitted him. Since Chunar secured his western frontier Sher Khan now turned to the east. Here he found Makhdumi Alam seditiously disposed towards his master Mahmud Shah who had succeeded Nasrat Shah in Bengal, and made friend-ship with him. He aided him against the king of Bengal, but could not save him. Sher Khan's alliance with Makhdumi Alam had made him the enemy of the king of Bengal and after the death of Makhdumi Alam he determined to attack Sher Khan. Meanwhile troubles were brewing for Sher Khan at home and he had become the object of court conspiracy in which the Lohani nobles, deprived of their jagirs and therefore burning in revenge had joined hands with Jalal Khan, who also had been smarting under the tutelage of Sher Khan (July-September 1533). Now it was decided that Jalal Khan should go and face the invader while Sher Khan remained in charge of the administration. The motive was that Jalal Khan with the malcontents should march out with an army; instead of fighting Mahmud Shah of Bengal he would join him; enter Bihar in combination with him; and then driving out his masterful deputy Sher Khan, become king both in name and in fact. The plan materialised in every detail except the last. After the desertion of Jalal Khan to the enemy (December 1533) Sher Khan became virtually the lord of Bihar. But Sher Khan had yet to meet the confederate forces of the two kings, i.e., Jalal Khan and Mahmud Shah. That came about at the battle of Surajagarh (March 1534) and be it said to his credit that he won a complete victory over the confederate forces. It was a moral victory for Sher Khan apart from anything else. By deserting to the enemy Jalal Khan had discredited himself and by defeating the enemy Sher Khan had become the saviour of the people. Now he was the real ruler of the country. But his position was some-what anomalous. He was a vassal of the Mughals and at the same time lord of Bihar. Yet Sher Khan did not tear off the screen of Mughal vassalage. This caution stood him in good stead and gave no room for the suspicion of the Mughals. That is why Humayun could with an easy heart start on his famous expedition against Bahadur Shah of Gujrat (February 1535).

But Sher Khan knew how far he could go with safety. He recalled his son as soon as the emperor started for Malwa. And if Humayun opened his campaign against Bahadur Shah in February 1535, Sher Khan opened his against Mahmud Shah of Bengal in May 1535. He conquered the whole of Monghyr district by July and when he realized that Humayun was in no position to return soon, he determined to follow up his victory after the rainy season. In January 1536 he marched on Gaur but finding the way through the Telia Ghari passes blocked by the Portuguese, who had been drawn into an alliance by Mahmud Shah and had been charged with the defence of the passes, Sher Khan abandoned that route, took another and less frequented one, called the Jharkhand route and appeared before Gaur by the end of February 1536. That frightened Mahmud Shah and inspite of the remonstrances of the Portuguese, he made peace with Sher Khan by offering him 13 lacs of gold and by ceding territories from Kiul to Sikriagali, 90 miles long and 30 miles broad. It was a brilliant achievement, and raised Sher Khan to the highest distinction among the Afghans.

This event synchronised with the flight of Bahadur Shah to Diu, to the Shelter of the Portuguese, and therefore all those who had found a refuge in his court now came and joined Sher Khan. He became the rallying point of the scattered Afghan nobility and this naturally increased his self-confidence. But a new danger threatened him. Humayun who had come back from his Gujrat and Malwa campaign looked upon with suspicion the proceedings of Sher Khan and Mahmud Shah was expecting help from the Portuguese. Sher Khan on the other hand was anxious to complete the conquest of Bengal for he had seen the richness of the prize and the weakness of its defenders. As he waited to watch the further developments, Humayun sent Hindu Beg, the governor of Jaunpur, to report on the conduct of Sher Khan; and Mahmud Shah sent Alfanso Vaz De Britto to Goa for help from the Portuguese viceroy. Since Hindu Beg's report was favourable and it lulled the suspicions of the emperor, Sher Khan embarked on his second invasion of Bengal (October 1537), and thus forestalled the designs of Mahmud Shah who was only waiting for the arrival of the Portuguese to commence hostilities. The latter arrived with 9 ships at Chittagong in the winter of 1537, but Sher Khan was prepared for it. He started by conquering the outlying districts of Bengal, especially Chittagong from its Portuguese governor and then besieged Gaur. But at this juncture an unexpected enemy appeared on the scene. The second invasion of Sher Khan had changed the attitude of Humayun and he started to punish him in the second week of December 1537. Sher Khan was in a fix. The siege of Gaur had just begun and the Portuguese though expelled from Chittagong had been watching for an opportunity to join hands with Mahmud Shah, while from the west Humayun was coming with all his fury.

Sher Khan made a quick decision of the course of action, he had to pursue, and determined to oppose Humayun at Chunar as long as possible in order that he might complete the conquest of Gaur undisturbed. It had been anticipated that Humayun would reach Chunar sooner, because the distance was shorter from Agra than from Gaur. Hence Sher Khan made all possible haste and before Humayun arrived there he had thrown a garrison into Chunar, provisioned it and removed from it women and children to Bahrkunda, a fortress in the interior. Now Humayun began the siege of the fortress in January 1538 and it was not before the middle of May 1538 that the fort surrendered. Of course Sher Khan had anticipated it, and therefore had removed the women and children still farther into the fortress of Rohtas, which he had acquired by treachery from its Hindu king. That was in March 1538 and on the 6th April Gaur surrendered to his son Jalal Khan and his general Khawas Khan, who had been conducting the siege in the absence of Sher Khan.

After the fall of Chunar there were peace-talks on both sides, but they fell through and Humanyun marched on to invade Bengal. On the way the fugitive king of Bengal—Mahmud Shah met him and tendered his allegiance. But Sher Khan was not prepared to allow Humaun a free passage into Bengal till he had removed the treasures of Gaur to Rohtas. Hence he deputed his son Jalal Khan to defend the pass and detain the Mughals. Jalal Khan carried out the commission and abandoned the pass when so directed by his father after the latter had returned from Gaur and deposited all the treasure at Rohtas (September 1538), Now Humayun entered Bengal and occupied Gaur without any difficulty. Then followed a period of six months' sensual torpor, when Humayun forgot his responsibilities, and when Sher Khan cut off the communication between Agra and Gaur and conquered the whole country right up to Benares and Jaunpur. Chunar was conquered from its Mughal governor and so was Benares. Only Jaunpur held out for long. About the end of December 1538 Sher Khan's rapid conquest and continuous interception of intelligence disturbed the repose of the emperor and he decided to quit Bengal. He made arrangements for the administration of the country and left Jahangir Beg with

5000 troops for the purpose, By the beginning of March 1539 he issued from Bengal and followed by Sher Khan came to a halt at Chaunsa. Sher Khan was encamped on the western and the Mughals on the eastern bank of a small stream flowing between Chaunsa and Baxar. From this position the emperor could neither attack Sher Khan with advantage nor could he continue his retreat. In this position both the parties remained till the rainy season set in, when they shifted to high positions. But for Humayun the situation was becoming critical. Though two months and a half had elapsed, no reinforcements arrived from Agra, whither had been sent Shaikh Bahol to persuade Hindal to come to the aid of his brother. Instead of helping Humayun his brothers—Hindal at first and Kamran later on, were indulging in ambitious schemes, prejudical to the interest of the dynasty. They even treated with scant attention the wise counsel of Mir Fateh Ali the governor of Delhi and Yadgar Nasir Mirza. Since no help was forthcoming from Agra Humayun sent one Shaikh Khalil to Sher Khan to negotiate for peace. Sher Khan dictated his terms, which included the surrender of Chunar with all the territories to the east of it. Humayun in consistence with his dignity could not accept them, and the negotiations fell through.

Now Sher Khan made secret preparations for a surprise attack for he had learnt from Shaik Kalil, whom he had bribed, that Humayun's army had become demoralised. Thus encouraged, he attacked the imperial camp on the morning of the 27th June 1539, routed and dispersed the army and captured the imperial family along with a large booty. Humayun escaped swimming across the river, assisted by a water-carrier and fled away towards the capital Humayun had lost all expcept life; Sher Khan had won all except the throne of Delhi. This was the first great defeat of the Mughals by the Afghans and the credit was entirely Sher Khan's. From Chaunsa Sher Khan returned to Bengal where he drove to destruction Jahagir Beg with all his 5000 Mughal veterans, systematically reduced the country to subjection and crowned himself king at Gaur with the style Sher Shah (December 1539). One phase of his rise was over. He had worked his way up from the position of a petty jagirdar of Bihar to that of the king of Bengal and

Bihar. He had fought on equal terms with the Mughal emperor and had defeated him. Such was his achievement of the past few years and that was not all. Still greater achievements and higher laurels were yet to be his.

King of Bengal and Bihar, vanquisher of the Mughal emperor, and the champion of Afghan independence, Sher Shah now aspired for the throne of Delhi and before trying to wrest it from Humayun he wanted to make adequate preparation for it. He sent two ambassadors, one to Malwa and the other to Gujrat, requesting the aid of their kings against Humayun. He perhaps had anticipated that since Humayun had, a few years back, over-run these two countries, their kings would now have no hesitation in creating a diversion in his favour by attacking Humayun from the south-west and thus the Mughal emperor would be harassed on all sides. But he was disappointed because Gujrat was in a state of confusion and in Malwa Qadir Shah became offended with him. Meanwhile Sher Shah had embarked on his expedition against the Mughals (February 1540) and had come as far as Prayag. There he detached his son Kutb Khan with a rather small army, because he had anticipated help from Malwa. Kutb Khan was to march up along the southern fringe of the Doab, while he himself marched along the northern fringe, thus taking Humayun on both the flanks. Kutb Khan, however, fighting single-handed was badly beaten at the battle of Kalpi and slain. Sher Shah met Humayun near Kanauj (17th May 1540), defeated him and put him to flight. This defeat of Humayun like the first was due to the short-sighted and selfish policy of Kamran. On the eve of the battle of Kanauj, Kamran left his brother to his own fate and went away with his 11,000 war-hardened soldiers to Lahore at a time when Humayun did not have an army worth the name with which to fight Sher Shah. Hence the inevitable came to pass. Defeated for the second time, Humayun fled away evacuating Agra and Delhi and reached Lahore with his family and two brothers Hindal and Askari. Behind him followed Sher Shah took possession of the capital and proclaimed himself king. With this began another chapter in the career of Sher Shah. He had redeemed the honour of the Afghans and had wrested the throne of Delhi for them. But the throne thus wrested had to be retained and the Mughals beaten had to be expelled from India. To the accomplishment of these he now turned his attention.

At Lahore, when all the brothers met and conferred together Humayun tried to persuade Kamran to combine their resources and oppose the usurper. But from the beginning, the spirit of the confernce was vitiated by the treacherous designs of Kamran, who had opened overtures with Sher Shah to seize and surrender Humayun in case he was allowed to retain the Punjab. This state of Mughal affairs emboldened Sher Shah and he attacked the Punjab and made a clean sweep of all these quarrelling brothers of whom Humayun, Askari and Hindal fled towards Sind and Kamran fled towards Kabul. He pursued them as far as Khushab and from there he returned to Bhira leaving Khawas Khan to pursue Humayun and Haibat Khan Niazi to pursue Kamran. From Bhira he wanted to subdue the country of the Gakkars extending on the west along the Indus from Kala Beg to Attock and on the east along the Jhelum up to the town of Khushab, for its strategic importance as well as for the professed loyalty of the Gakkars to the Timurids, of whom Kamran was established in Kabul and Mirza Haidar Doghlat in Kashmere. Since the chiefs of Gakkars, Sultan Adam and Sultan Sarang would not tender allegiance, an army was despatched against them. They were defeated and large numbers of prisoners were taken and sold as slaves. But a victory here and there was, he was told, not likely to be effectual. The country owing to its rugged features was extremely difficult to subdue and to this difficulty was combined an indomitable and warlike spirit of the people. Therefore it was decided that a strong fortress should be built at a spot from where the whole country could be dominated. The spot selected was given the name of Rohtas-Attock and Haibat Khan Niazi was put in charge of the construction of the fortress as well as of controlling the Gakkars with 50,000 troops. Sher Shah had to hasten back to Bengal where Khizr Khan his governor had assumed signs of royalty (March 1541).

Khizir Khan had married the daughter of the late Sultan Mahmud Shah and had thus strengthened his position in the eyes of the legitimists. But before he could mature his plans, Sher Shah arrived at Gaur (May 1541). His arrival completely dis-armed him and taken by surprise he tendered his submission. Sher Shah imprisoned him and re-organized the administration of Bengal so that there might be hardly any future possibility of a rebellion. He reduced the bulk of the province by fixing the western boundary along the line of the Koshi on the northern bank of the Ganges and the country between the Rajmahal hills and the Birbhum district on the southern bank of the Ganges. Then he divided the province into twenty-four small governor-ships, each under a Shiqdar and above them all he appointed a Qazi, styled Qazi Fazilat Amin-i-Bangala. These arrangements were completed by January 1542 and he returned to Agra meditating the conquest of Malwa. The conquest of Malwa was necessary to forestall the designs firstly of the Timurids, who might utilize Gujrat as a base and thence work through Malwa with the object of recovering their lost empire, and secondly of Maldeo of Marwar who was sure to find a willing ally in the Rajput leader, Puran Mal of Raiseen. Hence in July 1541, the siege of Gwalior had been ordered and after it surrendered (17th April 1542), Sher Shah sent an expedition into Malwa, desiring an amicable settlement with the chieftains of the country. And so it was. At Gagraon Puran Mal, at Sarangpur Mallu Khan known as Qadir Shah, and at Ujjain Muin Khan came and submitted. But Sher Shah in order to remove Qadir Shah from Malwa ordered his transfer to Gaur and this brought him out in true colours. He rebelled and fled away to Gujrat. This was followed by the imprisonment of Muin Khan, as a precautionary measure.

By the end of June 1542 Sher Shah returned to Agra. Here another important affair awaited his attention. Humayun frustrated in his attempts at the conquest of Sind, had come to Jodhpur invited by Maldeo and naturally this endangered the security of Sher Shah's throne. He therefore wrote a peremptory letter to Maldeo, demanding either to expel Humayun from his territory or to let Sher Shah do that; and followed it up by an expedition which he led himself to the frontiers of Maldeo's territory. The threat had its desired effect and Humayun was compelled by Maldeo to retreat. By September 1542 Sher Shah was back in Agra. Then he took up the affairs of Bihar and organized its governement. In the meanwhile Puran Mal had rebelled because in pursuance of his usual policy of administration Sher Shah had transferred him to Benares. Sher Shah was prepared for it and in January 1543 he took the field. Puran Mal was besieged at Raiseen, and brought to straits sued for peace. Sher Shah gladly accepted the proposal and a treaty was concluded by which the Rajputs were to be allowed to march out of the fort unmolested with their family and belongings while the Afghans moved two marches away. But as the Rajputs were marching out the Afghans of Malwa aided by a holy man Shaikh Rafiuddin Safwi, clamoured for breaking faith with Puran Mal on the score that the latter had enslaved many of their women. And Sher Shah yielded perhaps more for the purpose of preventing their joining and swelling the ranks of Maldeo than for satisfying the fanatic zeal of the Muslims. Accordingly the Rajputs were surprised, surrounded and despite their brave fighting butchered. It is a blot on the fair name of Sher Shah that he behaved with perfidy.

After the reduction of Malwa, Sher Shah turned his attention to Sind. Its conquest was necessary partly for preventing the possibility of a Timurid attack from beyond the Bolan Pass—either by Humayun who had gone to Persia to seek aid from the Shah or by Karman who held Qandahar, and partly for hemming in Maldeo by a ring of imperial territories as a preliminary for any attack on him. No sooner resolved than Haibat Khan Niazi was ordered from the Punjab. In the early part of 1543 Upper Sind was conquered and in October and November 1543, Lower Sind was occupied. It is after this that Sher Shah started to destroy Maldeo. The first great difficulty was the choice of a suitable route for there were two, one via Ranthambor and Ajmer, the other via Nagore and Mirtha. He however chose the latter and came as far as Mirtha, where Maldeo had taken a strong position. Since Maldeo would not take the offensive, Sher Shah had to wait full one month and his position was fast becoming critical. He was in the enemy's country 260 miles away from his base of operation, Narnol, and he could not attack with advantage the position of Maldeo. Hence he tried a trick. He wrote a number of letters in the name of Maldeo's nobles and contrived them to fall into the hands of Maldeo. That accomplished what Sher Shah could not have by force. Inspite of the solemn assertions by his nobles of their good-faith Maldeo decamped. But his general Kumbha did not. He remained with 12,000 of his brave Rajputs to give proof of his fidelity. The next day he made a furious attack on the Afghans and but for their superior number and artillery, he would have defeated them. At any rate Sher Shah won a splendid victory and promptly followed up his advantage. He divided his armies into two sections, one he himself led against Ajmer and the other led by Khawas Khan, Isa Khan and other chiefs moved upon Jodhpur. Ajmer opened its gates without resistance to Sher Shah who then made for Mount Abu and occupied it. Pali, a rich market place was looted and a rich booty taken. In the meanwhile the other army had taken possession of Jodhpur with ease since Maldeo had evacuated it and had retired to Siwana. This completed the conquest of Marwar, and Sher Shah hastened back to his capital where all sorts offalse rumours were spreading about his fate. In June 1544, after a short stay at Agra, he rejoined his army at Ajmer and then made a move upon Chittor. His approach put the usurper Banbir to flight and Chittor was occupied and left in charge of imperial officers. This actually gave a finishing touch to his Rajput policy. He had crushed Maldeo and had planted his power at the four most strategic points of Rajputana viz. Ajmer, Mt. Abu, Jodhpur and Chittor which were strongly garrisoned. From these four points he dominated Rajputana which he never wanted to conquer and bring under his direct control. What he wanted was a complete "political and geographical isolation" of the Rajput houses from one another, which would make combination impossible. In fact his policy was one of coercion not relieved by concilliation and forms a contrast to that of Akbar. It is clearly brought out by an incident which typifies Sher Shah's Rajput policy. After the occupation of Chittor he made an armed demonstration by making triumphant march through Jaipur as if "to impress the Rajputs with the resistless might of the rejuvenated empire of Delhi."

Back from Rajputana, he undertook the siege of Kalinger, because its Raja Kirat Singh had given him offence by sheltering a recalcitrant chieftain. The fortress was of strategic importance also. He started the siege in November 1544 and vigorously carried it on in person till on the 22nd May 1545, the day the fort was captured, he got severely burnt owing to an explosion of a heap of rockets and expired. Thus expired a great king, a great warrior and a great administrator. He left behind him enduring monuments of his genius. His system of administration framed on efficient bureaucratic lines, his excellent army organization his public and philanthropic works, his police system and coinage, all these bear testimony to his greatness. Indeed he had achieved more during the five years of his rule than what many others would do in a life-time . And all unwittingly he had built up a system of administration, which was best suited to the ideal of absolute kingship of the Timurids. In a way he had laid the foundations for the Mughal empire.

Sher Shah was succeeded by his son Islam Shah (1545-53) whose ambition centred round two things. The one was to establish himself on the throne to the prejudice of his elder brother Adil Khan; the other was to reduce the power of the great Afghan nobles, and thereby to make the royal power absolute. The trouble started very early owing to his suspicious and perfidious conduct towards Adil Khan and this eventually merged into a war of extermination of the four prominent nobles Kutb Khan, Jalal Khan, Isa Khan and Khawas Khan, who aided Adil Khan. He however succeeded in driving them to destruction and then securely sat on the throne of Delhi to the prejudice of his brother. His suspicion next fell on others like Sujjat Khan, but with less disastrous consequences to themselves. About 1548 he entered the Gakkar country and remained for two years to see the fort of Rohtas completed, and further ordered the fort of Mankot to be constructed. Having thus secured his northern frontier against future attacks either of Humayun or Mirza Haidar Doghlat, he returned home.

In 1552 occurred an incident that might well have made him proud of his position. Flying from his pursuers and expelled by Humayun from Kabul, Kamran, who had behaved most treacherously with his brother, came to the court of Islam Shah. He considered it extremely lucky, for with Karman as a tool he could frustrate all aggressive designs of Humayun on his kingdom and if circumstances permitted he might be a king-maker. Hence he entertained Kamran in his court, but at the same time kept him under surveillance. It proved galling to Kamran and he managed to escape back to the Gakkars who surrendered him to Humayun (1553). By now Islam Shah's days were numbered and he soon expired (1553) worn out by constant campaigns and disease.

"In person he was handsome and powerful. He possessed a competent degree of learning and is said to have treasured up in his memory the chief works of the best Persian poets. He was intelligent, acute, fond of the society of the learned men and of the pious divines, and remarkable for his skill in extempore poetical composition as well as for his wit and ready repartee." He too like his father was a great king, and did much not only to retain but to improve the system of government established by his father. But his successor and brother-in-law, Muhammed Shah Adil, who had ascended the throne by murdering the twelve-year old son of Islam Shah, proved extremely incapable. Rebellions started in different parts of the empire. His two brothers-in-law Sikandar Sur and Ibrahim Khan Sur proclaimed themselves king in the Punjab and Agra respectively. He himself had to shift from Gwalior which was the capital to Chunar, to suppress the revolt of Taj Khan Kararani. When the kingdom was thus rent by civil war, attacked Humayun from the north, occupied Lahore, defeated an army of Sikandar Sur at Machhiwara and then captured Delhi and with it, his lost throne. Thus came to a close the second phase of the struggle, heralded by the downfall of the Sur dynasty and re-establishment of the Mughal dynasty in India.

This period from 1540-1555, apart from the expulsion of the Mughals from India and revival of Afghan power was a period of remarkable achievements. Far-reaching policies of government were enunciated, an efficient system of administration was devised, and philanthropic works were undertaken on an extensive scale. The first two Surs were unique amongst the rulers of medieval India in many ways and were really the precursors of Akbar. Almost the first among the emperors of Northern India Sher Shah was fairly free from religious or sectarian rancour. His love of justice was such that he would not spare his own son when he violated the honour of a commoner's wife. In administration the Hindus used to be associated and merit not birth was the chief consideration. In fact as Prof. Qanungo remarks "he stands by the side of Akbar as a grand nationbuilder." His administrative system framed on bureaucratic lines was characterized by energy and efficiency. Centralization of authority was the keynote of his government, Revenue, police, civil and crimial justice, coinage and public works, all received equal attention and bore the stamp of his genius. What he had done was continued by his son Islam Shah. About his administrative policy Erskine remarks that "he endeavoured to concentrate all power in his own person. He deprived the Amirs of all their war-elephants leaving them perhaps only a bad female one for carriage...... Reports came in to him regularly from every part of his territories and in return he wrote mandates concerning every matter and thing whether relating to religion, civil government or revenue.........These mandates whether agreeable to law or not, it was necessary to conform in their minutest particulars No reference to Qazi or Mufti was allowed......He seems to have kept something like a standing army which his plan to bring all the revenue directly into the public treasury must have assisted in doing. He was anxious to keep the dread of his power unceasingly before his great officers; and justice in civil cases was administered not by the Mufti or Qazi but by a Munsiff or Amin." Thus we see he tried to carry out two principles in his administration, the first was the centralization of authority and the second was the establishment of political sovereignty unhampered by religious or sectarian interest. That Akbar profited by these activities of the first two Surs, there is no doubt. What the Mughals wanted most was to supplant the Afghan power and make their authority enduring in India. To accomplish the first, Akbar had to resort to Rajput alliance and the second depended upon how far the dissociation of the political from the religious interest could be effected; for so long as the Islamic church-state persisted in India, it could not commend itself to the acceptance and far less to the support of the majority of their subjects, i.e. the non-Muslims. And since the Mughals were foreigners in India, they needed the support of the people more than the Afghans, to make their power enduring. Hence the state had to be divested of all its sectarian bias, and a beginning had been made in this direction by the Surs. Thus Akbar's task was facilitated. The Mughals not only got from the Surs a system of administration that admirably suited their ideal of absolute monarchy; they also got the idea of establishing a non-sectarian polity, that was calculated to perpetuate their power.

The third phase of the Mughal-Afghan struggle for supremacy opened with the death of Humayun and succession of Akbar (14th February 1556). When Humayun died Akbar was far away in the Punjab, campaigning against Sikandar Shah Sur with his guardian Bairam Khan. The death of Humayun six months after his occupation of Delhi had left the Mughals in a precarious condition in Hindustan. He had not made his position secure on the Delhi throne; he had not established a government in Hindustan. He had distributed the provinces of Hindustan among his nobles no doubt, and Akbar had Hisar Firoza, Bairam Khan Sirhind with the neighbouring districts, Shah Abul Maali the Punjab, Tardi Beg Mewat, Muhammad Haidar Khan Biana, Ali Quli Saistani Sambhal, and Sikandar Khan Uzbeg Agra. But he had not clearly defined the boundaries of provinces nor had he posted armies at their head-quarters, as he had planned. Further, the Mughal nobility lacked confidence owing to his premature death and the Mughal army numbered barely 30,000 including the reinforcements from Hindustan. But this was not all. Akbar's minority and the lack of any possibility of military assistance from Kabul, that was at this time in the throes of an invasion by the ruler of Badkshan Prince Suleiman, aggravated the situation. And if the Mughals were thus hampered by their own unsettled condition they were harassed by a host of other factors for which they were not responsible.

A series of revolts had shaken the foundations of the Sur authority and given rise to a number of claimants to the throne. One was Sikandar Shah Sur, who though defeated by Humayun still had his hold on the Punjab and was gathering strength for a coming contest. Ibrahim Shah Sur, another claimant to the throne, had been defeated successively by

Sikandar Shah and Himu Muhammad Shah Adil's general, and had gone first to Punna and then to Malwa invited by the Afghans. He however soon disappeared from the scene, and there was one rival less for Akbar. But there was one other, more formidable than Ibrahim, and that was Himu, the powerful and victorious Hindu general of Muhammad Shah Adil, who, nominally the servant of Adil Shah, was really conquering for his own interest. He had risen from the low position of a shop-keeper in Rawari in Mewat to the highest office in the state by "great and commanding talents." Of him it is said that "though his frame was so feeble that he could not ride on horse-back and even in the field was forced be carried about in a litter or on an elephant, yet such was his spirit that he maintained stout contests with the enemies of the king and by his determined courage was victorious in many battles and achieved exploits worthy of the highest reputation" He had already won twenty-two victories for his master and now as he proceeded with 50,000 men supported by about 1000 war elephants by way of Gwalior upon Agra and Delhi, they were abandoned by the Mughals who fled to the Punjab and joined Akbar and Bairam Khan. That the Mughals should have thus abandoned their post in terror when they were expected to act with cool courage and determination was rather ominous. Equally ominous was it for them when Himu proclaimed himself emperor of Delhi under the style of Raja Vikramajit. This spread a panic in the ranks of the Mughals who had all gathered at Sirhind. They had now to fight a king, not a general. Hence, when Bairam Khan called a council of war to moot the question of fighting Himu, none seemed to approve of it. But Bairam Khan with his characteristic vigour forced his view on all and it was decided that the empire of Hindustan was worth fighting for. This resulted in the second battle of Panipat (5th November 1556) in which Himu was defeated and captured, and Akbar got rid of his most redoubtable antagonist. He was also slain by Akbar at the instance of Bairam Khan. The victory gave Akbar Delhi and Agra and almost the whole of the Doab. The Punjab was firmly secured after the defeat and surrender of Sikandar Shah Sur at Mankot (May 1557). About this time Muhammad Shah Adil was killed in a battle with the king of Bengal (1557). Thus one after another all the rivals of Akbar disappeared leaving him the sole occupant of the throne, The Sur dynasty had come to a tragic end, after a brief but brilliant career. But the end of the Sur dynasty did not wipe out Afghan opposition. It died hard in the Mughal empire and the last ebullition of it was experienced in the reign of Shahjahan. In the mighty empire of the Mughals, it took the shape of rebellion and that was all. They could never distrub the general peace and prosperity.

Akbar's reign started with the regency of Bairam Khan. The latter however masterful, niggardly and sectarian, was not selfish and always tried to promote his master's cause. It was he who after the extermination of the Afghan rivals of Akbar and the occupation of the Doab, determined to attack the Afghans in Malwa. Malwa was at this time under Baz Bahadur, the son of the trusted and capable general of Sher Shah, Sujaat Khan. Sujaat Khan had become independent during the reign of Muhammad Shah Adil and died in 1555-56. His death had been followed by trouble in Malwa, and hither had gone Ibrahim Shah Sur to fish in troubled waters. He failed and Baz Bahadur secured himself on the throne. He had allowed the kingdom to decline while he uindulged in sensual pleasures. No wonder that this state of affairs encouraged the Agra government to attack. In the autumn 1560, Adham Khan assisted by Pir Muhammad Khan, led an expedition and defeated Baz Bahadur near Sarangpur (1561). The victors disgraced themselves by perpetrating cruelties after their victory. Akbar's surprise visit stopped their proceedings and later on Adham Khan was recalled. Pir Muhammad Khan remained alone in charge of the affairs, and won another decisive victory and expelled Baz Bahadur beyond the Narmada. He ultimately fled to the shelter of Rana Udai Singh of Chittor and after Chittor was attacked and taken (1568) Baz Bahadur chose to surrender (1570-71). He was made a Mansabdar and thus the Afghan rule in Malwa came to an end.

There was one other province besides Malwa where the Afghans were yet supreme. That was Bengal. In the time of Sher Shah, Afghan chiefs held the country; Suleiman Khan, an Afghan of the Kirani or Kararani clan being then governor of Bihar. In 1564 Suleiman occupied Gaur, the capital of the Bengal kings, and so founded a new and short-lived Bengal dynasty."[1] He scrupulously avoided giving offence to Akbar. In 1568 he attacked Rohtas, which held out for the emperor. But as soon as Akbar sent an army he withdrew. He even sent valuable presents to Akbar from time to time and thus kept him in good humour. After his death in 1572, his son Daud Khan succeeded to the throne. He found a large treasure, a powerful army composed of 140,000 infantry, 40,000 cavalry, 20,000 guns, 3600 elephants and several hundred war-boats and a rich and prosperous kingdom left by his father. This turned his head and he "foresook the prudent measure of his father and assuming all insignia of royalry ordered the Khutba to be proclaimed in his own name through all the towns of Bengal and Bihar and directed the coin to be stamped with his own title, thus completely setting at defiance the authority of the emperor Akbar."[2] But Akbar, busy at this time in the conquest of Gujrat would not have minded it had he not given him offence deliberately by attacking the fort Zamania, that marked the eastern frontier of the Mughal empire. As soon as Akbar heard about it he ordered Munim Khan, the governor of Jaunpur, to attack the aggressor. He did as he was bid, but failed to make an impression on the enemy. Hence Raja Todar Mall was ordered, but Akbar, who had returned from Gujrat embarked on an expedition during the height of the rains. Patna was reached in August 1574, and Akbar's presence so encouraged the imperialists that they captured Hajipur and Patna from the enemy, who next fled away into Bengal. Akbar then returned to the capital (January 1575) having ordered for vigorous offensive against Daud, under the sole command of Munim Khan. Monghyr, Bhagalpur, Colgong and the Teliaghari pass were seized in succession, and the Mughals pursuing their advantage over-ran Bengal and drove Daud from place to place till at last they caught up with him at Tukaroi, now in the Balasore district of Orissa and defeated him at a decisive battle on 3rd March 1575. On the 12th April Daud made his submission and inspite of the remonstrances of Todar Mall, was granted liberal terms. He

1. Akbar the Great Mogul by V. A. Smith p. 123.
2. Stewart's History of Bengal p. 151.

was to retain Orissa in entire independence. But, for the folly of the Khan-i-khana the Mughals had to pay dearly a little later. There arose rebellions in the Ghoraghat region (now in the Dinajpur district) and Munim Khan shifted his head-quarters to Gaur. Soon after there prevailed a pestilential fever and he, along with many others died. His death was followed by a scene of confusion amongst the Mughal officers, and taking advantage of this state of affairs Daud Khan attacked. He soon over-ran Bengal, but in the mean while Akbar had deputed Khan Jahan, Hasan Kuli Khan, Governor of the Punjab, against him. After winning a series of successes Khan Jahan met Daud at the battle of Rajmahal (July 12, 1576) and defeated and killed him. His head was sent to Akbar and with his death disappeared the independent Afghan kingdom of Bengal.

The Afghan independence disappeared no doubt, but their hostility did hot. It used to rise at times, and indeed during the last days of his life Akbar was troubled by the recrudescence of Afghan pretensions in Bengal. That was the rebellion of Usman. Usman revolted about 1600 A.D. during the governorship of Man Singh. The latter, who used to stay generally at Ajmer, at once hastened to Bengal to quell the situation. The rebel had already defeated several imperial officers and occupied a large part of Bengal. Man Singh's arrival improved matters quickly and the rebel was defeated at Sherpur Atai most decisively (1604). After that Man Singh returned to the court and was raised to the mansab of 7,000, so far reserved only for the members of the royal family. But the province did not become quiet. Usman continued to trouble the government. In the mean while Man Singh's place had been taken by Islam Khan and he, inspite of his vigour had to strive several years in vain before he could crush Usman. It was on the 12th March 1612 that he met Usman at Nek Ujyal, and defeated him wounding him on the head. The wound became fatal and he expired a few hours after the battle. One after another of his leaderless followers submitted to the emperor and the situation became quiet. Jahangir adopted a policy of clemency and employed them in the Government. It is said of Jahangir that he paid so much attention to them that they abolished all further treasonable designs from their mind and thought themselves bound to continue subservient and attached to him even to the sacrifice of life.[1]

But this was not to outlast Jahangir. At the start of Shah Jahan's reign there occurred another Afghan rebellion. Shortly after the coronation of Shahjahan, Khan Jahan Lodi, the viceroy of the Deccan was summoned to the court. He received the greatest consideraion at the hands of the emperor but misconstrued it for a deliberate plot against him and left Agra one nigt without leave. He was pursued by an imperial army and flying into the Deccan made friendship with the Maratha leader Shahji and Murtza Nizam Shah II. This compelled the emperor to come in person to direct operation in the Deccan (1629) for it was a formidable combination. Within two years the allies had been worn out. Shahji deserted to the emperor and Khan Jahan was forced to fly for shelter at first to the king of Bijapur and then into Bundelkhand, whither he was hotly pursued and at last died fighting at Kalinger (1631).

This was the last Afghan rebellion in the Mughal empire. The Afghans had by now become reconciled to the Mughal rule and hence no further troubles arose. But indeed they had nourished their enmity for long and it is a little more than a century after the advent of the Mughals that Afghan hostility was completely crushed. This die-hard nature of Afghan hostility had led to the adoption by the Mughal a policy of conciliation towards the Rajputs.

1. Jahangir by Beni Prasad p. 215.

CHAPTER III

THE RAJPUTS AND THE MUGHALS

The rise and fall of the Rajputs unfold a story of exceeding romance and pathos, of valour unsurpassed and honour unsullied, of great sacrifices inspired by a deep sense of patriotism and yet, of abiding discord, moral degeneration, and physical exhaustion. The flower of Indian chivalry and the epitome of national greatness, the Rajputs were, inspite of their great qualities, clannish and conservative in their vital sentiments. Their indomitable courage, wreckless bravery, and love of independence were inspired by a religious sense of personal glory. They lived and died first for their clan, then for their king, and last for their country. They seldom employed their sterling qualities for the achievement of that glorious ideal, the liberation of Hindustan, or Northern India, from the clutches of the Muslims, which remained for ages the dream of the poet, the ideal of the philosopher, and the prayer of the people. Hence after centuries of struggle they fell, achieving little for the permanent good of the people, and contributing little for the political growth of India. They had a long span of political power extending over centuries, but here we are concerned only with that period of their history which marks their decline and fall. That was the period of the Mughal rule in India. For, it was the Mughals who most successfully conquered the Rajputs, yoked their fiery energies to the foundation of their empire, and left them so exhausted that by the end of the Mughal rule they fell an easy prey first to the Marathas and then to the British. Such was the culmination of their Mughal connection.

When the Mughals conquered Hindustan from the Afghans, they had to reckon with one other enemy viz. the Rajputs. The Rajputs had not ceased to be a factor in the politics of Hindustan. Undisturbed in the inhospitable regions of Rajputana they ran the obscure course of their tribal history, without substantially influencing the rise and fall of empires in Northern India. Bounded roughly by the Indian desert on the west and Bundelkhand on the east, by sandy tracts on the north and the Chambal on the south, Rajputana was often a terror to the invader, the trouble of the statesman, and the keystone of the empire of Hindustan. She baffled the Turks when they tried to conquer her by force; she frowned indignantly when the Afghan forged fetters for her. To the Mughals, however, she bowed her head, not only because the Mughals knew how to respect her susceptibilities, but also because she had become exhausted by centuries of warfare and internal discord, and the Mughals were mighty soldiers. Her decline had begun when the Mughals started empire-building in India, and the process was accelerated, and her fall completed, at the height of the Mughal glory. That was towards the end of Shahajahan's reign. The war of succession amongst the sons of Shahjahan exposed the degradation of the Rajputs, and more than forty years before, the last of the Rajput Kings, the proudest of the ruling princes of India, the Rana of Mewar had submitted to the Mughals. Towards the end of Aurangazeb's reign they made an attempt to revive their past glory. It was only a feeble attempt, which spent its force in the terrible convulsions that shook the Mughal empire to its foundations. On this basis the dealings of the Rajputs with the Mughals could be broadly divided into two periods : (i) the period of decline, and (ii) the period of downfall. The first recorded the struggle of the Rajput states to maintain their independence till one after another they succumbed; the second marked the subservience of the Rajputs when they conceded to merge their interest in those of the Mughal government and accordingly shed their blood to consolidate and perpetuate the empire. The former extends from 1526 to 1614; the latter from 1614 to 1707.

There were eight states in Rajputana, great and small, of which the three premier ones, Mewar, Marwar, and Amber played a leading part in her history. When the Turks established their empire in Hindustan, with the capital at Delhi, they did not venture to conquer and annex Rajputana. They remained content with the occupation of the three border fortresses viz. Ajmer, Gwalior and Kalinjar, that formed the line of frontier between Rajputana and Hindustan, and by which they could dominate Rajputana. They did not like to penetrate further inland, and up to the end of the Delhi sultanate period that line of forts formed the south-western limit of the empire of Hindustan. When the disintegration of the empire set in towards the end of the 14th century Rajputana still lay "deathless and indomitable". The century and a half following the invasion of Taimur destroyed the last vestiges of the Delhi Sultanate, and witnessed a remarkable revival of the Rajput power. At first Mewar attained to a pre-eminent position in Rajputana during that period of revival, and her glory filled the whole of the 15th and the first quarter of the 16th century. When her sun set on the field of Khanwa, that of Marwar rose to shine in splendour till the middle of the 16th century. The rise of Sher Shah eclipsed her glory, and in the reign of Akbar her subjection was complete. She formed a part of the empire. Again in the days of Marwar's downfall and Rajput disgrace Mewar raised her head in utter defiance of the Mughals. When one after another the princes of Rajputana paid homage to Akbar, Mewar alone waged a war of independence for a quarter of a century, and maintained her independence at a heavy cost. But she too fell during the reign of Jahangir. After that, the subjugation of the Rajputs was complete, and they became the prop of the empire, and obedient and trustworthy vassals of the Mughal emperors. Thus they remained for about three quarters of a century, till at last lashed to rebellion by the reactionary measures of Aurangeb, Marwar and Mewar formed an alliance, and dealt a severe blow at the empire, that accelerated its fall, and with it their own also.

Thus the fates conspired to give ascendancy alternately to Mewar and Marwar over the states of Rajputana at different periods of the later middle ages. Unfortunate Amber could never aspire for ascendancy because she was too near the headquarters of the conquerer of Northern India, and this left for her no option except the recognition of Muslim suzerainty. The Afghans and the Mughals could never suffer the slightest pretensions on her part to independence. Hence she remained in perpetual bondage to the foreign rule established in Hindustan. That in short is the brief outline of the political importance of the Rajputs in the Mughal period.

Now to the details. At the dawn of the 16th century, when Babar was fighting, conquering, and losing in the region of Central Asia, and the Afghan empire was at its height, Rana Sanga ascended the throne of Mewar. One of the greatest of his race, he raised Mewar to the pre-eminent position in Rajputana, and formed a well-knit confederacy that even threatened the Afghan empire in its palmiest days. When however the latter declined Mewar loomed large in the political horizon of Hindustan. After he had defeated the kings of Malwa and Gujrat singly as well as combined Rana Sanga also measured swords with Ibrahim Lodi twice, and once defeated him with immense slaughter. He had won in all eighteen pitched battles against his adversaries. "Eighty thousand horse, seven Rajas of the highest rank, nine Raos, and one hundred and four chieftains bearing the title of Rawal and Rawat with five hundred war elephants followed him into the field. The princes of Marwar and Amber did him homage, and the Raos of Gwalior, Ajmer, Sikri, Raisin, Kalpi, Chanderi, Bundi, Gagraon, Rampura and Abu served him as tributaries or held of him in chief."[1] Biana became the northern boundary of Mewar and the Sind river the eastern. He had successfully interfered in Malwa, and the north-eastern portion of it had fallen into his hands. He bestowed it upon his allies, Silahdin and Medini Rai, both Rajput chiefs; the former getting Raisin and Bhilsa, the latter Chanderi with its dependencies. On the south therefore his dominions spread far into Malwa. On the west he had pushed his frontiers as far as the impenetrable barriers of the desert and the mountains. When Sangram Singh was thus adding to his glory, Ibrahim Lodi was gradually undermining the strength of his empire by his attempts to exterminate the feudal nobility. The dissension and disaffection that reigned everywhere could not have escaped the keen eye of the Rana. He viewed it with internal delight and perhaps invited Babar to invade Hindustan and take Delhi, while he himself engaged to take Agra.[2] It was an excellent move on his part. He had already pushed his frontiers up to Biana, and Agra was only a few miles off.

1. Tod, Annals Vol. 1, Pages 348-49.
2. Babar's Memoires p. 339.

An attack on Agra from Biana as his base could not fail to be effective. But the agreement, as Babar complains, was broken by him; Babar won the battle of Panipat while Sanga did not move on Agra; and hence the empire of Hindustan fell to the share of Babar alone.

But before the empire of Hindustan became his, Babar had to subjugate the Afghans in the north-east, and the Rajputs in the south-west. He took immediate steps to crush the former, and did not care for the latter, perhaps because he had not expected that he should have to cross swords with the Rana. Why the Rana waited for full one year after Babar won the battle of Panipat, and why he did not engage him immediately are riddles unsolved by recorded history. It cannot be said that he was not fully prepared. He was then at the height of his power, and could not have been wanting the sinews of war. He could not have also put a premium on Babar's victory at Panipat so that he would be unnerved at the very thought of meeting Babar, for is it not that he himself had defeated Ibrahim Lodi once ? Hence it is safe to surmise that his delay was due to his watching the movements of Babar. He perhaps had anticipated that Babar like Muhammad Ghori and Mahmud of Ghazani or still recently Amir Taimur would go back after plundering the fairest parts of Hindustan. But when he found that Babar was in no mood of returning to his country he prepared to drive him out by force. Another incident hastened the outbreak of hostilities, and that was the fall of Biana to the Mughals. The Rana could not tolerate this, because it had long been his frontier outpost and a splendid base for threatening the ruler of Northern India. Hence before he met Babar on the field, he made it a point of taking Biana a task which was facilitated by the alliance of Hasan Khan Mewati. It is also significant of the power of the Rana, that the news of his movement was sufficient to bring about the surrender of Biana, Gwalior and other fortresses that had lately submitted to Babar.

The fall of Biana and Gwalior, the unholy alliance of Hasan Khan Mewati, and the determined advance of the Rana for a trial of conclusions forced Babar to take the field in person on 11th February 1527. He had called back Humayun from his campaign against the Afghans, in order that he might have all the available troops to muster against the Rana. He had hardly marched out when came the disconcerting news that Rabiri had been seized by Hasan Khan Lohani, Chandwa by Kutub Khan, and Kanauj and Sambhal had been abandoned by his troops. Further his own troops lost their morale at the tales of Rajput bravery, of which they had bitter experience at the skirmishes previous to the battle. Under such circumstances Babar despaired of a happy termination of the struggle. He had many misfortunes in life, and now that another, and perhaps more terrible than all the rest, was staring him in the face he repented for his past folly, and made amends for it by renouncing wine and promising to abolish the Tamgha or stamp tax on the Muhammadans in his dominion. Then he exhorted his men to screw up courage and face the situation. It made a great impression on his men, and "master and servant, great and small" swore on the Quaran that they would not desert him in the moment of his supreme peril. With such preliminaries, Babar could not have been very hopeful about the end of the battle, and might have agreed that "the Pilakhal at Biana should be boundary of their (Babar's and Rana's) respective dominions,"[1] and that the Rana should have an annual tribute from him. It is impossible to ascertain how far that was true on the evidence of Mughal records, for neither Babar nor the Mughal historians, who had a bias against the enemies of the imperial dynasty are likely to make any mention of these proposals, because they were very humiliating. But the Annals of Tod contains a different version. It seems the proposals were rejected, and the events moved forward to end in the battle of Khanwa. It was a decisive defeat, and cost the Rana all but his life. Even his life stained with defeat he did not long enjoy. On the battlefield he left dead some of his most veteran commanders and faithful allies. Rawal Udai Singh of Dongarpur, Ratna of Salumbar, Raimal Rathod of Marwar, Ramdas of Sonigira, Uja of Jhalawar and many other princes of note, were slain. Babar also paid dearly for his victory, but its decisive nature and far-reaching consequences more than made up for all his losses. It shattered the Rajput confederacy and removed the danger of Rajput predominance

1. Tods Annals Vol. I. p. 356.

in Hindustan once for all. Consequently Babar's position on the throne of Delhi became secure, and his days of wandering in search of a fortune now come to an end. In fact with the defeat of the Rana was laid the foundation of the Mughal empire in Hindustan.

After the defeat and flight of the Rana, Babar occupied Biana. He then planned a regular invasion of Rajputana as a sequel to his victory but had to abandon it owing to the approaching hot weather, and the opposition of the nobles, who counselled discretion. At any rate the project was never taken up afterwards, and perhaps that is significant of the wholesome impression left on the mind of Babar by the Rajputs.

After the hot weather he determined to make a move towards Malwa. The importance of Malwa for the ruler of Northern India is very great. Its conquest serves two purposes, one, of facilitating the subjugation of the Deccan and Gujrat, the other, of limiting the expansion of Rajputana states southwards. For Babar the latter was the greater necessity. His territories already lay on the north-east of Rajputana, and if Malwa was conquered there would be a fence of imperial provinces on three sides of Rajputana and thereby, the Rajputs would be held under greater control. That was exactly the policy of the Delhi Sultanate. In Decebmber 1527, he led an expedition against Medini Rao of Chanderi, the kingmaker of Malwa, and ally of Rana Sangram Singh. He took his position before the fortress of Chanderi on the 21st January 1528, and offered him favourable terms if he submitted. But since the terms were rejected Babar stormed the fortress on the 28th January after hard fighting, in which the Rajputs showed their usual bravery. After the fall of Chanderi, Babar had to hasten back to repulse the Afghan rebels, who were advancing into the Doab, and there was an end to Babar's fighting against the Rajputs.

Babar was lucky with regard to Mewar due to the death of Rana Sangram Singh. Smarting under the defeat he had retreated towards the hills of Mewat, with the vow that he would return to Chitor only after winning a victory over his enemy. This he was never destined to achieve, for "he died at Baswa on the frontier of Mewat not without suspicion of poison,"[1] and it is said his own ministers had hastened his end. After him there ensued a scramble for power, amidst plots and counter-plots so common in a polygamous household. The mother of the second son intrigued with Babar and promised in order to supplant the lawful heir, Ratan Singh to surrender to him Ranthambor, and the crown of Malwa king preseved in Chitore as a trophy. Inspite of her intrigues, Ratan Singh, succeeded, but had a speedy end owing to his folly, (1530). After him the second son of Sanga, Vikramajit ascended the throne. Already intriguing with a foreign foe to supplant his own brother, he had no hesitation in acknowledging the suzerrainty of Babar now. Since Babar wanted Ranthambor in continuation of his policy in Malwa, Vikramajit surrendered it in exchange for Shamsabad and seventy lakhs of rupees.[2]

So far with regard to Mewar. Of the other Rajput chiefs Bihari Mal of Amber was the first to pay homage to Babar. Nothing more is known about Babar's dealings with the Rajputs. Babar's attitude towards them was, on the whole, non-interfering. He had a bitter experience of his first contact with the Rajputs, and he had learnt to keep them at a respectable distance till the Mughal power in Hindustan had not been firmly established. He could not afford to quarrel with them at a time when he had to encounter the Afghans. And since the Mughals, unlike their predecessors the Afghans and the Turks, had to wrest the sovereignty of Hindustan from two enemies viz. the wily Afghan and the valiant Rajput, Babar like a statesman proceeded very cautiously, constantly taking care that he encountered only one of the two. This policy reached its perfection by a felicitious transformation in the hands of Babar's grandson. Humayun had not the genius of Akbar, and hence failed to profit by the example of his father.

Humayun did not make a wholesome impression on the Rajputs either as a soldier or as a statesman. In 1534, when Rani Karnavati of Chitore sought his help, he did not make the best use of the opportunity. In fact the Rani had sent him more than a mere request; she had sent him the tenderest token

1. Tods Annals, Vol. I. p. 357.
2. An Empire Builder of the XVI century, p. 167.

of her regard, her bracelets as a sister does to her brother. That was in keeping with the Rajput character full, of generous and noble sentiments. Karnavati had made him her bracelet-bound brother, and according to Rajput custom. Humayun ought to have shown sufficient chivalry in going to rescue the Rani from Bahadur Shah, who was besieging the fort of Chitore, and against whom Humayun's help had been sought. But Humayun weakly responded to the request, and went as far as Gwalior, and from there he demanded the withdrawal of Bahadur Shah. His threats, unbacked by force, availed the princess nothing, and she had to purchase peace from the invader. Humayun's attitude in this affair was not only improper, but also impolitic. He violated the moral obligation that he owed as a sovereign to his vassal—the obligation of defending Mewar when it was attacked by a foreign foe. By withholding his aid to the Mewar queen he not only did not act as a chivalrous gentleman, but did not act as a responsible sovereign also. Hence he did not win the love and loyalty of the Rajputs.

But Amber continued to be loyal, and Raja Bihari Mal "received from Humayun the Mansab of five thousand as Raja of Amber."[1] Nothing more is known about his dealings with the Rajputs till he entered Marwar as a fugitive seeking the help of Maldeo to recover his lost throne from Sher Shah. About July or August 1541, Maldeo had invited him to come at once, and with his assistance, to invade Delhi and Agra, because Sher Shah was then away in Bengal. Maldeo had thus aimed at the role of king-maker, and there was nothing startling about it. Ascending the throne in 1532, that very year he had conquered Nagore and Ajmer, and then had gradually extended his sway over a large part of Rajputana. His kingdom comprised thirty-eight districts, and extended as far as the Salt Lake of Sambhar. His extensive dominions and constructive genius had combined to make him one of the greatest rulers of Marwar, and one of "the most powerful of the Hindu princes, who still retained their independence."[2] Supreme in Rajputana, he wanted to be the king-maker in Hindustan. Hence he

1. Tods Annals Vol. III. p. 137.
2. Brigg's Ferista. Vol. II. p. 121.

offered his help to Humayun, and if the latter had come in time perhaps he would have achieved considerable success. But attracted by false hopes he delayed in Sind, and when he came into Marwar in July 1542, it was already too late. For, Sher Shah, who had an inkling of the designs of Maldeo, had hastened back to the capital from Bengal, and re-organised his resources before Maldeo could be of any help to Humayun. Marching with a considerable army as far as Nagore, situated on Maldeo's frontier he sent a message to Maldeo in the first week of August "offering him the alternative of either himself expelling Humayun from his territories or suffering it to be done by the Afghans i.e. in plain words, giving battle."[1] Thus Maldeo was brought to a very uncomfortable predicament at this time. He had Sher Shah on his northern and Humayun on his western frontier. The one had come to chastise him, the other to seek his assistance. Hence he had to make a quick decision between peace and war, and perhaps he thought, a peace was precarious and a war perilous. But in fact, a war at this time would have been more to his advantage than to Sher Shah's, for Sher Shah was still unsettled in Hindustan, and his army was divided in several provinces between Bengal and the Indus. Maldeo did not utilize the occasion, did not offer a battle; and that was because Humayun had brought no army with him. Noticing that his real designs had been detected by Sher Shah, he changed his attitude towards Humayun, and gave no assurance of assistance to Humayun's agent, Shamsuddin, who had been sent in advance to ascertain his intentions. Hence the party of Humanyun retreated, and Maldeo sent an army to pursue it, in order that Sher Shah might get the impression that Humayun had entered his state without his consent. The fugitive emperor had to bear untold hardships while retreating throug the waterless and inhospitable desert country, along with the empress, Hamida Banu Begum, then in an advanced state of pregancy. On the whole Maldeo's conduct was ungenerous and incompatible with Rajput character. Crossing the desert, he found a safe assylum in Umarkot, with another Rajput prince Rana Pratap. Shortly after he attempted the conquest

1. Qanugo's Sher Shah pp. 275-76.

of Sind with his help, but ill-luck dogged him there, and he was ultimalely forced to quit India towards the end of 1543.

Such is the history of Humayun's dealings with the Rajputs. He failed to impress them as a conqueror and as a King and had not the genius to utilize their strength to cover up his own weakness. Irresolute as a leader, and short-sighted as a statesman, he amply deserved expulsion from India. When he once again sat on the throne of Hindustan, his days were numbered and he could not punish Maldeo for his treachery. His son, however, was destined to do what he could not.

"Akbar was the real founder of the empire of the Mughals the first successful conqueror of Rajput independence. To this end his virtues were powerful auxiliaries, as by his skill in the analysis of the mind and its readiest stimulant to action, he was enabled to gild the chain with which he bound them." True, but the way had been shown by Sher Shah, who by an effective combination of war and diplomacy had fettered the independence of the Rajputs. His is a new note in the foreign policy of Delhi kings, and Akbar not only utilized it, but improved upon it. Akbar's policy towards the Rajputs was one of coercion relieved by conciliation. Like Sher Shah he wielded the two potent weapons of statecraft, force and diplomacy, with consummate skill. But while Sher Shah, after conquering the Rajputs, by war and diplomacy left them sullen and smarting under his yoke, Akbar after conquering them by the very same methods, not only reconciled them to his rule, but made them supporters of his sovereignty. Unlike Sher Shah Akbar, was able to gild the chain with which he bound the Rajputs, and established the tenderest of human relationships to serve that end. Akbar treated them as friends and relations, while Sher Shah had treated them as mere vassals.

This difference in the policy of these two kings of India was due to the different problems of empire-building that faced them. For Sher Shah the problem was to drive out the Mughals, and once that was done, the Afghan rule in India was revived, and there was no other difficulty. The people were already familiar with the Afghans, whom they were accustomed to obey, and whose rule was for them an accepted fact. Sher Shah could easily have their support. Hence he did not care whether the Rajputs were reconciled or not. Akbar, on the other hand, had not only to revive the Mughal rule, he had to make it acceptable to the people. He had to make the Mughal sway an established fact in Hindustan. The Mughals had lost their empire only fifteen years after its foundation to recover it fifteen years later. The Mughal restoration had hardly lasted for six months, when Akbar succeeded to the throne. He did not inherit an empire; he inherited the troubles of a disputed succession, and internal disorder. He had to crush the Afghans before he became the master of the situation; he had further to subdue the unruly and establish order. And all the while he was labouring under the great disadvantage that he was a foreigner in India. The people of Hindustan looked upon the Mughals with some suspicion. Hence when he conquered the Rajputs he strove to blot out all traces of bitterness, born of conquest, which might rankle in their heart. friendship and good-will made ample amends for the sword and blood; and his respect for their religion and racial susceptibilities endeared his rule to them. To crown all, matrimonial relationship bridged the gulf between the conqueror and the conquered.

"Whether the mother of Prince Akbar stimulated by the recollection of her misfortune, nursed his young animosity against Maldeo for the miseries of Umarkot, or whether it was merely an act of cautionary policy to curb the Rajput power, which was consistent with his own, in S. 1617 (1561 A.D.) he invaded Marwar"[1] Malkot or Mirtha was besieged, and captured after a sanguinary fight in 1562. The important castle of Nagore also fell, and both of these were conferred upon Ray Singh of Bikaner (belonging to a younger branch of the same family) who had early submitted to Akbar. After the fall of these important fortresses besides Ajmer, which had alrady become an integral part of the Mughal empire, Maldeo realized the necessity of submitting to Akbar, and in 1569 sent his second son Chandra Sen with customary gifts to the court of Akbar. The latter graciously received him, but resented the conduct of Maldeo, who did not come to pay homage in person. He therefore punished Maldeo by conferring Jodhpur upon Ray Singh of Bikaner. He even went further and proclaimed him

1. Tod's Annals Vol. II, p. 958.

as the chief of his race. Chandra Sen, a spirited youth resented the high-handed proceedings of Akbar, and left his court without leave. But Akbar was not the person to take this insult lying low. Hard on the heels of Chandra Sen was despatched an army, under Husain Kuli Khan, to besiege and capture Jodhpur. Maldeo offered a stubborn resistance but to no avail. When Jodhpur was captured, the old Rao submitted, but brave Chandra Sen would not. He retired to Siwana at the western exteremity of the state, and there lived for seventeen years, fighting for the honour of his house and disputing the claim of his elder brother Udai Singh to the throne.

In the mean while the broken-hearted and old Rao Mal Deo, had to send his eldest son Udai Singh to pay homage to Akbar on his behalf. Udai Singh succeeded in winning the favour of the emperor, and soon won the nick-name of "Motā Rajā" for his growing obesity. He was enrolled as a Mansabdar of one thousand, and recognised heir to the throne. In 1569 or 1570 died Maldeo, and was spared the humiliation of personally attending the court of Akabar. The last days of this hero of the desert was a contrast to the glory of his younger days, when the whole of Rajputana echoed his name. Had he lived but one more decade, he would have had Pratap by his side to fight for the cause of independence.

After his death Udai Singh succeeded him, and rendered signal services to the emperor, who held him in great esteem. He gave his daughter Jagat Gosain in marriage to Prince Salim, and on this happy occasion Akbar not only restored all the districts taken from Maldeo but granted several new ones in Malwa, so that the revenues of the state doubled. Yet in spite of the wealth and honour that the Rathor chiefs obtained from their Mughal connection they felt the degradation and this feeling often found expression in the presence of the suzerain.

In his old age Udai Singh grew so fat that he could not render military service, and hence deputed his son Sur Singh to represent him both in the court and the camp. In his last days he showed signs of licentiousness, and in spite of his twenty-seven queens cast covetous eyes on the daughter of a Brahman. He died in 1595 leaving thirtyfour sons and daughters to multiply his race.

The news of his death reached Sur Singh the eldest of his sons, while he was at Lahore with the imperial force. Owing to his exceptional achievements in wars, and resourcefulness he had been given the title of "Sawai Raja" even in the life-time of his father. When commanded to reduce the Raja of Sirohi, he did it so thoroughly that "the Rao had not a pallet left to sleep upon".[1] He was then associated with Khan-i-Azam in the campaign against Muzaffar Shah Gujrati in 1583-84. After the successful close of the campaign Khan-i-Azam was made the Khan-i-Khana and Sur Singh got a sword, a khilat, and a grant of fresh lands and increased Mansab. He succeeded his father in 1595, and on the outbreak of the Deccan war he was ordered to join the imperial army. "He obeyed, and with thirteen thousand horse, ten large guns, and twenty elephants, he fought three grand battles".[2] Thus the Mughal relations with Marwar, at the time of Akbar were extremly cordial. The Raos of Jodhpur became trusted allies and powerful vassals after they were subdued by Akbar and thus they remained till the reign of Aurangzeb.

On the occasion of Jahangir's coronation Sur Singh attended the court in company with his son Gaj Singh. Gaj Singh as his father's representative at the imperial court and camp rendered brilliant services to the empire. When charged with the conquest of Jalor from the rebel Bihari Pathan, he achieved it in three months killing seven thousand Pathans and taking rich spoils from the fort. Then in 1613, when Prince Khurram was deputed against Rana Amar Singh of Mewar, Gaj Singh was ordered to serve under him with the Marwar contingent. But since the Raja submitted there was no need of his services, but nevertheless his services were recognised and rewarded. In all Sur Singh had received sixteen fiefs from the emperor and had to maintain thirteen thousand horse for the imperial service. After his death in 1620 his son Gaj Singh succeeded. In the imperial army Gaj Singh had played a brilliant part in the sieges and battles of Kirki garh, Asir and Satara and had won for himself the title of Dalthamban or controller of the army. In recognition of his achievements his horses were exempted from the imperial dāgh or branding.

1. Tod's Annals Vol. II, p. 969.
2. Tod's Annnls Vol. II, p. 970.

When Prince Shah Jahan, after murdering his elder brother Khusrau, wanted to exclude Parvez from succession and sought Raja Gaj Singh's help, the latter turned a deaf ear to all his importunities, because Parvez was the son of his father's sister. During the rebellion of Prince Shah Jahan, Jahangir made an appeal to all the Rajput princes to support him in crushing the rebellious prince. There was a ready response and Gaj Singh showed such a great enthusiasm, that Janangir kissed his hand in the open court. That was no oridnary honour, and Raja Gaj enthusiastically led his troops to take part in the Battle of the Tons. The imperialists were led by Mahabat Khan, and according to his plan, the Kachhwa prince Mirza Raja of Amber was to have the command of the vanguard. The proud Rathod resented this arrangement because the post of honour which was his right had been given to his rival, and therefore he refused to fight and withdrew to a distance. It would have been fatal to the imperialists, had not Prince Shah Jahan sent a message either to join his cause or draw his sword. That was more than he could bear. Already he was burning to avenge the murder of his friend Govind Das perpetrated by Shah Jahan and now this message made him blind with rage, and forgetting the slight of Mahabat Khan he joined the ranks, he had just deserted. He fought with such a dash that the imperialists got victory and he wreaked his vengeance by killing Shah Jahan's friend Bhim Singh of Mewar.

The whole life of Gaj Singh was spent in fighting, and in 1638 he was killed in an expedition in Gujrat. He left two sons Amra and Jaswant. Amra, the elder was very turbulent and therefore in 1634 he was banished from the state. He entered the service of Shah Jahan but even there he proved unruly and was killed in a fracas in the imperial audience hall.

Jaswant Singh succeeded his father in 1638. Three years before (1635) he had taken an active part in the campaign against Jhujhar Singh of Bundelkhand. Twenty years after he ascended the Gaddi, the war of succession broke out amongst the sons of Shah Jahan and Prince Dara raised his Mansab to five thousand and sent him to check the northward advance of Aurangzeb and Murad. He took the commission and fought the battle of Dharmat on the 15th of April 1658 and sustained a defeat at the hands of the Princes. After Dharmat, Dara, was decisively defeated at Samugarh (29th May 1658) and then Jaswant Singh joined the standards of Aurangzeb. In the battle of Khajwa (14th January 1659) he behaved treacherously towards Aurangzeb and instead of taking part in fighting withdrew to his own kingdom. There he opened overtures with Dara, who was staying with Shah Nawaz Khan, the Governor of Gujrat, and was in sore need of help to regain his hold on the kingdom and promised to join him against Aurangzeb near Ajmer. Relying on his words Dara came to Ajmer, only to find that he had been forced to remain neutral by the threats and concessions of Aurangzeb. Single-handed he had to face the imperialists, led by his mortal enemy Aurangzeb at the pass of Deorai and after a deadly contested battle raging for full three days he was defeated (14th March 1659). He was pursued through Rajputana and Sindh, with relentless vigour and ultimately was captured at the mouth of the Bolan pass. In this war of succession Jaswant had showed himself as wantingin those virtues which mark out a Rajput from all others.

As regards Amber, it has been noticed, that Bihari Mall was the first Rajput prince to receive a Mansab of five thousand from Humayun. He was also the first Rajput prince to give his daughter in marriage to Akbar. Perhaps he was constrained to do that to Safeguard his interest against the hostility of Sharf-ud-din who had espoused the cause of Suja his elder brother Pooran Mal's son claiming Marwar for himself. Or perhaps the suggestion might have come from Akbar. It would be more in the fitness of things to credit Akbar with the suggestion. His foresight apart, he must have taken this cue from Humayun, who after the re-conquest of Hindustan "enjoined his nobles to enter into matrimonial alliance with the zamindars of the country, and after marrying the elder daughter of Jamal Khan, he asked Bairam Khan to marry the younger one".[1] Akbar must have extended the meaning of the "zamindars of the country" to include the Rajput princes. This is a remarkable feature of Mughal empire. At any rate Akbar's marriage with Bihari Mall's[2] daughter (1562) produced two important results. It united the interests of the Mughal

1. Ain-i-Akbari p. 334. (Trans. by Blockman).
2. I think Bihari Mall is more appropriate than Bharmal.

dynasty and of the Kachhwa princes of Amber; it created a bad precedent for other Rajput rulers, inasmuch as their giving a daughter became the *sine qua non* of their political submission. But this alliance had some grace and dignity about it. The bride was not converted to Islam. She followed her religion all her life and was the mother of Jahangir.

After the death of Bihari Mall, his son Bhagwan Das succeeded him in 1575, and ruled till 1592. In 1572 he saved the life of Akbar in the battle of Sarnal, and gave his daughter to Prince Salim in 1587, when he was created a Mansabdar of five thousand. In 1592 occured his death, and he was succeeded by his nephew and adopted son Man Singh. Before he became the ruler of Amber he had taken a prominent part in the affairs of the empire, and had rendered signal services to the emperor in different capacities. It was through his help that Akbar was so successful in his Rajput policy. The surrender of Ranthambor was brought about by means of his clever strategem (1569). In 1573, at Surat, when Akbar, intoxicated with wine, was about to kill himself it was Man Singh who saved him. The next year he accompanied Akbar to Bihar, and took an active part in the campaign against Daud. In 1575 he brought about the war with Rana Pratap, which lasted for about a quarter of a century. He held the governorship of Kabul, Bengal and the Indus provinces, and conducted important campaigns in that capacity. As the governor of Bengal he conquered Orissa, and made Assam tributary to the Mughals. Owing to all these brilliant achievements, he was raised to the Mansab of seven thousand towards the end of Akbar's reign. He was thus placed "above every Muhammadan officer, though soon after Shah Rukh and Aziz Koka were raised to the same dignity."[1]

After the death of Akbar, he supported Khusrau against Jahangir for the throne, but it was of no effect. After his coronation Jahangir loaded him with honours, to remove all bitterness from his mind. In 1611, he was sent along with Khan Jahan, against Rana Amar Singh of Mewar, and in 1615 died in Bengal.

After Man Singh his two successors Bhao Singh (1615-

1. Ain-i-Akbari, p. 341.

1621) and Maha Singh (1621-1625 A. D.) proved unworthy of his great reputation and achievements. They were weak and dissolute, and attained no distinction in the imperial service. Nor did they do anything substantial for the welfare of their own state.

Maha Singh was succeeded by Jai Singh (1625-1667 A.D.) popularly known as Mirza Raja Jai Singh, who equalled his great predecessor Man Singh in military talent and diplomacy. He played an inglorious part in the war of succession, and betrayed the cause of Dara after the battle of Bahadurpur, when he refused to accompany Suleiman Shukoh to the assistance of the vanquished Dara. It is significant that, but for the treachery of two powerful Rajput princes Jaswant Singh and Jai Singh, the cause of Dara would not have been lost and that of Aurangzeb triumphed. The war of succession, one of the most disgusting episodes of Mughal history reveals the depth of moral degradation into which the brave and noble Rajputs had fallen. At any rate Aurangzeb bestowed upon Jai Singh a Mansab of six thousand for his meritorious services and a few years later when the imperial generals failed one after another against Shivaji, sent him into the Deccan. He arrived in the Deccan in February 1665, and so cleverly did he manipulate the affairs that Shivaji felt the pressure of his diplomacy as much as of his force. Shivaji opened overtures for a peace, and it was concluded on the12th June 1665, by which he gave up the major part of his conquests to the emperor and acknowledged his suzerainty. He further prersuaded Shivaji to visit the court of the emperor in 1665. This remarkable achievement would have been the precursor of much good to the empire had not Aurangzeb spoiled the original plan of Jai Singh by treacherously imprisoning Shivaji at Agra. When he escaped, Jai Singh was suspected of being a party to it, and his son and representative at the court was disgraced. This came as a great shock in his old age and he died on the 2nd July 1667 at Burhanpur.

His place in the imperial service could never be filled by his successors, and consequently other Rajput princes snatched away the distinction that the Jaipur princes enjoyed since the time of Akbar. His successor was so unworthy of the Rajput name and fame, that when in 1679 the Rajput war broke out owing to the outrageous proceedings of Aurangzeb he did not raise a finger to help the league of the Rajput princes. In 1699 succeeded Sawai Jai Singh to the Gaddi of Amber, and his personality was remarkable in so many spheres of life. Great as a warrior, shrewd and far-seeing as a statesman, deeply concerned in the welfare of his subjects, and incomparable in his time as a scholar and scientist, he has left an immortal name behind. His learned treatise on astronomy, and his observatories still standing, are more enduring monuments of his glory than his political achievements. He took an active part in the war of succession after the death of Aurangzeb. When Bahadur Shah marched into the Deccan, he formed a league of Rajput princes to withold their allegiance to the Mughals, and stop giving their daughters to them. He however failed to carry out his scheme, but later on helped the ascendancy of the Marathas under his friend Baji Rao, and thus brought about the downfall of the Mughals. That in short is the history of the dealings of the Mughals with the Amber princes.

Rao Jodha, the founder of Jodhpur had fourteen sons, and as all of them could not be provided for in the desert country, they were permitted to conquer foreign lands. The sixth son Bika conquered the country, to the north of the state, and founded the city of Bikaner in 1488. The first among the Rathor princes of Bikaner to submit to Akbar was Raja Kalyan Mall, who was a friend of Bairam Khan, and paid his court to Akbar at Ajmer about 1571-72. He held a mansab of two thousand, and did not play any conspicuous part in the empire. His son however had a more distinguished career, and obtained the first charge of trust when in 1573 Akbar started to crush the Gujrat rebellion. He was ordered to hold Jodhpur as a precautionary measure during the campaign. Two years later he went with Shah Quli Maharam to crush the rebellion of Chandra Sen, son of Maldeo. He failed, and therefore was recalled. When Muhammed Hakim Mirza invaded the Punjab in 1580, Rai Singh along with other nobles was sent in advance of the imperial army. He was employed against the Baluchis, and against the Rana Amar Singh of Mewar. He outlived Akbar and became a mansabdar of five thousand at the succession of Jahanagir. When Khusrau rebelled and

Jahangir pursued him into the Punjab, he was in charge of the imperial harem. Since he left his charge without the permission of the emperor, Jahangir determined to chastise him. But he returned to his allegiance in a year, and regained the royal favour. He gave his daughter to Jahangir and died about 1612.

After Rai Singh none of his successors rose to the eminence he had attained, though the dynasty freely shed its blood for the good of the empire. Karan Singh (1632-1669) showed some insubordination, and was punished by Aurangzeb in 1660. Of his four sons three were slain in the Deccan in the imperial service, and the fourth Anup Singh succeeded his father. He was a loyal servant of the empire, and held a mansab of five thousand. His successors were of little importance, and left no impress on the history of the Mughal empire.

Nothing particular is known about the dealings between the Rawals of Jaisalmer and the Mughals, except that in 1615 Sawai Singh held the state as a fief from the Mughals, and he and his successors continued to render loyal services to the empire.

"With Rao Surjan commenced a new era for Bundi (1554). Hitherto her princes had enjoyed independence excepting the homage and occasional service on emergencies which are maintained as much from kinship as vassalage."[1] The homage was rendered to the Ranas of Mewar. Rao Surjan of Bundi was the commandant of the fort of Ranthambor for the Ranas of Mewar. After taking Chitor Akbar invested it in February 1569 in person, and found that it was impossible to capture it by force of arms. Hence in consultation with Man Singh and Bhagwandas, he resorted to a strategem, and effected his purpose without wasting time or resources. He entered the castle disguised as the mace-bearer of Man Singh; was recognised and accorded due respect by Surjan Rao's uncle, and won over the commandant by fair promises of reward and royal favour. On the spot a treaty was drawn up, the main provisions of which throw light on the Rajput policy of Akbar. The terms were (i) that the chiefs of Bundi should be exempted from that custom degrading to a Rajput, of sending

1. Tod's Annals, Vol. III, p. 1480.

a Dola (bride) to the royal harem; (ii) that they should be exempted from the Jazia or poll tax; (iii) that they should be exempted from the obligation of sending their wives and female relatives to hold a stall in the Mina bazar at the palace, for the festival of Naoroza; (iv) that they should have the privilege of entering the Diwan-i-aam or hall of audience completely armed; (v) that they should not be compelled to cross Attock; (vi) that their sacred edifices should be respected; (vii) that they should never be placed under a Hindu leader; (viii) that their horses should not be branded; (ix) that they should be allowed to beat their kettle-drums in the streets of the capital as far as the Lal Darwaza or red-gate; (x) that they should not be commanded to make the prostration, or sijdah, on entering the presence; (xi) and that their capital Bundi should never be taken away from them.[1] In short Akbar promised to respect all the national susceptibilities of a Rajput. The integrity of Bundi was never violated but Ranthambor formed a part of the imperial territory and was included in the Subah or province of Ajmer.[2] Afterwards he was appointed governor of Garha-Katanga, from where he was transferred to the province of Benares, with a mansab of two thousand. He lived in Benares, to a good old age, and added many beautiful temples to the city. Two of his sons took a valiant part in the Gujrat campaign as well as in the Deccan wars. He died in 1593, and was succeeded by Rao Bhoj. He was full of Rajput pride, and resented Jahangir's proposal to marry his grand-daughter, i.e., the daughter of his daughter, married to Man Singh's son Jagat Singh. "Hence Jahangir resolved to punish him on his return from Kabul. But Rao Bhoj in the end of 1016 A.H. (1607) committed suicide."[3] It is therefore said that Rathor and Kachhwa princesses were married to the Timurids, but not the Hara princesses. He was succeeded by Rao Ratan, his eldest son. He helped Jahangir against his rebellious son Khurram. It was during his time that Kotah was separated from Bundi, both of which used to be

1. Tod's Annals, Vol. III. p. 1482. Though a different version has been given by Dr. Srivastav in his Akbar the Great, I am inclined to agree with Tod and Smith.

2. Smith's Akbar, p. 100.

3. Ain-i-Akbari p. 458.

called Haravati. He gave Kotah to his second son Madho Singh, because he had rendered meritorious services to the emperor. In 1652 Rao Chhatrasal succeeded his grand-father Rao Ratan, and played an important part in the war succession of 1658. He was a staunch partisan of Dara, and was killed in the battle of Samugarh (29th May 1658). He "had been engaged in fifty-two combats, and left a name renowned for courage and incorruptible fidelity."[1] He was succeeded by his son Rao Bhao Singh (1658-1678)and since the father had supported Dara, the son was punished. His state was ordered to be devastated, but since he bravely defended it, and defeated the imperial troops, Aurangzeb pleased with his courage, pardoned him, and bade him come to the court. He complied and was granted the government of Aurangabad under prince Mauzzam. Owing to his great deeds of valour and the erection of many public edifices, he was well known in Aurangabad. He died sometime between March 1677 and February 1678, and since he was childless his brother's grandson succeeded him under the style Rao Anirudh Singh. He accompanied Aurangzeb into the Deccan, and rendered signal services there.

On the whole the relations of the Haras with the Mughals, were cordial, and they distinguished in battles as no other Rajputs did.

Thus all the Rajput princes were won over without much difficulty. One after another they were lured into the dignity of office and courtly ease, and most of them materially profited, but instead they had to barter their honour and independence. That was the result of their lack of unity and common purpose. But amongst them there was one house, which did not submit without making vigorous and almost superhuman efforts to retain its independence. The glories of Mewar far surpassing those of other states had kept alive in the heart of the Sisodias that flame of patriotism, which defied danger and death in order to keep the honour bright. Even in the days of craven Udai Singh Chitor was not an easy conquest. According to the Tod's Annals, Akbar twice besieged that fort, the first time he could not take it because of the masculine courage of the Rana's concubine, and the second

1. Tod's Annals, Vol. III, p. 1492.

time he took it inspite of the heroic defence of Jai Mall and Patta. Rana Udai Singh fled away, and spent his days in pleasure and unconcern on the banks of Udai Sagar. Four years did he live in ignoble ease, and when he died there ensued a quarrel among his sons on the question of succession. At last Pratap, the greatest of that great race of Rajputs, was acknowledged as the King, and succeeded to a kingdom whose capital had been conquered, whose resources had been crippled, and whose allies had been lured into service of the Mughals. He had only the unsullied honour of his house, the unflinching devotion of his followers, and his own unfathomable love for the country as his only assets. With these he determined to defy the Mughals, and liberate his country from their clutches. While the princes of Marwar, Amber, Bikaner, Bundi, and his own brother Sagarji made common cause with the Mughals against him, while the resources of the fair and rich empire of Hindustan were employed against him, and while the armies from the hills of Kabul, the highlands of Central Asia and the sands of Rajputana were ranged against him, he could only count upon the indomitable courage of the Sisodias and his capacity to lead them into the battle for freedom. And despite his advantage Akbar lost and Pratap won.

So long as Akbar's hands were full with other works he could not direct his energies against Mewar. In 1575 his conquest of Northern India was completed by the annexation of Bengal and in this year the Rana gave offence to Man Singh by refusing to dine with him. Rana's reasons in doing so were, that Man Singh had defiled his caste and degraded his family by entering into matrimonial relations with the Mughals. Man Singh reported the conduct of the Rana to Akbar, who already offended at his unbending attitude, was sufficiently exasperated to declare war on him. "But the first considerable fight was disastrous to the cause of liberty" and that was the battle of Haldighat or Gogunda (June 1576).[1] The Mughal army was under the command of Man Singh, who was assisted by Asaf Khan the second, and other officers of note. At the pass of Haldighat "Pratap was posted with the flower of Mewar and glorious was the struggle for its mainte-

1. Smith's Akbar, p. 151.

nance. Clan after clan followed with desperate intrepidity, emulating the daring of the prince."[1] But this desperate valour of the Rajputs was of no avail against the Mughal artillery. The Rana fled away leaving the bulk of his army dead on the field. But if he was defeated in battle, he was not dismayed in his fight for independence. He continued the war through stress and strain, and gave no rest to himself and his enemies so long as he was alive. In his struggle, against the greatest of the Mughals, extending for about a quarter of a century there were times when darkness and danger thickened around him, and his cause seemed lost for ever. But all these he bore with admirable courage, and the last years of his life were comparatively peaceful and glorious, for he recovered all Mewar excepting Chitor, Ajmer and Mandalgarh, and Akbar could not carry on the war owing to his stay for thirteen years away from his capital. In 1597, before Akbar returned to his capital, died the great Rana, leaving a name that is immortal in the history of India, that is even now idolized by every Rajput, and revered by all.

But on his death-bed he was restless to think that his son Amar would not be able to maintain the independence, for which he had fought all his life. He had not that immeasurable store of fortitude, which triumphs over tribulations, and so did it prove to be in the end. In the reign of Jahangir several expeditions were sent against Mewar, and the first impulses of the Rana were for politic submission. Wearied out at last he submitted in 1614, and was very honourably treated by Prince Khurram. Thus ended the struggle for independence of the last great house of Rajputana. The submission of the Rana was only a "bare recognition of the imperial suzerainty" and a precarious independence was at last bartered for ignoble peace.

But Rana Amar Singh did not like to reign after the loss of independence. He abdicated in favour of his son Karan Singh, and secluded himself in the sylvan retreat of Nauchauki (1620). According to the terms of the treaty, the Ranas were to be exempted from personal attendance, and their only mark of submission would be to receive an imperial Farman

2. Tod's Annal. Vol. I. 270.

outside their capital at the time of their accession to the Gaddi of Mewar. Nevertheless the Rana felt the indignity of Mewar being called a fief or Jagir, and himself, a jagirdar of the empire. Jahangir himself of Rajput blood, and a great admirer of Rajput valour spared no pains to mitigate the indignity and placed "the heir-apparent of Mewar immediately over all the princes of Hindustan." He also got two life-size marble statues made, one of Rana Amar Singh, the other of his son Karan Singh, and placed them below his Jharokha or audience window. The Sisodias did not fail to appreciate the generosity of Jahangir, and henceforth their interest became indentical with those of the empire. When Prince Shahjahan rebelled owing to the undesirable domination of Nurjahan, he was aided by a Mewar prince, Raja Bhim Singh a younger brother of Rana Karan. He saved Shahjahan from sustaining a crushing defeat at Bilochpur in March 1623, and stood firm by him, when men like the Khana-i-khana Abdur Rahim deserted him. He fought bravely at the battle of the Tons, and was there killed covered with wounds. Mahabat Khan when driven to desperation by the enmity of Nurjahan, was sheltered in Mewar, whence he opened overtures for friendship with Prince Shahjahan, and ultimately joined him. Rajput tradition fondly narrates how, when Prince Shahjahan was worsted by Mahabat Khan and a few years after he took shelter in Mewar, the Rana built for him a sumptuous edifice "adorned with a lofty dome crowned with the crescent."[1] It was gorgeously decorated, and the prince lived here till, a short time before his father's death, he left the Rana's shelter to retire into Persia. But he returned from Sindh, and along with Mahabat Khan awaited his chances for the throne.

Rana Jagat Singh succeeded Rana Karan in 1628. After Jahangir died, and the throne was secured for Shahjahan by his father-in-law, Asaf Khan, the new Rana "sent his brother and a bard of Rajputs to Surat to form cortege of emperor, who repaired directly to Udaipur; and it was in the Badal Mahal of his palace that he was first saluted by the title of Shahjahan."[2] It is said that the new monarch restored five alienated districts, and presented a very valuable ruby

1. Tod's Annals, Vol. I, p. 431.
2. Tod's Annals, Vol. I, p. 432.

to the Rana before he left Udaipur. Whether he permitted to fortify Chitor is doubtful, but certain it is that he was very favourably disposed to the Ranas of Udaipur, and when sheltered there as a prince, had exchanged his turban with Rana Karan, as symbol of fraternity. The reign of Jagat Singh is primarily an epoch of constructive work. The state began to thrive in peace; beautiful palaces and garden-houses bedecked the capital and the lakes that give a special charm to Mewar.

Rana Jagat Singh died in 1652, and was succeeded by Rana Rai Singh, whose reign was as disturbed as his father's was peaceful. Only two years after his accession, he began to fortify Chitor in violation of the treaty between the Ranas and the Mughals, and was promptly punished by Sahajahan, who sent an army against him, and he had to tender an apology to the emperor. On the eve of the war of succession, each of the four sons of Shahjahan wrote to him seeking his aid, and he was inclined towards Dara, as did many other Rajput princes. But sword became the supreme arbiter of the claims of the rival princes, and it made Aurangzeb the emperor. Dharmat, Samugarh and Deorai decided the fate of Dara as did Khajwah of Shuja; and Murad was executed in the prison fortress of Gwalior. The support of the Rajputs was of as little avail to Dara, as all the resources of Bengal to Shuja.

But the victory of Aurangzeb was the victory of Islamic orthodoxy. He had fought the war of succession, and had driven his brothers to destruction because they were, one and all, degenerate Muslims, and of them Dara was an apostate from Islam. With inexorable consistency Aurangzeb followed, in the plenitude of his power, a policy, that was at once indicative of the man, and destructive of the stability of the Empire. It reversed and in a way resembled, the policy of Akbar, a century before. Akbar had insulted Islam, Aurangzeb insulted Hinduism; and both indulged in the coercion of a creed. In 1579 Akbar's religious policy had precipitated the most formidable rebellion in his reign and in 1679, Aurangzeb's reactionary measures resulted in the Rajput war, which proved very harmful to the interests of the Empire. In this war Maharana Raj Singh played an important part. Aurangzeb had started his reign by offending the Hindus, and in 1669 had issued a general order "to demolish all the schools and temples of the infidels, and to put down their religious teaching and practices."[1] Even before this his senseless bigotry had goaded the peasants of Mathura to rebellion, and a little later followed the rebellion of the Satnamis and the Sikhs. Not perturbed by these outrages he planned a fresh outrage on the most devoted servants of the Empire viz, the Rajputs. When on the 10th of December 1678 Maharaja Jaswant Singh of Jodhpur died at Jamrud, Aurangzeb eager to annex his state, immediately appointed Muslim officers to take charge of the government of Jodhpur, and on the 9th of January 1679 himself left for Ajmer "in order to be close enough to Jodhpur to opposition, and direct the military operation that might be necessary."[2] He remained there till the end of March, and invested Indra Singh, chief of Nagore and a descendant of the family of Jaswant, with a mock royalty, as the head of the Rathors and the Raja of Jodhpur. In the meanwhile the news that one of the Jaswant Singh's widows had given birth to a son reached Aurangzeb on the 26th of February 1679. On the 2nd of April he returned to the capital and on that day he imposed Jaziya on the Hindus, as if he was not content with injury only, and wanted to add insult to it. This was resented by all the Hindus, and Maharana Raj Singh, and Shivaji wrote to Aurangzeb emphasising the inexpediency of the order. But Aurangzeb was not to be moved from his resolve. Equally inexorable was he in his determination to annex Jodhpur, when two deputations of Rathor chiefs waited on the emperor, and pleaded the claims of Ajit Singh, the posthumous son of Jaswant Singh. The family of Jaswant Singh had by that time returned to Delhi and the emperor demanded that baby Ajit should be left in his care, and since the Rathors and their great leader Durgadas demurred, he ordered an army to surround the residence of Jaswant Singh's Ranis. These proceedings of Aurangzeb maddened the Rathors into fury, and their leader Durgadas determined to rescue the sole heir of his dead master from the clutches of the emperor. Thus resolved, he cut his way through the Mughal troops, by a series

1. Sarkar's Aurangazeb Vol. III, p. 265.
2. Ibid. p. 326.

of rear guard actions, and carried the baby prince with his mother in safety to Marwar (22nd July 1679).

"Ajit grew up in strict concealment among a monastic brotherhood on the lonely rock of Abu. But his escape from Delhi had become known, and his name became the rallying cry of the Rathor legitimists."[1] Aurangzeb's officers in Jodhpur found it hard to tackle the situation, and poor Indra Singh proved utterly incapable to check the surging sea of the fierce Rathors. Hence Aurangzeb dismissed or degraded the former, and dethroned the latter. It appeared as if Aurangzeb had been baffled but he was not the man to own a defeat so easily. He therefore proclaimed that Durgadas' protege was an impostor, and that the genuine prince Ajit Singh, was being brought up in his own palace. The latter however was no other than a milk-maid's son. Soon after he despatched a strong force under Sarbuland Khan to take Jodhpur (17th August 1679), and a fortnight later he himself went to Ajmer to direct military operations from there. Large reinforcements flooded the country of the Rathors, and they were slowly but steadily dislodged from all their strongholds. Their country was ravaged, and their religion insulted. That at once threatened the religious liberty and political safety of Mewar. For, Marwar annexed the annexation of Mewar was only a question of time, and on the revival of Jaziya the Maharana had been asked to enforce it in his state. To add to it came the appealing entreaty of the mother of Ajit Singh, herself a princess of Mewar for the protection of her baby boy. All these considerations provoked the Maharana to make common cause with the Rathors. By the end of November the war assumed greater magnitude with the entry of the Rana into it. But Aurangzeb was not unprepared for a contingency like this, and he was the first to strike. Leaving Ajmer on the 30th of November 1679 he occupied the pass of Deobari early in January 1680, and almost immediately, the capital of Udaipur. The Rana had prepared to meet the Mughal attack by ordering the complete evacuation of the plain country the capital included. The triumph of the Mughals seemed to be a barren one, for the Mughals shrank from penetrating

1. Sarkar's Aurangzeb Vol. III, p. 334.

the hilly regions, whither the Rana had retired with his people. The Rajputs fought a guerilla war but Aurangzeb glutted his vengeance by destroying 236 temples in Udaipur and Chitor alone. When he returned by the end of March, Prince Akbar was left in occupation of the Chitore district as the Mughal base with a strong army. But the Mughals' positions in Mewar and Marwar became separated by the Aravalis, and the Rana, who had held the crest in force, could easily make surprise attacks on the Mughals, eastward or westward, as it suited his convenience. On the whole the Mughals felt hard pressed in the two theatres of war, chiefly because they could not successfully meet the guerilla tactics of the Rajpus, and did not know the ins and outs of that hilly country. In June Prince Akbar was transferred to Marwar front, and Prince Azam took his place in Chitor. A grand campaign was planned to close the cordon of Mughal armies round the hilly retreat of the Maharana, but it failed. The Rathors and Sisodias literally tired out their opponents, and made themselves so dreadful, that on one occasion Tahawar Khan refused to enter the hills. Even when he entered he suffered heavy losses at the hands of Bhim Singh, the second son of the Maharana. Nevertheless, Aurangzeb did not budge an inch from his resolve, and the operations continued with great vigour. But from September 1680, a suspicious slackening of Prince Akbar's activities was noticeable, and the prince was listening to the overtures of Durgadaṣ and Rajsingh, who pointed out to him that his father's bigoted policy was about to sap the foundations of the empire, and that the most advisable step for him should be to seize the throne with their help. The negotiations had not taken a final form when the Maharana died (22nd October, 1680) and a month had passed before his son and successor Jaisingh could resume the negotiations. In December definite agreements were reached. Akbar promised to treat the Rajputs with honour and justice, while the Maharana agreed to send half of his army to his help. The prince crowned himself as emperor on the 1st January 1681, and on the 2nd, marched on Ajmer to capture it. But instead of a dash on Ajmer, he delayed on the way covering a distance of 120 miles in thirteen days. His dilatory proceedings came to his father's rescue, for he could call back several divisions from contiguous regions, and collected a respectable army of sixteen thousand men. When Akbar approached Ajmer, Aurangzeb met him at Deoraha, four miles from Ajmer. But as the two armies lay face to face, Aurangzeb wrote a letter commending the cleverness of his son Akbar in luring the Rajputs into a snare, where they could be easily destroyed; and contrived it to fall into the hands of Durgadas. Durgadas did not believe it, but when he went to prince Akbar for ascertaining the truth of the matter, he could not enter his tent, as it was past midnight, and the prince had given strict orders that he should not be awakened. Then he sent his men to Tahawar Khan, the right-hand man of the Prince, and he was reported to have gone to the imperial camp. He therefore felt convinced of the truth of the letter, and three hours before dawn, he rode away at the head of all his troops towards Marwar. When the silly Prince Akbar awoke in the morning after the revelries of the night he found to his surprise that all had deserted him except a devoted band of his old retainers, and he too fled away in the track of the Rajputs giving up all hopes of wresting the peacock throne from his father.

It was only when Prince Akbar joined Durgadas that the latter discovered the trick played on them and since Akbar was relentlessly pursued in Mewar and Marwar, he was conducted by Durgadas into the Court of the Maratha King Sambhaji, where he was safe. But the flight of the prince, who had made an attempt to get the throne on the strength of Rajputs, and failed, was likely to prove dangerous in alliance with the Marathas who were the sworn enemy of Aurangzeb. The rebel son of Shahjahan could not rest in peace because his own son had rebelled against him, and he became anxious to make peace with the Rajputs in order that he might come to the Deccan to prevent Akbar from further mischief. On the other hand the Rajputs had been fighting against tremendous odds to retain their honour and independence. Their country had been ravaged and the resources ruined by the Mughals. Starvation stared them in the face. It was only their indomitable courage and fortitude, that had sustained them in their darkest hour. Hence they too were eager for peace. On the 14th of June 1681, Maharana Jai Singh made peace. For the Rathors, an honourable peace was out of the question, and hence in Marwar the war dragged on for more than a quarter of a century till after the death of Aurangzeb, when Ajit Singh's claims were recognised by his successor Bahadur Shah.

But Aurangzeb was not mindful of Marwar now and as he withdrew into the Deccan in September 1681 the Mughal pressure on the Rajputs was relaxed. In the end the Rathors vindicated their honour. They had shown great courage, wonderful tenacity of purpose and admirable fortitude, which equalled the glory of the Sisodias under Pratap. But at this national crisis the Sisodias showed unworthy of their great traditions, and betrayed the cause, for which the Rathors shed their blood freely for thirty years. The Maharana made a mistake in concluding peace without reference to the people of Marwar. The impolicy, however, of Aurangzeb proved disastrous to the interests of the empire, and damaged the imperial prestige to an unprecedented degree. Nearly all the Rajput clans, except the Kachhwas refused to serve in the imperial army, and therefore Aurangzeb was immediately handicapped in his Deccan War. Indeed nothing could be a greater folly than to provoke the Rajputs to rebel at a time, when the Afghans on the northern and the Marathas on the southern frontier had not been mastered. The hostility of the Rajputs was never pacified and after Aurangzeb's death, it helped to hasten the downfall of the Mughal Empire.

That in short is the outline of the relations of the Rajputs with the Mughals. It was the Mughals, who immensely profited by their Rajput connection, for they employed the Rajputs in war and diplomacy and through them endeared their rule to the Hindus in general. The Rajputs marched as the standard bearers of the Mughals to distant corners of India and settled there as the sentinels of their empire. But the Rajputs ruined their man-power thereby. Poor and sterile, Rajputana could not shed her life-blood perennially for the sake of the empire and send out colonies of warriors without depopulating many of her thriving localities. The Rajputs spread all over India, but their expansion destroyed their vitality and traditions, owing to their detached life in foreign lands. Thus the Rajputs, whose man-power had constantly been exploited by the Mughals for a century and a half, absolutely broke down at the decline of the Mughal empire. So complete had been their national exhaustion, that they had to submit to the Marathas, and to the British after the Marathas, without a show of opposition. The fall of the Mughals therefore heralded the fall of the Rajputs. After that, they ceased to count as a factor in the politics of India.

CHAPTER IV

THE GENESIS OF THE DIN-I-ILAHI

The sixteenth century is a century of religious revival in the history of the world. The grand currents of the Reformation compare favourably with the surging-up of a new life in India. India experienced an awakening that quickened her progress and vitalized her national life. The dominant note of this awakening was Love and Liberalism—Love that united man to God, and therefore to his brother man, and Liberalism, born of this love that levelled down the barrier of caste, creed and calling, and took its stand on the bed-rock of human existence and essence of all religions, universal brotherhood, With glorious ideals it inspired the Hindu and Muslim alike, and they forgot for a time the trivialities of their creed. To the Muslim as to the Hindu, it heralded the dawn of a new era, to the Muslim with the birth of the promised Mahdi, to the Hindu with the realization of the all-absorbing love of God.

The beginning of the sixteenth century recorded the advent of two new peoples into India—the Mughals and the Europeans, the one as conquerors, the other as partly conquerors and partly traders. They brought with them their own culture, and tried to impose it on the country; but the Mughal succeeded, and the European failed. That was due not only to the enormous political power that backed the Mughal culture, but to its essentially kindred nature, that endeared it to the people and its suitability to the needs of the time and genius of India. At this time however, India was evolving one of her own, and her task was facilitated by her contact with the Mughals. They supplied the leaven, and the result was the splendid outburst of the literary and artistic genius of India. Indeed in the whole length of Indian history we do not come across another century within whose compass such a gamut of religious movements rose to blend their notes and enrich each other. The Vaishnavas, the Mahdavis and the Roshnis propounded great truths and inspired men with new hopes and ideals. They sang of their immortal themes, and preached their priceless realizations with an earnestness and eloquence, that made the very atmosphere throb with feeling. The transient joys and sorrows of life were to be consecrated, the limitations of mortality to be transceded and the follies of man to be forgotten, such were their inspired teachings. Into such an elevating atmosphere entered the Mughals bringing with them their great heritage of culture and refinement. Drinking freely of the fountain of Sufism, they always took a broad and liberal view of life, and developed the habit of thinking freely and thereby detaching themselves from the narrow bounds of orthodoxy. Thus they aided the trend of the times, and exercised a synthesizing influence, helping to produce a new culture, that has lived through centuries, long after their sceptre crumbled to the dust.

Babar and Humayun showed this trait of their character, but neither of them lived sufficiently long and in peace to make any impression on or take the impress of Indian thought. But Akbar did both; he took the impress of, and left this impress on, India. In this sense Akbar was essentially an Indian monarch, though a foreigner in India. He inherited great traditions of culture and conquest, and like his father and grandfather had come into close contact with the Sufis. Intelligent to an uncommon degree, with a mind alert and inquisitive, he was best fitted by birth, up-bringing and association to feel most keenly those hankerings and that spiritual unrest which distinguished the century in which he lived. Thus he was not only the child of his century, he was its best replica. To ascertain therefore the variety of influences that moulded his character, and eventually impelled him to found a novel faith—Din-i-Ilahi, the outcome of his eclecticism, an outline of his heredity and environments is necessary; for the former endowed him with those qualities of head and heart that prepared him to receive the impress of his environments, and reflect it in the best possible way.

The descendants of Taimur have been not only mighty warriors and empire-builders but were men of enlightenment and scholarship. Their zeal for conquest and achievements in the field has not obliterated the aesthetic side of their life. Taimur himself was an ideal for his house. If he made wide conquests to increase the glory of his name, he extended his patronage as widely to men of learning. Poets and painters, sculptors and historians, philosophers and scientists, all graced his court, and he felt equally at home in their company as in that of his war-hardened soldiers. If he conquered kingdoms, he did so to enrich Samarkand and Bokhara, which became not only the seats of culture in Asia but boasted of beautiful palaces and extensive parks, public baths and garden-houses, colleges and mosques. Even the country around became one stretch of smiling green owing to a network of canals. His unwearied zeal for conquest found ample leisure for conversation with scholars and artists, and great as a builder of empire, he was equally great as a builder of the seats of culture. His son Shah-rukh inherited his father's great qualities. Besides being the ruler of a vast empire he was a great lover of the peaceful pursuits of life. 'Through India China and Tartary and even some western countries went his emissaries of peace, gathering knowledge for him, inviting scholars to his court, and by well-doing only spreading the fame of the peace-loving Shah-rukh'.[1] Ulugh Beg, his son proved himself not unworthy of his house. He was a great soldier but his achievements in the field have been eclipsed by his achievements in science. He encouraged the cause of science by building an observatory at the foot of a mountain in Samarkand, that was three stories high, and very well equipped. He also contributed to the advancement of astronomy by compiling some astronomical tables. Abu Sayyid Mirza of Samarkand and Sultan Hussain Mirza of Herat were also famous for their high attainments, and patronage of art, literature and science. As for Babar it is difficult to exaggerate his many-sided genius. Great as a soldier, great as a conqueror, great as a man, he was equally great as a scholar, as a poet and as a writer of spirited prose. Wherever he went, he went to win the love of the people and to make their country beautiful. In Hindustan, in the din of war, he found time to lay out beautiful gardens. In his tempestuous life he snatched moments of peace to write not only his monumental autobiography, but a Turki diwan (collection of odes), a tract on Turki prosody, and several commentaries in the same language. He was also a skilful musician and a *connoisseur* of art. He was thoroughly conversant with Sufism, the Masnavi being a source

1. Von Noer, vol. i, p. 134.

of perennial interest for him. Such a combination of wonderful accomplishments has seldom been noticed in any monarch, eastern or western. Though not as accomplished as Babar, Humayun had inherited his faculties in no inconsiderable degree. Besides being a lovable man, essentially good and kind at heart he possessed a competent knowledge of geography, history, chemistry, music and poetry, as known in those days. He was also a poet of some reputation. And the son of Humayun, grandson of Babar, and the descendant of Taimur could not fail to inherit those talents, and tendencies for culture, which are rare among the rulers of men.

But he claimed descent from Chingiz Khan also. Chingiz Khan, the greatest conqueror known to history, was not an errant barbarian. He was a learned law-giver, and well-versed in the arts and sciences of the age. Kublai Khan, his descendant, was not only a great conqueror but a versatile scholar. He was no mean linguist, being conversant with Persian, Arabic, Tibetan, Chinese and even Latin. He took immense interest in the progress of art and science, which flourished under his patronage. Yunus Khan, the maternal grandfather of Babar, was again an all-round scholar. His culture had almost wiped off the traces of his Mongol ancestry. He was a poet, painter, penman, musician, scientist, and what not ! Akbar's own mother was the daughter of a Persian scholar, who was the descendant of a celebrated saint of Persia. Such were the traditions of the house in which Akbar was born. The culture of the house softened the edge of orthodoxy, and in their attitude towards religion, the later Timurids, especially Babar and Humayun allowed a degree of latitude, that was tantamount to toleration. This was due chiefly to their association with Sufi mystics, many of whom were poets. In order to understand the full significance of the influences of Sufi mysticism on the Timurids, a brief outline of the cult will not be out of place here.

'Most of the Asiatic poets are Sufis' and 'they prefer or profess to prefer, the meditations and ecstasies of mysticism to the pleasures of the world".[1] Their mysticism is based upon the doctrine that God alone is the absolute reality, that the

1. *Rose Garden of Persia*, p. 44.

human soul is an emanation from His essence with which it is to be reunited, and that 'the universe is nothing more than a combination of accidents united in a single essence in the Truth.[1] God is immanent in all things, and to feel His hallowed presence in them was the heart-felt desire of the Sufis. For this they lived a pure and noble life, and discarded all material attachments, and practised deep contemplation or Mushahdah. They had no faith in rituals and, imbued with a deep love for God, they 'held that divine illumination and grace were imparted directly to every soul, and not through the channel of external observances.'[2] That was why Jalal-ud-din Rumi declared 'fools exalt the mosque while they ignore the true temple in the heart.' Their pure and fervent love of God impelled them to reject all hopes of reward either in this world or in the next and the cheap worldly righteousness that consists in the scruptulous observance of ablutions, prayers fastings, etc. They aspired for the beatific vision or union with God in an ecstatic state, which has been considered as the quintessence of all happiness. But the true Sufi should not rest content with the union only. He must try to live continuously in that ecstatic state. As the great Sufi theologian Ghazali said 'you must know that the beginning of the path is the journey to God and that journey in God is its goal, for in this latter, absorption in God takes place. At the outset this glides by like a flash of light barely striking the eye; but thereafter becoming habitual it lifts the mind into a higher world when the most pure essential Reality is manifested, and the human mind is imbued with the form of the spiritual world, whilst the majesty of the Deity evolves and discloses itself.' This in the Hindu mysticism is the highest stage of Yoga. This state is to be attained by continuous striving, by trying to feel constantly His presence in everything, by purging one's own thought, and centring it on God. Such in brief, are the beliefs and practices of the Sufis.

Inspired by the divine presence in everything, the Sufi poets wrote beautiful verses, that breathed celestial beauty. Thrilled by the touch and sight of their Beloved, they forgot the whole world, and sang immortal songs depicting their experience that is at once so evanescent and so eternal. Maddened

1. *Lawaih translated by Whinfield and Kazimi*, p. 33.
2. *Ibid.*, Preface xii.

by the wine of His love they saw life transformed into one unending dream of joy in which the evils of life, its sorrows and tears, had no existence at all. They expressed these ecstatic experiences of theirs through the medium of a symbolism that smacks of sensuousness to the uninitiated. They used wine or wine-cup as a symbol of faith or fervent love for God; the cup-bearer as a symbol of God Himself. God is also symbolized as the rose or rose-garden, and the devotee, the nightingale. Through these symbols the Sufi gave form to his sublimest, and therefore the most impalpable feelings of his heart. Whether it be Moasi, the king of poets (eleventh century) singing of his 'lovely fair' or Sadi the 'nightingale of the groves of Shiraz' (thirteenth century), the great Maulana of Rum (twelfth and thirteenth centuries) or Omar Khayyam (twelfth century) singing of his wine-cup, roses and fair maidens, the inimitable Hafiz (fourteenth century) or the exquisite Jami (fifteenth century) singing of the love of Zuleika for Yusuf, it is the same theme throughout. Consumed by a deep celestial love, they made everything they touched, lovable, and because of them Persian poetry has become so rich to-day. This poetry breathing the sublimest emotions of the poets, and couched in a form of the highest lyric beauty produced wonderful impression on the reader. The Timurids in general, and Babar, Humayun and Akbar in particular, were deeply imbued with the spirit of this poetry. Cultured as they were they appreciated the liberal and sublime creed of the Sufis and learned to look at the facts of life from their angle of vision. That was how Sufism influenced through its beautiful poetry the mind of the early Mughal Emperors of India.

But far more than this was their personal contact with Sufis. The rise of the Safwi dynasty in Persia inaugurated a period of persecution for all creeds other than Shiaism. The Safwis rose to power as the champions of this faith, and their orthodoxy and zeal to spread it even outside their dominions were obvious in their dealings with Babar and Humayun. From the dominions of such fanatics as these fled away many a Sufi and found shelter in the more congenial atmosphere at first of Samarkand, Bokhara, Hirat and then of Kabul. Babar must have entertained them in his court after those dominions fell under the sway of the Uzbegs and the Persians. Many might have come to the court of Humayun after 1545 attracted by his love of culture and literary patronage. Further, Balkh a famous centre of learning and culture was under Babar and Humayun for some time, and Khorasan, the birth-place of Jami and Hatifi is close by. Prince Suleiman, a kinsman and a contemporary of Babar, Humayun and Akbar, was a great Sufi master, and tradition has it that he had attained to that coveted stage of mystic progress which is called Sahibihal. While Governor of Badakshan, Humayun might have come into contact with the Sufis, and imbibed their teachings, so that we find him often falling into a frame of mind which inclined him to renounce the worries of the world and retire into a secluded life to spend his days in the pursuit of learning or in the company of holy men. He was kept steady however by the reprimands of his father. Akbar, when young, must have associated with Sufis in the court of Kabul, so that he could recite verses from the Masnavi, and Diwan of the 'Mystic tongue' i.e., of Hafiz.[1] Later on he came into contact with Abdul Latif 'a paragon of learning', who was appointed as his tutor by Bairam Khan. Abdul Latif was noted for his moderate views on religion. The guiding principle of his life was 'Sulh-i-kul' i.e. peace with all, and this he must have imparted to his young pupil then only sixteen.

But when Akbar was being prepared by heredity and early associations to rule successfully over diverse peoples of an extensive empire, of which he was the real founder, a great religious ferment was going on in the country. The Bhakti and Mahdavi movements had taken a strong hold of the popular mind and they were supplemented by another of the Roshnis. They all taught, and were founded on, one great truth, voz., the brotherhood of man. The Vaishnav's was an emotional creed, while the Mahdavi's and the Roshni's was an austere creed. While the former thrilled to think that everything was his Beloved and therefore his very life was a consecration, the latter enjoined rigorous practice of asceticism and constant warfare with the flesh to attain to the beatific vision. These creeds must have exerted tremendous influence on the mind of Akbar. For aught we know of his keen interest in the things about him, it

1. *Akbarnama*, vol. i, p. 520.

may be surmised that Vaishnavism might have impressed him by its similarity with Sufism, and the Mahdavi and Roshni might have prompted him to assume the role of a prophet—the promised Mahdi. A brief outline of these movements therefore is essential here.

The Bhakti movement or Vaishnavism 'owes its origin to the stream of thought which began with the Upanishads and culminated in the east in Buddhism and Jainism, and arose about the time of the latter.[1] It was based upon 'the ideas of a Supreme God and devotion to Him as the mode of salvation.' This system was started as a counter-blow to the atheistic and rigidly ethical religions like Buddhism. In the fourth B.C. Megasthenes referred to it as the religion of the people of Sourasena. The most eloquent exposition of its principles is in the Bhagwad Gita, and 'the programme that it proposes is, on the one hand that we purify our minds purging them of all attachments and passions by dedicating all the fruits of our actions to God; and yet on the other hand that we continue to perform all the duties belonging to our particular caste or stage of life.......A life dedicated to God and lived for and in love of Him, is a life which is inevitably ennobled to the highest degree."[2] Self-surrender to and concentration on God are enjoined just as in the Yoga system of Patanjali, but in this idea of love of God, the emotional side is entirely absent. In the Vishnu Puran is depicted the wonderful Bhakti or devotion of Prahlad to Hari for its own sake, not for any reward; but even here the feeling element seems to be absent. Further, the great controversialist of the ninth century A.D., Shankara laid the axe at the root of all emotional love of God and piety when he expounded his famous Maya doctrine, and proved that the world is unreal. Ramanuja however, in the eleventh century most successfully controverted Shankara and laid stress on devotion or Bhakti, in which contemplation and communion were more prominent than any exuberance of feeling.[3] About the same time (eleventh century) we meet with a new idea of this Bhakti in the Bhagwat Purana where it is said to be the supreme source of spiritual enjoyment. It 'is no longer the old contemplation

1. *Vaishnavism and Shaivism*, by Bhandarkar, p. 9.
2. *Hindu Mysticism*, by Das Gupta, p. 117.
3. *Ibid*, p. 121.

or meditation of God stirred by a deep-seated love. It is the ebullition of feelings and emotions of attachment to God. It manifests itself in the soft melting of the heart and expresses itself in tears, inarticulate utterances of speech, laughter, song and dances, such as can be possible through a mad intoxication of love.[1] Two principles henceforth form the creed of faith of the Vaishnavas, the one is self-surrender to God, the other a life of God-intoxication. The latter, i.e. the emotional side of Bhakti made a strong appeal to the people, and it permeated the whole society especially when it was presented to them through the symbolism of the love of Radha and Krishna. The mode of presentation was extremely human in its setting, and that was noticed for the first time in the teaching of Nimbarka in the twelfth century. With Nimbarka the way to the eternal beatitude is the Bhakti for the lotus-like feet of Krishna.

'A spirit of sympathy for the lower castes and classes of Hindu society has from the very beginning been the distinguishing feature of Vaishnavism'.[2] But it was Ramananda (1300-1411 A.D.) who for the first time gave the most liberal scope to this sympathy by admitting all classes and creeds into his fold, and by adopting the vernacular of Northern India to teach his doctrines to the common folk. Of his disciples Kabir was one, Rohidas another and Padmavati a woman, still another. Some of his disciples founded different schools and spread the worship of Rama and Sita over an extensive portion of Northern and Central India. At this stage we discern two branches of Vaishnavism—the Rama cult and the Krishna cult. But while the former was based essentially upon the conception of God as the father, supporter and lord, the latter was on the conception of God as the beloved, the nearest and the dearest. Naturally the Krishna cult appealed more readily to the people and attracted more men than the Rama cult. 'The episodes of Krishna's life in Brindaban are spiritualized.......They are interpreted as the eternal, timeless and spaceless play of God with His own associates and His energies, with whom he eternally realizes himself in love and friendship.'[3] This LILA of Krishna made his devotees mad with love and joy and Vallabha

1. *Hindu Mysticism*, by Das Gupta, p. 124.
2. *Vaishnavism and Shaivism*, by Bhandarkar, p. 66.
3. *Hindu Mysticism*, p. 128.

(fifteenth and sixteenth centuries) and Chaitanya (1485-1533 A.D.) were the two greatest exponents of this cult. It spread far and wide into all the parts of India, and wherever it went, it proved irresistible in its fascination for the people. Brahman and Sudra, prince and peasant, Hindu and Muslim, all went mad in love for the cowherd of Brindaban. From the Muslim lady Taj to Raskhani, from the princess Mira Bai to the beggar Sur Das, all were inspired by a love that levels all distinction of sex, caste, creed or calling. All were equal because they all loved Krishna, and had their being in Him. A reign of all-absorbing love and equality was going to be established and with this great promise dawned the sixteenth century in India.

By the year 1540 all the great religious teachers had passed away. Vallabha must have been dead a few years before or after Chaitanya. Kabir the greatest of the rationalists and a disciple of Ramananda died in 1518. Nanak the founder of Sikhism died in 1538. Thus in this early part of the sixteenth century lived and preached some of the greatest religious reformers of India. They all taught one great cult—the cult of love, and one great truth,—the brotherhood of man. But after the great Gurus or Masters were gone, arose no less illustrious poets who broadcast their teachings in a more homely manner, and through the more effective medium of vernacular poetry of considerable lyric beauty. They appealed to millions and melted their hearts into love of God. Tulsi Das himself a great Vaishnav, wrote his monumental work of Ramcharitmanas, in which he depicted Rama as full of the milk of of divine mercy and love, and brought him closer to the perception and therefore to the realization of common men. What Tulsi Das did with Rama as his hero, Sur Das did with Krishna. Besides these two great luninaries of the poetical firmament, there shone many a modest star, that added to their lustre. Imbued with a deep love they poured forth their feelings in elegant poetry and furthered the cause of Vaishnavism. Keshav Das, Raskhani, Mira Bai, and a whole gamut of poets sang of the celestial love of Radha and Krishna, the verdant groves of Brindavan, the amorous diversion of the Gopis, the Shrawan swing under the Kadamba tree, and a thousand other themes of the enchanting LILA of Krishna. The intense love that the great gurus or masters had felt for God and men, was now objectified, and reproduced in a more homely way which delighted and elevated the toiling peasant, the leisured wealthy, the cloistered scholar, the witty courtier and even the monarchs of the country.

At such a time when the country was thrilling with the glowing ideals of love and human brotherhood, when the scriptures and outward forms of religion were denounced, and sincerity, devotion and purity of heart were exalted, when the poets sang of the sublime truths of life in the most touching way, came Akbar to the throne of India. Surcharged as the atmosphere was with these ideals, unsophisticated and inquisitive as Akbar was by nature, indifferent as he was to orthodoxy or fanaticism by heredity, and imbued as he was with the spirit of Sufism, it is no wonder that he made a radical departure from the religious policy of his predecessors in India.

But side by side with Vaishnavism there was another movement agitating the minds of the Muslims. That was the Mahdavi movement, based on the belief that at the close of a millenium, after the birth of Muhammad, a Messiah or redeemer of the sins of mankind would come upon the earth. The belief became very strong towards the close of the fifteenth century and throughout the sixteenth century, and there was a great deal of sensation in Arabia, Persia, Khorasan, Transoxiana and Hindustan. In Hindustan the movement was started by Sayyid Muhammad of Jaunpur (born about 1443) who proclaimed himself to be the promised Mahdi. To his numerous followers he was the guide, whom they were to love and obey. They believed that he got inspiration directly from God, and therefore was equal in authority with Muhammad. The Quran, revealed to Muhammad, was to be explained by the Mahdi. The Mahdi taught that the goal of life was the attainment of the beatific vision by meditation on God and of ultimate identity with Him. Like Sufis, they also aspired for the self-annihilation in God. The devotee should renounce all the worldly attachments, lead a poor and chaste life, and depend entirely upon the mercy of God for the attainment of the desired object. The injunctions of the Quran were not binding upon him unless confirmed by the Mahdi, and in fact the rituals had no value for him. The followers joined into a brotherhood in which the members had equal rights and equal shares in the possession of each and all. They were ready to fight if persecuted, and considered as infidels all those who did not believe in the Mahdi. Resembling the Sufis in many of their fundamental doctrines, they differed from the latter so far as their creed was austere and militant. But on the whole theirs was a faith that did not fit in with the ways of the society and the demands of the state. The spirit of brotherhood and equality, obedience to the authority of the Mahdi alone on earth, communistic tendencies with regard to property and aspiration for super-mundane attainments cut at the very root of the society and state. The believers generally abandoned their household and lived in groups professing poverty and practising austerities. They had no anxiety even for the satisfaction of the barest needs of life. In everything they depended upon God, and fasted for days together when they did not get anything by way of charity. 'But in spite of their destitute condition they always went armed, carrying a sword and shield or other arms, that they might repel enemies. And whenever they saw any person do what was contrary to their notions of right they, in the first instance, mildly warned him to desist ; but if he persisted they proceeded to compel him by force and violence to alter his conduct.[1] Thus they took justice into their hands whenever there was an occasion for it without waiting for the state to interfere or take action.

This faith made rapid progress in India because of the two successors of Sayyid Muhammad, viz. Shaikh Abdulla Niazi an Afghan, and Shaikh Alai his disciple. Shaikh Abdulla was a disciple of Shaikh Salim Chisti. After completing his education he made an extensive tour through all the Muhammadan countries, and during his travels adopted the doctrines of Mahdavi faith. Coming back, he settled down in Biana in the neighbourhood of the lowly and poor, and preached his faith with such an earnestness and zeal that he soon won numerous converts. In Biana lived another holy man, Shaikh Alai, a profound scholar and a teacher of the aspirants for the spiritual path. When he came to know of Shaikh Abdulla he met him and became a convert to his views. With him nearly all his followers embraced the new faith, and then began the remark-

1. Erskine's *History of India*, vol. ii.

able career of Shaikh Alai. His persuasive eloquence, burning faith, profound scholarship and sincere zeal made a deep impression on everyone who heard him, and the followers of the faith increased every day. On his way to Mecca he halted at Khawaspur, and converted the celebrated general of Sher Shah, Khawas Khan along with his troops. When Islam Shah ascended the throne, the Shaikh was called to the court, admonished for his heretical doctrines and banished to Handia. At Handia, he converted its governor Bihar Khan Sarwani, with the greater part of his troops. Hence he was again called to the court, condemned as a pretender and preacher of heresies, and sentenced to death in 1553. But before his death he had spread his faith extensively both in Hindustan and the Deccan, and had won numerous converts to his faith. In Ahmadnagar, the movement had a good number of adherents. Shaikh Mubarak the father of Abul Fazl and Faizi was a believer in the Mahdavi faith with strong leanings towards Sufism. He was a learned man and a reputed teacher of Nagore. He had many disciples, who shared his views, and when he came to the court of Akbar, along with his brilliant sons, he exerted considerable influence on him and had a fair share in the religious experiments of Akbar.

But side by side with the Mahdavi movement in Hindustan there was flowing in Afghanistan, another tide of religious movement that was like the former, an offshoot of Islam and based upon almost similar principles. That was the Roshni movement. The Roshnis as the followers of the faith called themselves, believed in the coming of a Messiah. They held that God is the absolute reality, from whom emanate 'the Universal All-Reason', and 'the primal elements time and space', i.e., the individual existence and phenomenal universe, and that to God will all these return. 'This return of the sparks of reason after amalgamation with matter, to the pure All-Reason, which is the first emanation of God, is facilitated by an indispensable approach from both sides, first from the All-Reason, and secondly from the soul of the world. Corresponding to this gradation, first the souls of Divine Incarnation absorb the full force of the All-Reason, then those of the Prophets whom the first enlighten, and so in descending measure, the souls of the apostles and emissaries of prophets. As in men and with similar systematic gradation, these same spiritual powers dwell in celestial phenomena ; first in sunlight, secondly in rain'.[1] These divine souls incarnate or manifest themselves as historical persons, epoch after epoch and it is the duty of the enlightened to discover or recognize him and proclaim him amongst men. He thus helps individual souls in their return to the source from which they sprang. Thus the Messiah or the divine incarnation is virtually the God on earth and therefore greater than any prophet, e.g. Muhammad, who subordinated himself to God. They, like the Sufis, believed in ecstatic communion with God to be attained by spiritual practices. These practices carry a man forward in the path, and there are eight stages in it before the goal is reached. These doctrines were first expounded by Abdullah Qadah, who flourished in the ninth century A. D. The creed developed and won numerous converts in and outside India. In the sixteenth century, there was one great exponent of this creed at Kalinjar by name Mulla Suleiman. He became the spiritual preceptor of Shaikh Bayazid, the 'Pir-i-Raushan' or apostle of light of the Roshnis. Bayazid came of a saintly family and early in life gave proof of great spiritual predilection. Starting life as a horse-dealer he travelled widely, and on one occasion met Suleiman at Kalinjar. Having become his disciple, he returned to his native country Kaniguram in the Afghan hills between the Gomal and the Kurram and practised austerities to behold God. At last he had the revelation and was commanded to teach the truth to men. He proclaimed himself the representative of God and 'the guide of those who err.' Persecuted in his native district, he fled away to that of the Pustus and there he gathered a large following. He meant to unite the scattered tribesmen of the frontier hills, and like Muhammad he assumed the role of the spiritual and temporal head. He issued circular letters to the following purport : 'Come unto me, for I am a perfect Pir ; whoever lays hold of the skirt of my garment shall obtain salvation, and whoever does not, shall utterly perish.'[2] Thus he preached not only a new creed but a crusade against all other creeds. Like the Mahdavis, he drew a line of distinction between his faith and

1. Von Noer, vol. ii, pp. 144-45.
2. Von Noer, vol. ii, p. 157.

others, and considered the followers of the latter as less than men, and when harmful, as wolf tiger, serpent and scorpion. Therefore these were fit for slaughter. Thus the creed of the Roshnis was militant like that of the Mahdavis.

Here was another aberration from Islam, another instance of a man posing himself as God's representative, and playing the role of both spiritual and temporal head. These two movements at the head of each of which was a Prophet—a God's representative, might have suggested to Akbar, that neither of them was the real representative of God and further that if they could pass for Prophets, he also could pass for one and make a new religion and thus become the head of the state and 'church.' But Akbar's idea was really to ensure indivisible allegiance—in matters spiritual as well as temporal, for himself, and here lay his stumbling block. He wanted to make a religion to suit his political needs, and therefore to be acceptable to his subjects professing various creeds. In his anxiety to substitute one creed for the many, he was led to adopt an eclecticism that found expression in the Din-i-Ilahi.

In an age characterized by such intellectual ferment and religious ebullition, lived and moved Akbar. Born with a mystic temperament, endowed with an all-comprehending genius, and destined to rule over the most powerful and richest empire of the day, his religious views and political ambition took a deep colouring from the tendencies of the times. His intense interest in human affairs coupled with some sort of a spiritual hankering landed him on a false belief in his prophethood. But in his attitude towards the religions of the Empire he was actuated by a number of cognate motives. Like a great statesman he had early foreseen that in a country where the Mughals were to stamp out the Afghan power and subjugate the Hindus—Rajputs, he could not afford to make the former his political enemy, and the latter religious helots. If he was to build up an Empire in India, he could not offend both. While his co-religionists, the Afghans were to be overthrown, his Hindu subjects should not be persecuted for their religion. The policy that inclined him to conciliate the Rajputs, so that the might successfully hold his own against the enemies of the Mughals in India, led him on to inaugurate a policy of toleration towards the Hindus. With this object in view he remitted the Pilgrim tax in the eighth and the Jaziya in the ninth year of his reign. That must have been also the real cause of his Rajput marriage earlier. By having Rajput wives he came into intimate touch with Hinduism, for they were allowed freedom of worship within the palace. He must have watched his favourite wife Maryam Zamani performing the Homa or fire-sacrifice and worshipping in her own way in the temple still standing in Fatehpur Sikri, as a witness to his policy of toleration, and must have had many a discussion on Hinduism with that intelligent and learned lady. Thus he must have learnt a good deal about Hinduism.

Apart from his contact with the Hindus, he came into personal relations with a man, who was destined to influence him in no inconsiderable degree. That was Abul Fazl, whose father was a Mahdavi by conviction. He was a prodigy as a boy and a talented scholar and theologian in youth. He was introduced to Akbar about 1574. Before that time his father and elder brother Faizi had come to the court. These two became by their learning and views the eyesore of the ecclesiastical heads of the kingdom. It was therefore one of the aims of the latter to ruin the family of Shaikh Mubarak. So it is just possible that when Abul Fazl came to the court and secured the friendship of Akbar, he, like his father in 1573, might have suggested to Akbar the idea of overthrowing the authority of the spiritual heads . Be that as it may, there is no gainsaying the fact that one who aspired for communion with God and spiritual consummation of his life, might have won the admiration and confidence of Akbar. Himself a mystic, Akbar must have appreciated the same characteristic in Abul Fazl. And Abul Fazl who could say 'my mind felt no rest and my heart felt itself drawn to the sages of Mongolia or the hermits of the Lebanon; I longed for interviews with the Lamas of Tibet or with the Padris of Portugal and the learned of the Zendavasta' surely was no narrow sectarian, no hair-splitting theologian. He considered all religious as various expressions of man's quest for the truth, of his quenchless yearning for God. He knew that in their essentials all religions taught the same truth. Hence he realized the greatness of all religions, and was at home with the saints of all religions. He was thus the prototype of Akbar, mystic like him, eclectic like him. His association therefore must have made a considerable contribution to the religious development of Akbar. And it is significant that the year after his arrival at the court, i.e., 1575, Akbar ordered the construction of Ibādat-Khānā for holding philosophical and theological discussions. Whether, in doing so, Akbar imitated the example of Suleiman Kararani or whether the idea originated from him, there is no means of ascertaining. To this Ibādat-Khānā were invited at first learned Ulamas representing different schools of religious thought, and Akbar found ample food for religious speculation from their discussions. On Thursday evenings the debates used to commence and continue till late next morning, and the assembly generally consisted of the Shaikhs, Sayyids, Ulamas and Amirs seated according to the order of precedence. Akbar used to listen with rapt attention, and sincerely believed in Islam so far. But when he found that these theological discussions often degraded into vulgar rancour, morbid orthodoxy and personal attacks, he instinctively felt that the heads of religion—Mukhdum-ul-Mulk and Shaikh Abdun Nabi, were not only in error, but were not of great understanding and attainments. He must also have felt that Islam alone could not satisfy his curiosity. Hence just as on the one hand he realized that the Ulamas had no capacity to comprehend the highest principles and deepest truths of religion, he concluded on the other that Islam was certainly not the best of all religions. He naturally wanted to converse with the learned exponents of other religions to know what these contained, and invited them to the Ibādat-Khānā. Hence as Abul Fazl remarks, the assembly consisted of 'Sufis, philosophers, orators, jurists, Sunnis, Shias, Brahmans, Jatis, Sinnas, Charbaks, Nazarenes, Jews, Sabians, Zoroastrians and others'.[1] Whether all these men were there or not, certain it is however that Akbar learned a good deal about Christianity, Jainism and Zoroastrianism from the exponents of these religions.

In 1576 Akbar invited Julian Pareira, the Portuguese Vicar-General of Bengal living at Satgaon, to come to the Court. Akbar questioned him about Christianity but he failed to satisfy his keen curiosity. Next year, therefore, another Portuguese, Pietro Tavares was sent for, but with no better result. In 1578 Antonio Cabral was invited from Goa, and he too failed to give

1. *Akbarnama*, vol. iii, p. 366.

him full satisfaction. Hence in 1580 came to his court at his request, a Jesuit Mission consisting of Aquaviva and Monserrate with the Persian interpreter Enriquez. If dissatisfied with Islam (not because Islam was at fault, but because its exponents were not the right type of men) he admired Christianity, much to the annoyance of the Muslims; he did not confine his attention to the latter faith only. He wanted to learn the estentials of Zoroastrianism and Jainism. Impelled by an insatiable thirst for the truth embodied in these religions, he invited to the court in 1578, Dastur Meherji Rana, the religious head of the Parsis at Navsari. He was allowed to take part in the debates, and hold private discussions with Akbar. His influence on Akbar was soon felt to an amazing extent and the latter adopted many practices of the Zoroastrians, e.g., sunworship, fire-worship, etc. Inheriting a love for everything Persian, he observed their festivals also. A little later, i.e., 1582 the Jains were also invited. Of the three exponents of Jainism, Hira Vijay Suri, Vijay Sen Suri and Bhanu Chandra Suri, the first exerted considerable influence on Akbar, and it was at his instance that Akbar attempted to stop the slaughter of animals in his kingdom.

In the meanwhile he was not neglecting Hinduism. He used to invite a learned Pandit at night to listen all alone, to his discourses on Hindu philosophy and religion. It is said, since the Pandit would not sit near a Mlechha nor would he enter his apartments, he (the Pandit) used to be seated on a charpai or cot, and pulled up the balcony, where Akbar used to rest for the night . There suspended between the heaven and earth he would explain in all solemnity the unfathomable mysteries of Hinduism to the intently listening emperor. Already in intimate contact with the Hindus, he soon learnt to appreciate a good many of their practices and favoured Hinduism in various ways. Thus his dissatisfaction with Islam prompted him to study other religions by means of discourses and debates, which eventually resulted in his eclecticism.

But his eclecticism led to another result. It has been suggested that he felt disgusted at the mode of the discussion between Makhdum-ul-Mulk and Shaikh Abdun Nabi, and concluded that they were no good as the heads of religion. He was conscious on the other hand of his own superior intellect, magnetic personality, and genuine love for the Truth. These were further wedded to a spirit of robust optimism and boundless self-confidence bred by an unchequered career of conquest in Northern India. Beginning with a precarious claim to the throne and a negligible portion of Hindustan, he had in a score of years fought and conquered powerful enemies, suppressed dangerous rebellions, triumphed over great hardships and established an empire embracing the whole of Northern India. He had, by this time, impressed the people with his genius as a great king and conqueror. At such a time there came a suggestion from Shaikh Mubarak that head of the state as he was, he might be the head of the religion also. It was not an unworthy or novel suggestion. There were at this time so many who called themselves Prophets or Mahdis in different parts of the country. Could he not—Akbar might have thought now—make himself one? Perhaps he was not a whit inferior to them. This idea proved very fruitful in the mind of one, whose domineering nature prompted him constantly to impress his personality on all the activities of man.

But apart from this, Akbar had some political interest to serve by assuming headship of religion. For it is not only that 'so long as the spiritual supremacy over the recluse, which is called Holiness, and supremacy over laymen which is called Sovereignty, were distinct, there was strife and confusion among the children of Noah', but that the authority of Ulamas served as the only effective check to Akbar's absolute or unrestrained political supremacy in Hindustan. According to the fundamental principles of Muhammadan polity, the government ought to be in consonance with the Quranic injunctions; and as such the interpretation and application of these injuctions were the province of the Ulamas. They gave the religious sanction to the temporal authority of the king by reading the Khutba in his name. Thus with the king they laid a parallel claim to the obedience of the people. It would have been extremely galling to Akbar, a man of domineering nature as he was, that he could not command the indivisible allegiance of his subjects. Further, it was a veritable canker to the healthy development of the state. Akbar realized it, and therefore determined not to be thwarted by the parasitical ecclesiastics in the exercise of his absolute sway over the subjects, or in enunciating new policies, that might be expedient but not in consonance with the Quranic laws. In this departure from the beaten track of Islamic statecraft, he was not the solitary exception. He had many an illustrious predecessor like Alauddin Khiliji, and others, but Akbar proved far more shrewd and capable, and therefore attained complete success. Hence he had taken the suggestion of Shaikh Mubarak in right earnest, and set to destroy the authority of the Ulamas so that he might step into their place.

But Akbar's ambition for establishing his spiritual headship did not outrun his discretion. He proceeded step by step, broke one link after another of that chain which bound him to the priesthood. He took the first definite step in 1579. A year had passed since he fell into that spiritual trance, that ecstatic communion with God, at the time of the Kamargha hunt in May 1578. He perhaps felt strong enough to defy the religious traditions, and took the place of the preacher at the chief Mosque in Fatehpur Sikri and recited the Khutba in his own name so as to emphasize his new role as the spiritual leader of the nation, i.e., Imam-i-Adil. That was in June 1579, and that was the first blow at the authority of the Ulamas.

The second blow was not long in coming. In September 1579 a document was drafted 'with honest intentions, for the glory of God and propagation of Islam' by which the principal Ulamas and lawyers resigned into the hands of Akbar their authority in matters spiritual. This was the Infallibility Decree. It placed Akbar's dispensation and wisdom in matters spiritual and temporal above those of the Mujtahids, and therefore it was laid down that 'should in future a religious question come up regarding which the opinions of the Mujtahids are at variance, and His Majesty in his penetrating understanding and clear wisdom be inclined to adopt for the benefit of the nation and as a political expedient, any of the conflicting opinions which exist on that point and should issue a decree to that effect, we do hereby agree that such a decree shall be binding on us and on the whole nation.' Akbar's decision was to be final because he would be able to square 'the benefit of the nation' with religious requirements, political expediency with the interest of Islam. Thus according to Akbar the political and religious well-being of 'the nation' was to take precedence over purely religious interest. Hence this Infallibility Decree made him supreme in temporal and spiritual matters.

But many took alarm at this interference in religion. Men like Badaoni thought that he was a humbug, for the time was long past when he 'spent whole nights in praising God', or when 'he would sit many a morning alone in prayer and meditation on a large flat stone of an old building, which lay near the palace in a lovely spot with his head bent over his chest, gathering bliss of the early hours of dawn,'[1] and now his political ambition eclipsed his love for God. But he was not a pretender. He did not mean to assume the spiritual leadership of 'the nation' without having spiritual experience. That he believed, he had the mystic communion with God with all sincerity, is a fact; that he fancied he had attained the beatific vision, is a fact; and therefore, that he believed in his superior guidance in matters spiritual, is also a fact. From start to finish, from ascending the pulpit at Fatehpur Sikri to the propagation of Din-i-Ilahi, Akbar was intensely sincere. His only fault was that he utilized his spiritual experience for political purposes.

The time chosen for this was not inopportune. As has been indicated, on all sides there was a religious upheaval; new cults were preached and new ideals were upheld: the time itself was the revolt embodied-revolt against the old and orthodox creeds. There was nothing novel in Akbar's attitude. Further, a king claiming spiritual headship was not a new thing in the Muslim world. The Caliphs had combined political power and spiritual guidance in their own person, and the Great Prophet himself had set the example. Akbar knew that the people resented his interference. But if he became the Prophet of a new creed, then he would be on an equal footing with Muhammad, and then the incongruity of spiritual and temporal supremacy would disappear. Hence the next logical step would be the foundation of a new religion. That would place Akbar's authority beyond the reach of mortal men and establish his complete supremacy. In this too Akbar was sincere, for he earnestly believed that just as all his subjects paid homage to one sovereign, and lived under one government, so they should obey one Prophet and follow one religion. That would put an end to the rancours subsisting between different religions, and

1. Badaoni, vol. ii, p. 203.

to the divided allegiance between the king and the priesthood. Since Akbar was to be the King and Prophet of India, he should suppress Islam and its claims on the obedience of the king. Islam appeared to be the most uncompromising of all the religions of India, and therefore he determined to render it innocuous before he propagated his Divine Faith, proclaimed his prophethood, and established his indivisible sovereignty.

Having thus determined, he dealt blow after blow at the priesthood in such quick succession that it was prostrate in no time. The year after the Infallibility Decree, Akbar forbade the name of Muhammad in public prayers. Early that year (1580) he got rid of Makhdum-ul-Mulk and Shaikh Abdun Nabi by sending them on a forced pilgrimage to Mecca. In the place of Abdun Nabi the Sadr-i-sadr, was appointed Khwaja Naqsbandi, who proved a pliant tool in the hand of Akbar and bowed to his will in all matters. This step was followed by a remarkable innovation in religion, and that was the substitution of 'There is no God but God, and Akbar is His Vicegerent' for 'There is no God but God, and Muhammad is His Prophet.' If Akbar was the Vicegerent of God on earth, then people must pay devotion to him. In 1580 therefore the four degrees of devotion to His Majesty were prescribed, and they consisted in the readiness to sacrifice property, life, honour and religion for the emperor. At this time Akbar ordered that 'Allahu Akbar' should be substituted for 'Bismillah'. This he did because it means 'Akbar is God' besides meaning 'God is Great'. Side by side, a committee was instituted to inquire into the rights of the holders of Siyurghals. That was the hardest blow to the material interests of the Ulamas.

All these created a smouldering but almost universal discontent, which aggravated by the Fatwa of Muhammad Yazdi and disaffection of Bengal and Bihar officers owing to the reduction of their allowances, blazed up into a formidable rebellion. The rebels had actually aimed at the subversion of Akbar's sovereignty, and substitution of Muhammad Hakim's. The rebels had invited Muhammad Hakim, tried to seduce several high officers like Khwaja Shah Mansur and Kasim Khan from their allegiance to Akbar, and attacked and killed no less a person than the Governor of Bengal, Muzafar Khan Tarbati. All this happened in 1580, and towards the end of it and beginning of 1581, Muhammad Hakim invaded from the North-west. Now was the most critical time for Akbar, and never was his resourcefulness better displayed than at this crisis. Starting at the head of an enormous army on February 8, 1581 from Fatehpur Sikri he struck terror into the heart of the invader, who not only retreated but evacuated Kabul and fled away into the hills to allow Akbar to enter it safely and to avoid a meeting with his brother. Simultaneously, his generals in India defeated the rebels and broke the back of the rebellion in the eastern provinces of the empire. When Akbar returned from Kabul and stepped on the soil of the Punjab, the rebellion had been crushed in blood. This was the last and perhaps the greatest of his triumphs, and naturally enough engendered in him boundless self-confidence and convinced him of his divine destiny. He signalized his triumph by proclaiming the abolition of the office of Sadr-i-sadr. In full flush of triumph, he turned to teach a lesson to the ecclesiastics, and specially the arrogant ones. Shaikh Abdun Nabi and Makhdum-ul-Mulk died under highly suspicious circumstances;[1] Mir Muiz-ul-Mulk and another Mulla got watery graves because their boat foundered; and 'one by one he sent all the Mullas against whom he had any suspicions of dissatisfaction to the abode of annihilation.'[2] Thus did the priesthood lie prostrate under the blows of Akbar.

Now that all opposition had been completely overcome, Akbar resolved, as Bartoli says 'to make himself the founder of a new religion, compounded out of various elements, taken partly from the Quran of Muhammad, partly from the scriptures of the Brahmans, and to a certain extent, as far as suited his purpose from the Gospel of Christ.'[3] In order to do this he summoned a general council of theologians and Mansabdars, and impressed upon them the expediency of uniting all the discordant creeds and customs of his peoples, so that they might live in peace and prosperity. 'We ought' he said 'therefore to bring them all into one, but in such a fashion that they should be both 'one' and 'all', with the great advantage of not losing what is good in any one religion, while gaining what is better in another.'[4] That was his idea about a new religion.

1. A. N. iii, 406, note by *Beveridge*; Badaoni ii, 321.
2. Badaoni ii 285.
3. Smith, pp. 211-12.
4. *Ibid*, p. 212.

He wanted to found a religion, just as he had founded an empire. He would piece together the brilliant bits of every religion, and make a new one out of them, in the way he had conquered and annexed province after province of India, and built up one great empire. In his folly he forgot that religions are never made; their elements are not borrowed and pieced together. The great founders of religions, i.e., the prophets never meant to found them. They in their intense love of mankind, sought to impart it their own realizations, their own knowledge about the Truth, God and mysteries of life, and it was their followers who formed themselves into distinctive groups, and thus creeds came into being. Akbar was doing just the other way; he began where religions end. He planned and arranged the details of his Divine Faith, after enunciating its basic principles.

A number of fantastic regulations were issued in 1582, and a large number of Shaikhs, and Fakirs who resisted even then, were exiled to Qandahar and exchanged for horses. The Sijdah was now declared to be the due of the emperor. The fast of Ramzan, the pilgrimage to Mecca and the study of Arabic, of Muhammadan law and of Quranic exegesis were forbidden. Certain rites were prescribed for the converts, who, when they performed these became Darshaniyas or disciples of His Majesty. Many came attracted by material gains, but the faith did not gain popular support in spite of the attempts of Akbar, Shaikh Mubarak, Abul Fazl, and a host of other prominent nobles, and soon after the death of Akbar his universal religion, Din-i-Ilahi or Divine Faith disappeared.

Thus the Divine Faith constituted out of many faiths, was one of the many institutions of Akbar. His political institutions were more lasting than this, because he was essentially a king, a stateman, a born ruler of men, and superficially a spiritual guide, a dabbler in religion. He was no doubt a mystic by temperament, and had imbibed a good deal of it from his environments; he was a freethinker by birth; he was domineering because of his wonderful talents; and the century in which he lived breathed into him a spirit of revolt against all creedal coercion. What was still wanting was supplied by his unchequered career of conquest. Out of these elements grew the Din-i-Ilahi, and from the nature of its constituents could not survive its maker.

THE DECCAN AND THE MUGHALS

PART I

"At a time when the force of the first Islamic penetration of Northern India was spent, the Muslim expansion there was arrested...,and the Pathan monarchy was seized with decay and dissolusion, Indian Islam started on a new career of expansion in the South." This could as well be said of the Mughals. By the end of the sixteenth century Akbar had not only conquered but consolidated the whole of Northern India. Then following the policy of his house and the tendency of the Timurids, he naturally turned towards the North-west, the cool hills of Kabul, the fruitful valleys of the Oxus and the cities of Central Asia, viz. Samarkand, Bokhara and Hirat. For full thirteen years he had been taking note of every change in the political condition of those countries. But when he realised that so long as Abdullah Khan was at the head of the Uzbegs and so long as Shah Abbas was the sovereign of Persia, he could not hope for any brilliant prospects in that direction. The time was not ripe for him to interfere in Trans-Oxiana, and he was not a man to indulge in possibilities. Hence he turned his attention towards the south. It was not a policy pre-conceived, but a policy followed after the failure of his central Asian policy. It is true that "he desired the subjugation of the Sultanates for its own sake because the mere existence of any independent power in territories accessible to his armies was an offence to him, and he loved the wealth and power acquired by his victorious arms." But when Dr. Smith says that because Akbar "regarded the existence of all the Portuguese settlements on the western coast especially that of Diu and Daman in his provinces of Gujrat as an offence and always cherished hopes of destroying the Portuguese dominion" and because his early direct attacks on their settlements in Gujrat had failed, therefore "Akbar percived that the subjugation of the Sultanates of the Deccan plateau was the necessary preliminary to a systematic assault in force on the European possessions along the coast," he is certainly going beyond what could be warranted by facts. For, although it is possible that he might have cherished the idea of driving them out when the Deccan Sultanates were conquered, it is too much to say that the conquest was "the necessary preliminary to a systematic assault in force on the European settlements on the coast", or that "at the back of his mind he always had the further plan of driving his christian friends into the sea."[1] If Akbar could not conquer the two minor settlements of Daman and Diu lying in his own province of Gujrat, how could he expect "the subjugation of the European settlements" after the conquest of the Deccan Sultanates? Obviously it is far too problematic to be taken as the cause of the conquest of the Deccan. A man of practical commonsense as Akbar was, he could not have undertaken the conquest of the Deccan so as to drive out the Europeans after the conquest was complete, when the complete conquest was only speculative.

The real cause was perhaps something else. After the disintegration of the Bahmani Empire, five Sultanates were founded on its ruins. Of these five Sultanates, Ahmednagar had the hegemony in the whole of the sixteenth century and Bijapur in the seventeenth. "The greatness of Ahmednagar filled the sixteenth century; but the first quarter of the seventeenth century saw its final extinction."[2] In these two states lay some of the most famous ports of the west coast. Dabhol, Chaul, Rajapur and Goa furnished splendid outlets for the Deccan; and the Muhammadan kingdoms maintained a brisk communication with the western Muhammadan countries, Persia, Arabia and Egypt. But Akbar was specially jealous of their connection with Persia. The Shahs of Persia were the hereditary rivals of the Timurids. In Akbar's time the rivalry was very keen because by 1595 the frontiers of the two empires had touched. But Akbar's designs on the Deccan were not dictated solely by the religious allegiance of the Deccan Sultans to the Shah. Neither was he very keen about the Deccan in the beginning. When the mighty kingdom of Vijayanagar fell he did not hear anything about it. Sometime after the only news that he had was what an envoy of Raja of Cochin

1. Smith's Akbar, p. 264.
2. Sarkar—Aurangzeb Vol. IV, p. 2.

could communicate to him. As far back as 1576 Raja Ali Khan of Khandesh had acknowledged the suzerainty of Akbar in order that he might secure his hold on the throne as against the legal heir, the minor son of Miran Muhammad Faruqi, whom he had deposed. Then in 1583 the civil strife between the Deccanees and the Foreigners in Ahmednagar led several of the latter to revolt and of these, two, viz. Mir Murtaza Khan and Khudawand Khan came to the court of Akbar. The same year arrived Burhan-ul-Mulk in his court. He had, before that time, made two unsuccessful attempts to secure the throne, had gone to seek the support of the ruler of Khandesh, and at last had come to the emperor. The same year saw the power of Akbar at its zenith. He had, a year back, crushed the great rebellion of 1580; he had shattered the forces of the rebels; chased Muhammad Hakim Mirza from Kabul and had struck a decisive blow at the religious authority of the Ulemas by abolishing the office of Chief Sadr on the day he crossed the Ravi (November 1581). In 1582 Akbar resumed the discussions of Ibādat Khānā. In 1583 the prestige of his arms and the authority of his office both as the emperor and the religious head were unrivalled. And in this year came to him these fugitives from the Deccan. There was hardly any trouble in the trans-frontier regions. He could have very well undertaken a campaign in the Deccan. But no; it was for the present farthest from his intentions. He had been looking forward to the troubles convulsing Badakhshan, and he was more concerned in the issue of those troubles. "He hoped when firmly established in Kabul and Badakhshan, to win back the ancestral territories of Transoxiana, from which his grandfather Babar had been expelled early in life; and lastly he meditated subjugation of Bijapur and other kingdoms of the Deccan plateau."[1] And we find this order, maintained in the sequence of his conquests.

The next year 1583-84 occurred the Gujrat rebellion. "The time seeming favourable for interference, the emperor in 1585-86 ordered Aziz Kokah, the Khani Azam to effect the conquest of Berar."[2] The mutual jealousies of the commanders were responsible for the inactivity and ultimate dispersion

1. Smith p. 23-24.
2. Akbar by Von Noer, Vol. II, p. 296.

of the armies. But at the time another and a greater concern was engaging the attention of Akbar. Badakshan had fallen into the hands of Abdullah Khan Uzbeg, and while on the 6th August 1585 he was consulting with the Khan-i-Khana about his foreign policy, "dropped the news of Muhammad Hakim's death" and he seized the opportunity he had been eagerly looking for. That Akbar had projected the conquest of Badakshan is clear from the accounts of Nizam-Ud-din; that Mirza Khan had heard of it and had also offered himself to join the army. The Khan-i-Khana wrote from the Deccan "since the emperor has determined to attempt the conquest of Badakshan, the desire to kiss his feet has possessed me, in order that I may accompany him in this expedition."[1] This was in the 33rd year of Akbar's reign. But at the end of his prolonged stay at Attock and Lahore, he felt that "the Uzbegs were strong in that direction and that project must wait, whereas the Sultanates of the Deccan were comparatively weak and always at variance one with the other." Hence he determined to follow "an adventurous policy in the South. If fortune should favour him and if his life should be prolonged he might after wards undertake the conquest of Turan, the regions in Trans oxiana where his ancestors had ruled long ago."[2]

Again it was not that he had entirely neglected the Deccan; his was an all-comprehensive mind. He would not pursue one policy to give up another. He had been watching the condition of affairs in the Deccan; he had been casting about for plans. In 1590 he summoned Burhan-ul-Mulk from his jagir of Bangash and offered him his armed assistance to disposses his son Ismail of the throne of Ahmednagar. Burhan declined his offer with the explanation "that a Mughal army would alarm the Dakshinis but if allowed to gather his adherents on the frontier he would endeavour to win the Nizam Shahis by conciliation."[3] The emperor therefore gave him Hindia at the frontiers of Berar and asked Raja Ali Khan of Khandesh to assist Burhan-ul-Mulk in his project. The time chosen was extremely favourable. The insane and imbecile king Murtaza Nizam Shah had been murdered in 1588 by his

1. Muntkhab Ut Tawarikh by Al Badaoni, Vol. II, p. 373.
2. Akbar by Smith, p. 246.
3. Akbar by Von Noer, Vol. II, p. 300.

son Miran Husain, who in turn had been deposed in less than a year by his minister Mirza Khan who had raised Ismail, son of Burhan-ul-Mulk to the throne. Mirza Khan was the head of the foreigners and hence this act of king-making was resented by the Deccaness amongst whom was Jamal Khan the Mahdavi. Jamal Khan won over the king to his side and thus became Prime Minister of the state. His enlightened rule was marked by partisan persecution and consequent alienation of the greater part of the people. Nevertheless he had defeated Salabat Khan and had driven out the foreigners from the kingdom. When therefore the kingdom was distracted by civil strifes and bitter persecutions, invaded Burhan-ul-Mulk with the help of Raja Ali Khan. In spite of the staunch adherence of his ten thousand Mahdavis, Jamal Khan was defeated and killed; his master and Burhan's son Ismail was taken and kept as a prisoner and the old Burhan-ul-Mulk occupied the throne. With his succession in 1590 the influence of the foreigners was restored and the Shiah, not Mahdavi faith was re-established as the state religion. Akbar thought, he had his own nominee on the throne of Ahmednagar and he must have felt delighted to find that without war or waste of his resources he had two vassal chiefs in the Deccan, viz. Raja Ali Khan of Khandesh and Burhan-ul-Mulk of Ahmednagar. He must have been encouraged thereby to think of securing the allegiance of the rest of the kingdoms by similar methods. But yet far away from the Deccan, he had not read the symptoms of the Deccan politics correctly, and he was soon disillusioned in his high hopes.

Akbar, determined to sound the bottom of the affairs, sent in August 1591 an embassy to the Deccan Sultans. Faizi had been directed to negotiate with Burhan-ul-Mulk and Raja Ali Khan as also with Bijapur and Golconda Sultans. The embassy returned at the close of 1593. Raja Ali Khan recognised the suzerainty of Akbar. Burhan-ul-Mulk, according to Akbar had not sent suitable gifts, i.e. only 15 elephants with certain textiles and a few jewels. The other two Sultans had refused to recognise Akbar's suzerainty. Hence the Deccan campaign was determined upon and at first Prince Murad was given the supreme command of an army of 70,000 horse. The time chosen was most favourable partly because Akbar was free from all trans-frontier troubles and partly because Burhan's position was almost untenable in Ahmednagar owing to his childish freaks. The conquest of Sind had been completed in 1592; Orissa had been annexed by Man Singh the same year. Kashmere had been conquered and Akbar had started on his second visit of that country about August 1592; the campain of Gujrat had been completed in 1593 and Muzaffar Shah had committed suicide. On all sides his arms had been victorious. As against these successes, the abortive embassy must have highly exasperated the emperor and to give effective vent to his indignation, he at once resolved to proceed to Agra where he would be able to organise a force for the Deccan. No sooner resolved than Prince Danyal was ordered to march and "Khan-i-Khana, Rai Rai Singh and many other nobles were ordered to accompany him. Shah Rukh Mirza, Shah Baz Khan and the other chiefs of Malwa were ordered to join with their forces. Raja Man Singh was also directed to march from Bengal."[1] But at the town of Shikarpur when the Khan-i-Khana was called to the presence he represented that it would be convenient to invade the Deccan after the rains when food and fodder could be easily procured. The counsel was accepted. Prince Danyal was recalled and thus there was a delay of another eight months. But "the emperor resolved to head the expedition himself at the conclusion of the rains." The resolution was not carried out but the lion had been roused. In 1595 Prince Murad was associated in command with the Khan-i-Khana, and the two generals were ordered to advance from Gujrat and Malwa to effect a junction and to march upon Ahmednagar. Raja Ali Khan faithful to the emperor as ever joined the Khan-i-Khana with his forces.

But never had the persons been worse selected. Prince Murad did not like the selection of the Khan-i-Khana, quarrelled with him, and was arrogant and addicted to wine. The Khan-i-Khana on the other hand was a Shiah and was not expected to act vigorously against the people of his own faith. In the beginning of the campaign, without effecting a junction in time, Prince Murad desired that the main body should move against Ahmednagar from his province while the Khan-i-Khana urged for an advance from Malwa. A dead-lock thus arose

1. Akbar Nama, Elliot Vol. VI, page 91.

and when they started the siege of Ahmednagar, the besieged so gallantly defended under Chand Bibi that the imperialist generals were glad to come to terms. Early in 1596 a treaty was concluded on condition that Bahadur, a son of Burhan-ul-Mulk should be elevated to the throne as a vassal of the emperor that "the province of Ahmednagar should be confirmed to him, and the province of Berar given up to the emperor and the jewels, the pick of the elephants and other things were to be sent as tribute to the emperor."

But this was looked upon as "unworthy" by the emperor and as a "disgrace" by the Deccanees themselves. Therefore Bijapur and Ahmednagar formed an alliance and fought a contested and indecisive battle with the imperialists at Supa on the Godavari about the beginning of 1597. Many commanders of note were killed and amongst them was Raja Ali Khan. But when the news reached the emperor he was highly enraged and sent Abul Fazal to bring the Prince back to the court. In the mean time Daulatabad had surrendered after a short siege; Nasik and Kherla too had fallen; and in May 1599 Prince Murad died at Dihbari on the Purta, twenty koss from Daulatabad.

Now late in 1598, Akbar had left Lahore for Agra. The news of Abdullah's death in 1598 had freed his hands in the north, and he now thought of making an end of the Deccan troubles by personal supervision. After the death of Prince Murad, Akbar left the capital in charge of Prince Salim and came to the south in July 1599. Having crossed the Narbada he took Burhanpur without opposition and commissioned Prince Danyal and Khan-i-Khana to operate against Ahmednagar. "Internal dissensions precluded the effective defence of the city and Chand Bibi the only capable leader was either murdered or constrained to take poison." In August 1600, the town was stormed and the young king was taken prisoner. He passed the rest of his life in the fortress of Gwalior.

Burhanpur was the capital of Khandesh. Sultan Miran Shah son of Raja Ali Khan had thrown off his allegiance to the emperor and after the occupation of Burhanpur, had shut himself in the fortress of Asirgarh. Akbar himself conducted the siege from April 9, 1600, but the siege had begun in February. It was extremely difficult to take the fort and five months after in August Akbar got the news of Prince Salim's revolt. Out of necessity Akbar lured the king into his power by promises of safety and liberty and then imprisoned the king. Even then the fort did not surrender. Hence as a last recourse he bribed the officials and on January 17, 1601 about ten and a half months after the preliminary operations had begun it capitulated. The sultan spent the rest of his days in the fortress of Gwalior, and Akbar hastened back to Agra to quell the rebellion of Prince Salim.

Thus the conquest of the Deccan was started by Akbar, and was carried on with considerable success after it had been realized that the recovery of the ancestral dominions of the Timurids in Central Asia was an empty dream. It is a new note in the foreign policy of the Mughals, and is certainly a land-mark in the expansion of the Mughal empire. Hereafter all the Mughal emperors made it their guiding principle, to carry to completion, what Akbar had begun. On this principle the Mughal rule in India, was destined to stake its all, and if the Mughals won an empire in Hindustan, they lost it in the Deccan. How this came about, how out of the dogged tenacity of the successors of Akbar and especially Aurangzeb to annex the Deccan, arose difficulties which the Mughals could not overcome, will be the main purpose of our study.

Jahangir adopted his father's policy in the Deccan, but Khusrau's revolt and the siege of Qandhar came in the way of his launching a vigorous campaign. When however he was left free to pursue schemes of conquest he was amazed at the wonderful ability and meteoric success of Malik Ambar. An Abyssinian by birth but a Deccanee by adoption, he had started life as a follower of Chingez Khan, "one of the greatest of Ahmednagar nobles and the conqueror of Berar."[1] He was the first man to discover the military potentialities of the Maratha people and organise them into highly mobile cavalry troops. These he utilized in guerilla warfare against the Mughals with deadly effect. He made Khadki the capital of the decadent Nizam Shahi dynasty, and determined to win back the independence and integrity of their kingdom, he made unremitting warfare against the Mughal usurpers. Aided by the wild nature of

1. **Beni Prasad's Jahangir, p. 259.**

the country his abilities and activities brought him great success and the Mughals were harassed and handicapped everywhere. To relieve the situation the Khan-i-Khana was deputed by Jahangir with 12,000 troops, and when he arrived in the Deccan he realized that the real cause of the failure of the Mughals lay in their mutual jealousies and insubordination. Jahangir tried to set the matter right by sending Asaf Khan and Prince Parvez but to no avail. Khan-i-Khana suffered reverses and was constrained to sign a "disgraceful peace." Ultimately Malik Ambar recovered Ahmednagar from its Mughal commandant and that was the apogee of Mughal humiliation. In great anger Jahangir called the Khan-i-Khana and ordered a grand offensive to be planned against the enemy. Abdullah Khan, who was the Governor of Gujrat was to march thence towards Nasik and Trimbak with an army of 14,000 and "keep in touch with the armies which were to advance under Khan Jahan Lodi, Man Singh and the Amir-ul-Umara from the sides of Berar and Khandesh. They were to hem in the enemy and destroy him by a concerted attack (1611)."[1] But the whole plan was frustrated by the selfish ambition of Abdullah Khan, who himself suffered owing to his reckless proceedings. He was miserably harassed in his march and forced to retreat from Daulatabad by the guerilla bands of Maratha light horse, and his retreat was only a signal for the other section of imperialists for similar action.

When this news reached Jahangir he was highly indignant and deputed Khan-i-Khana again to the scene in 1612. This time he achieved better results and retrieved the prestige of the imperial arms. "He continued in supreme command till 1616 and acquitted himself with credit, but he was still accused of being corrupted by Deccan gold."[2] Prince Khurram, who had won laurels in Mewar was anxious to go there in order that he might steal a march over Prince Parvez, who had been sufficiently discredited by now. The emperor, also desired to move down to Mandu, to be near the scene of operation. In November 1616, Prince Khurram, honoured by the title of Shah Jahan, marched into the Deccan and soon after he was followed by the emperor. The arrival of the formidable army

1. Beni Prasad : Jahangir, p. 267.
2. Ibid p. 270.

of Prince Shahjahan, backed from Mandu by Jahangir overawed Malik Ambar, and he readily came to terms with the imperialists. He had to cede to the Mughals all the high-land districts, he had conquered from them and surrendered Ahmednagar and other forts. That was the net result of all these years of campaign from 1608 to 1616. "The expenditure of millions of rupees and thousands of lives had not advanced the Mughal frontier a single mile beyond the limits of 1605."[1] Having accomplished this Prince Shahjahan left the Deccan and reached Mandu on 12th October 1617. Khan-i-Khana was appointed governor of the Mughal Deccan comprising Khandesh, Berar and Ahmednagar.

But the state of peace did not continue long. Malik Ambar was looking forward to an opportunity when he could strike again. In 1620 he broke the treaty, formed an alliance with Bijapur and Golconda, mustered an army of 60,000 troops and conquered or captured the Mughals districts and outposts so rapidly that within three months the bulk of Ahmednagar and Berar was in his possession. The humiliation of the imperialists was complete when Burhanpur was besieged and captured by the enemy, the Narbada was crossed, the surrounding districts were over-run, and the environs of Mandu were plundered. A new factor had appeared in Deccan warfare. The guerilla tactics aided by the hilly nature of the country had baffled the Mughals, and it was a real crisis, that Jahangir had to face in the Deccan now. Relying on the brilliant parts of Prince Shahjahan he deputed him once again and once again did he justify his selection by completely over-powering the enemy and by retrieving the lost prestige of the Mughal arms. Malik Ambar submitted near Daulatabad and this time his submission partially affected the independence of Golconda and Bijapur Sultans, who were his allies. A treaty of peace was arranged and according to its terms "all the imperial territory recently seized by the Deccanees during the previous two years together with 14 Coss of the adjoining territory was to be ceded to the Mughals. Fifty lakhs of rupees was to be paid as tribute......eighteen lakhs by Bijapur, twelve lakhs by Ahmednagar and twenty lakhs by Golconda."[2] Within six months of his arrival Shah Jahan had accomplished

1. Beni Prasad's Jahangir p. 285-86.
2. Beni Prasad's Jahangir p. 334-35.

this and indeed that was very creditable. But from the very nature of affairs i.e. the Mughal aggression and Deccanee resistance, it was not expected that peace would be lasting. The Mughals could not abandon their aggressive designs in the Deccan, nor could the Deccanees be expected to part with their freedom without severe struggles. Hence in spite of the glorious achievements of Shahjahan, they were not likely to endure. This uncertain tenure of peace was further aggraavated by the revolt of Shahjahan in the Autumn 1622.

Shahjahan's revolt threw the affairs of the empire into a temporary disorder and the Deccan also shared in it. By October 1623 king Adil Shah and Malik Ambar, had come to strained relations and each was seeking the assistance of Mahabat Khan "the temporary guardian of Mughal interests in the Deccan" against the other. But Mahabat was not in a position to grant his aid to any one of them for that was likely to drive the other to form an alliance with the rebel Prince Shahjahan, who was then in the Deccan. Hence Mahabat delayed his decision and after the departure of Shahjahan from the Deccan he extended his aid to the Adil Shah of Bijapur. Malik Ambar bore this insult with a patient shrug of shoulders and after the withdrawal of the imperialists under Mahbat Khan he formed an offensive and defensive alliance with Golconda and attacked Bijapur with all his fury. The imperial detachment that had proceeded from Burhanpur to the reliei of Bijapur, was defeated by Ambar and consequently Bijapur and Ahmednagar were subjected to a severe siege. At this juncture arrived Prince Shahjahan once again in the Deccan, defeated and driven out from the east. He was warmly welcomed by Malik Ambar and the two erstwhile enemies became staunch friends in their adversity. It was arranged that he should besiege Burhanpur while Malik Ambar managed Bijapur and Ahmednagar. With great enthusiasm the Prince started the siege, but before long arrived Mahabat and Prince Parvez on the scene, and that turned the tide against the confederates. Shahjahan had to raise the siege; he had been forshaken by friends; he had left his family behind; desertion and disloyalty dogged his footsteps; and he had been taken ill. Penitent and broken down he eventually wrote to the emperor begging for mercy and his prayer was granted (March, 1626).

But the rebellion of the Prince had disturbed the steady progress of the Mughal arms in the Deccan, and had given rise to the fateful dissension between Nurjahan and Mahabat Khan. While the proceedings of Mahabat Khan in the north had upset the harmony in imperial affairs, in the south the corrupt conduct and mutual jealousies of the Mughal officers affected the imperial interests there. Khan Jahan who had replaced Mahabat Khan was not a match for Malik Ambar. Starting badly he would have failed miserably, had it not been for the death of Ambar in May 1626. With his death ensued a scene of confusion and unsettlement which could have been best utilized by the imperialists, but Khan Jahan did not possess the requisite talent for it. He was at first prevailed upon by Ahmednagar nobles to accept terms of peace based upon allegiance to the Mughal emperor, but soon after was completely disillusioned when Hamid Khan, who had risen to power as the result of a domestic revolution in Ahmednagar, declared war on the Mughals. Khan Jahan opened a vigorous campaign, but seduced by enemy's gold in the shape of a bribe of three lakhs of Huns from Hamid Khan, he resigned the whole country of Balaghat as far as Ahmednagar and issued instruction to his officers to abandon their charge. At this time arrived the news of emperor's death, which changed the aspects of affairs there. Thus ended ingloriously the Deccan campaign of Jahangir, of which "the most distressing and disreputable features were the corruption and mutual dissensions of the Mughal officers."[1]

The Deccan campaign of Jahangir had been marred by Mughal corruption and dissension no doubt, but nevertheless, they had appreciably weakened the Deccan states—Ahmednagar, Bijapur and Golconda. With the accession of Shahjahan to the throne (early February 1628) the aggressive policy inaugurated by Akbar and continued by Jahangir was resumed and the work of conquest proceeded apace. Trouble started with the revolt of Khan Jahan Lodi, governor of the Deccan. A nominee of Nurjahan, he had been ordered early in 1627 to crush Shahjahan and Mahabat Khan who had become friends in their mutual adversity. After the coronation of

1. Jahangir by Beni Prasad, p. 425.

Shahjahan, he was invited to the court and was treated with the utmost consideration. But he looked upon the royal favour with suspicion and one night quit Agra for the south without the permission of the emperor. He was closely pursued by an imperial army and turning to give battle on the Chambal he was defeated. Flying for shelter he plunged into the wild country of Bundelkhand and thence he fled away into the Deccan, where he made friendship with Shahji and Murtaza Nizam Shah II, Shahji's master. Khan Jahan's presence in the Deccan where he had long served as a general, his great ability and his alliance with the enemies of the Mughals made the situation of affairs in the Mughal Deccan very unsafe. The emperor realizing the gravity of the situation proceeded to the spot in 1629 and fixed his headquarters at Burhanpur. He then divided his army in three sections, and they gradually wore out the enemy converging upon him from three directions. Khan Jahan was forced to seek shelter with Adil Shah, who refused to help him. At the same time Khan Jahan's ally Shahji deserted him and joined the imperial service. Khan Jahan was therefore constrained to fly for shelter and he retird into Bundelkhand, in order that he might foment fresh troubles there. But he failed in his designs, the local chiefs opposed him, and the Mughal army did not give him any rest. He was at last overtaken and died fighting to the last moment at Kalingar (1631).

With the death of Khan Jahan one thorn had been cleared. There still remained Murtaza Nizam Shah II, who was persisting in his enmity. In 1630, therefore, Shahjahan ordered Azim Khan to close with the enemy. At this crisis Muhammad Adil Shah of Bijapur sent his general Randula Khan to the help of Murtza Nizam Shah. But as the Bijapur general approached Ahmednagar he opened overtures with Azim Khan, who rejected them owing to his extravagant demands. He then turned to join the Nizam Shah, but before he could do so, he was severely defeated by Azim Khan. The Nizam Shah, driven to despair released Fateh Khan, son of Malik Ambar from prison, where he had been kept for some time and made him his minister only with the hope that he might successfully check the Mughal attack. The Mughal attack was not, however, destined to last long. When in June 1631 Mumtaz Mahal, the best-loved queen of Shahjahan died at Burhanpur, he became so disconsolate and distracted that he could not be persuaded to stay any longer at Burhanpur and left the Deccan in disgust never to visit Burhanpur again. Further the unhappy concidence of a severe famine in the Deccan made a campaign extremely difficult for the Mughals. Hence military operations were interrupted for some time.

In the meanwhile Fateh Khan had murdered his master Murtza Nizam Shah, and had set up on the throne his young son Hussain Shah with himself as the regent. These reckless proceedings made him extremely unpopular. In order to secure his power against his enemies, he opened negotiations with the imperialists and sent his son to the emperor to assure him that he had acted solely in the interest of the emperor, and that pending his approval, Hussain had been seated on the throne. Shahjahan was highly gratified,commended his proceedings and restored to him his jagirs, which had been taken away previously and conferred upon Shahji. But this introduced a new complication in the affairs of the Mughals. Shahji left the imperial service owing to the insult and entered the service of Bijapur. Now Adil Shah promptly sent him on his own suggestion, against Fateh Khan. The latter appealed to Mahabat Khan then in the Deccan for help; but Shahji was so quick to strike that before the Mughal reinforcement arrived, he had besieged Daulatabad and forced him not only to recant his submission to the Mughals but to make common cause with Bijapur against them. Fateh Khan was further to cede Sholapur and its five and a half districts, in return for which he was allowed to retain Daulatabad with rest of Ahmednagar. These settlements made Shahji throw a garrison into the fort of Daulatabad, and then he decamped in time to avoid meeting Mahabat Khan, who was on his way to Daulatabad. On arriving there he found that all had been upset by Shahji. But Mahabat Khan was not a man to despair. By a clever combination of force and diplomacy he forced Fateh Khan to sue for peace. Further a bribe of ten lakhs of rupees induced him to surrender his young ward Hussain Shah and enter the imperial service (1633).

But the imprisonment of Hussain Shah and betrayal of Fateh Khan did not ensure peace for the Mughals. Hardly had Mahabat Khan turned his back on Daulatbad and Mughal trenches been evacuated, when Shahji appeared before the fortress and besieged it with ruthless vigour. Mahabat Khan apprised of the activities of Shahji, rapidly returned and once again drove him away. But Shahji now discovered an infant descendant of the Nizam Shahi dynasty and proclaimed him king with himself as the Regent. He then secured the help of Bijapur and succeeded in defeating the Mughals at Parenda and in driving them out of Ahmednagar into Khandesh. The death of Mahabat Khan occurring at this time proved to be a real turning point, in-as-much as it encouraged Shahji and forced the emperor Shahjahan to come to the Deccan to direct operations in person. The alarming rise of Shahji, who was the most powerful Maratha general and the last king-maker of Ahmednagar, foreshadowed a future for the whole race of Marathas, that was likely to be at once great and glorious, even though Maratha power was an unknown quantity in the political equations of the contemporary Deccan.

On the 21st February 1636 the emperor arrived at Daulatabad. His long experience of the Deccan in younger days made him grasp the situation at once. He saw that unless Golconda and Bijapur were crushed, Shahji could not be crushed also. These three were the only factors in the Deccan and they had realized that upon the safety of each depended the safety of all and vice versa. Hence he directed three large armies to converge on Golconda and Bijapur and coerce the sultans to submission, while a fourth was ordered to reduce the Nizam Shahi forts of the north-west and occupy Junnar and Nasik districts. The plan succeeded wonderfully well. The timid Qutub Shah recognised the suzerainty of Shahjahan by promising to pay an annual tribute, strike coins and read Khutba in his name. Far otherwise, however, was the attitude of Adil Shah. Determined to vindicate his honour and dignity, he carried on a defensive warfare with cool courage and ruthless energy. Twice did the Mughals penetrate from three directions butchering and burning and plundering, and twice were they repulsed with fierce and desperate bravery. At last the parties weary of the war entered into a treaty of peace which was signed on the 6th May 1636. It was stipulated that Adil Shah would recognize the suzerainty of Shahjahan and pay a peace-offering of twenty lakhs of rupees. He was to respect the frontier of Golconds and with-hold his aid from Shahji. In return for all these he was to acquire a part of Ahmednagar. On the 25th June arrived a rich present worth forty lakhs from Golconda and on the 11th July the emperor left for Mandu. Three days later arrived Aurangzeb as the viceroy. The peace of 1636 left Shahji to fight all alone. He held out for a few months even though he was attacked by the Mughals and the Bijapuris, and at last surrendered in October 1636.

Thus closed one phase of the Mughal conquest of the Deccan. Shahjahan had so far reckoned with the three powerful Deccan states. Since two of them had been humbled, and the third completely destroyed and the Marathas as a people had not yet risen to power, the Mughals were free to turn their arms to the conquest of other less important kingdoms of the Deccan. Khan-i-Douran made a dash into the Gond country between the Wardha and the Wainganga and levied contribution. He next turned upon Nagpur, the fortress of Gond Raja of Deogarh, by name Kukia and besieged it with great vigour. This forced the Gond Raja to seek an interview on the 16th January 1637. He paid a peace-offering of one and a half lakhs of rupees in cash and 170 elephants, and promised an annual tribute of a lakh and a half to the emperor. Here was a new avenue of conquest opened by Khan Douran.

In 1644 Aurangzeb resigned his viceroyalty of the Deccan and it was not before eight years had passed that he was again appointed to that government. During this period Shahjahan had neither the energy nor inclination to pursue a vigorous policy in the Deccan, for he had to direct all that to the North-western frontier, where the imperial interests had received the most disastrous set-back. Consequently the Deccan affairs had to be neglected and in these eight years between the resignation and reappointment of Aurangzeb, as many as six viceroys had come and gone. The frequent change of viceroys had told upon the efficiency of administration and prosperity of the people. "Much cultivated soil had lapsed into the jungle, the cultivators had declined in number and resources and the revenues had fallen off greatly." Therefore when Aurangzeb was appointed to the government of the Deccan, he had been directed by the emperor to pay special attention to the condition of the countryside.

other for his son. Consequently Mir Jumla was appointed a commander of 5000 and his son Muhammad Amin a commander of 2000 (3rd December 1655). But in the mean time the latter with his family had been thrown into prison on the 21st November 1655 by the Qutab Shah because he was "guilty of some disrespect to the person. This treatment being resented by Mir Jumla, altercations arose between him and the king, which at length led to a formal petition on the part of the former for the emperor's protection."[1] Here was the opportunity for Aurangzeb's ambition and designs. He ordered the Qutab Shah to release the family and son of Mir Jumla who was now a Mughal servant and ordered Prince Muhammad to lead an army into the country to enforce obedience. The emperor apprised of the confinement of Muhammad Amin also wrote to the Qutab Shah on December 24th to release him. The letter when received by Aurangzeb (January 7th 1656) was with-held purposely for some time and the military forces were ordered into the kingdom on the plea that the Qutab Shah had refused to comply with the Imperial orders. When the letter of 24th December was forwarded to the Qutab Shah he released the prisoners but by this time Prince Muhammad was within striking distance of Haidarabad. He had been ordered to take the king unawares, bring him to an interview and if possible "lighten his neck of the burden of his head." Qutab Shah abandoned his capital and fled into the strong fortress of Golconda. On 24th January Prince Muhammad entered Haidarabad, the city was plundered and an immensely valuable booty fell into the hands of the Mughals. Aurangzeb himself had left Daulatabad on the 20th January to join his son, in February 1656. Resolved to annex the kingdom he rejected the repeated offers of peace of the Qutab Shah till the latter opened negotiation with Dara who was bribed to intercede in his favour. Aurangzeb however was urging Shahjahan to order annexation. At last persuaded by Dara, the emperor ordered Aurangzeb to settle terms of peace with Golconda (on 24th February.) This letter was suppressed in order that delay and suspense might extort more favourable terms from the Qutab Shah. At last when through the agency

1. Grant Duff's History of the Marathas, Vol. I, p. 152.

of Dara and Jahanara the emperor came to know of the true story of Aurangzeb's proceedings he ordered immediate cessation of war and directed Aurangzeb to quit Golconda territory at once. In disgrace the prince raised the siege on 30th March. But before he had done so he had forced the Qutab Shah to pay a heavy indemnity and cede a district and besides to agree to a secret treaty with Aurangzeb, by which he gave his daughter in marriage to Prince Muhammad Sultan and declared him as his heir-apparent.

The relations of Bijapur with the Mughals were more or less peaceful. The king, Muhammed Adil Shah ruled prosperously till 1656 and when he died on 4th November left a son of 18 to succeed him. On his death arose troubles with regard to the succession. It was rumoured that the boy was not the real son of Muhammed Adil Shah, that he was of obscure parentage and that the childless Sultan had brought him up in his harem. All sorts of disorder followed in the train of this rumour. Shahji Bhonsla disobeyed his master and the turbulent nobles showed clearest signs of disaffection. Aurangzeb seized this opportunity and reported the matter to the emperor and urged him to sanction an invasion. In anticipation of his orders he massed his troops on the frontier and himself moved to Ahmednagar.

Now he was not afraid of any hostile combination at the court to thwart his aggressive designs because there was his staunch friend Mir Jumla, holding the office of Prime Minister of the empire. He had come to the court on 7th July 1656, had been given a mansab of 6000 and raised to this high office of Prime Minister at once. His long experience in the Deccan affairs gave a weight to his opinion which would not be questioned by anyone in the court. When he supported the plan of Aurangzeb, the emperor naturally sanctioned the war and deputed the great wazir to help in the operations. The emperor's directions to Aurangzeb were that either he should attack and annex the whole of Bijapur or at least that portion of Ahmednagar which had been ceded to the Adil Shah in 1636 and demand a sum of 1½ crore of rupees and recognition of Shahjahan's suzerainty in lieu of the annexation of Bijapur territory. In the meantime Aurangzeb had been sparing no pains to corrupt the army and nobility of Bijapur and actually inducing them to desert. Thus as on the one hand he persuaded the emperor to sanction the war so on the other he had undermined the strength of the Adil Shah by alienating his army. Then came Mir Jumla, who, on account of his valuable experience in the Deccan affairs and reputed abilities as a general and strategist had been ordered to help Aurangzeb in his operations against Bijapur. He arrived at Aurangabad on the 18th January 1657 and on 2nd March 1657 Aurangzeb commenced the siege of Bidar aided by the reinforcements of Mir Jumla. At the end of three weeks on 29th March the fortress capitulated and then came the turn of Kalyani, which fell on 29th July. In the meantime Shahjahan had written repeatedly to close the campaign and conclude a treaty for the Bijapur envoy had agreed to pay 1½ crores of rupees and cede Bidar, Kalyani and Parenda, besides all the forts in the Nizam Shahi Konkan. But Aurangzeb was inexorable.

Soon after this however was received the news of Shahjahan's dangerous illness and perforce he had to close the campaign. So he accepted the terms of peace and determined to meet the situation. The royal princes were prepared for a deadly contest for the throne and Aurangzeb could not be behindhand in it.

Shahjahan however recovered and ordered Aurangzeb to send Mir Jumla back to the court. Aurangzeb encountered that step by arresting Mir Jumla on the pretext of disloyalty and Mir Jumla was no unwilling prisoner of Aurangzeb. After making full preparations he left Daulatabad on 5th March 1658, and was destined to come back once more in 1682 and never return again. His absence gave a free hand to Shivaji and he began to rise steadily. This requires a brief outline of the career of Shivaji and of the history of Maharastra that made the rise of the Marathas possible.

PART—II

Shivaji's rise to power was not an isolated phenomenon, it had been preceded by long of preparation and political training on the part of the Marathas. The happy coincidence of a religious movement in Maharastra i.e. the Pandharpur movement, that disseminated the ideal of universal brotherhood, the generous policy of the Bijapur and Ahmednagar Sultans in associating the Marathas freely in the army and administration, and the political decadence of the Deccan states due to the internal and external causes, supplied the requisite stimulus to the unity and political consciousness of the Maratha people. Their political and military importance could be best judged from the fact that Burhan Nizam Shah (1508-53) had a Maratha Prime Minister, that Ibrahim Adil Shah (1535-58) substituted Marathi for Persian as the court-language, that Malik Ambar, as has been said above, organized the Marathas into mobile bands of cavalry, which he employed with deadly effect in a guerilla warfare against the Mughals, and that Shahji was one of his trusted lieutenants, and after his death played the role of the guardian of the interests of the Nizam Shahi dynasty. Consequently there were many leading Maratha families in Ahmednagar and Bijapur states, e.g. the Jadhavas and Bhonsles in Ahmednagar and the Chandra Rao Moreys, the Nimbalkars, the Ghatgeys, the Gharpureys and the Sawants of Wadi in Bijapur. When the Mughals were trying to weaken and exterminate the three Deccan states, these Marathas actuated by a spirit of religious and political unity, naturally looked with suspicion upon the encroaching arms of Islam and a leaven to their determined action was supplied by their religious fervour, when emperors like Shahjahan and Aurangzeb initiated policies of religious intolerance and persecution. That is the keynote to the rise of Shivaji and of the Marathas. It was a process that extended over the whole of the 17th century and was facilitated by the destruction of Ahmednagar, Bijapur and Golconda by the Mughals. But apart from the religious stimulus and removal of the local rivalry, the geographical features of the country also came to their aid. The folds and mazes of the Sahyadri, (the Western Ghats) the deep and narrow valleys, the difficult passes, the low-lying spurs, the flat-topped hills, the terraced hill sides, the rugged and inhospitable soil—all these contributed to baffle the invader, and for the inhabitants to value their independence as something great and glorious.

The glory and greatness of Maharastra centres round the name of Bhonsles. Tracing their descent to a fugitive prince of the house of Mewar, they lived in obscurity till the rise of

Shahji Bhonsle. As has been noted already he rose to prominence in 1628, and played an important part in the conflict between the Nizam Shahi dynasty and the Mughals. In 1636, the kingdom of Ahmednagar was completely destroyed and he had to give up the cause of the Nizam Shahis and take service with Bijapur. Only ten years after this, his illustrious son, Shivaji started on his career of conquest, and mission of independence. Born in 1627, he grew up a brave, spirited and enterprising young man under the fostering care of Dadaji Konddeo. He chose a career of independence for himself, and gave signal proof of it during the weak and indifferent administration of Muhammad Adil Shah from 1646 to 1656. He conquered Torna in 1646 which was followed by the conquest of a good many forts from the Jagirdars of Bijapur Government. In the year 1656 his conquest of Jawali, by getting its chief Chandra Rao More murdered, synchronised with the death of the Adil Shah; and the scenes of confusion that arose in Bijapur and encouraged the attack of Aurangzeb, also substantially aided the ambition of Shivaji. So far he had wisely refrained from giving offence to the Mughals; but on the eve of Aurangzeb's war on Bijapur he had actually offered to join him. But soon he decided otherwise and determined to create a diversion in favour of Bijapur, by attacking the Mughal territories. This course of action was calculated to serve a double purpose. He would help to check the Mughal aggression into the Deccan by combining with Bijapur, and thereby induce the authorities to condone the murder of Chandra Rao More. Hence two Maratha captains were ordered to raid Mughal territories across the Bhima. But Aurangzeb's excellent arrangements circumscribed the activities of Shivaji, who was pursued and defeated in May 1657. Aurangzeb's officers further kept a watchful eye on his Marathas. When however Shivaji heard that Bijapur authorities had made peace he also wrote to Aurangzeb tendering his submission. Aurangzeb was then starting for the North to fight for the throne, and he could not afford to take stern measures against him. He accepted Shivaji's submission and granted him pardon, but directed the Adil Shah to expel him from all his possessions. Then he turned his back on the Deccan and that was the opportunity of Shivaji.

Shivaji now organized his resources and turned his arms into the Konkan, where the affairs were in a flux due to the distracted condition of Bijapur Government. He acquired Northern Konkan without much trouble and forced the Portuguese to pay an annual tribute. Thus steadily his power grew till in 1659, when the comparative peaceful conditions in Bijapur induced the authorities to take examplary action against Shivaji. Afzal Khan was sent at the head of an army ten thousand strong, commissioned to "effect the capture or murder of Shivaji by pretending friendship with him." But instead of capturing or murdering Shivaji, he himself was killed at the fateful interview at the foot of the hill-fort Pratapgarh, where he had come with evil designs. Treachery was met successfully by caution and Shivaji's gain was enormous. In the first place, it was a great moral victory, and next, he got an immense booty which added to his resources.

By this time Aurangzeb's attention had been turned on the Deccan, and he ordered Sayista Khan to crush Shivaji. The Khan captured a number of forts and ultimately occupied Poona. But Poona proved his ruin. He was surprised within his camp on the night of 5th April 1663 by Shivaji, accompanied by a light body of Marathas. He narrowly escaped being killed and was consequently transferred by Aurangzeb who condemned his incapacity and carelessness. Raja Jai Singh took his place in the Deccan and it was he who by a clever combination of force and diplomacy constrained Shivaji to come to terms with him. By the treaty of Purandar he resigned 23 of his forts, and lands yielding 4 lakhs of hun as annual revenues and retained only 12 forts and lands yielding one lakh hun (1665). He further made an engagement with the emperor that if lands yielding 4 lakhs of huns a year in the low lands of Konkan and 5 lakhs of hun a year in the uplands (Balaghat Bijapuri) were granted to him by the emperor and if he was assured by an imperial farman that these lands, after he wrested them from Bijapur authorities by his own troops, would accrue to him, then he would pay 40 lakhs of hun in 13 yearly instalments. Jai Singh accepted these proposals, for he wrote in explanation to the emperor that, that was the best means of formenting local rivalry between Shivaji and Bijapur.

"This policy" he wrote to the emperor "will result in a three-fold gain : first, we get 40 lakhs of Hun or 2 crores of rupees; secondly, Shivaji will be alienated from Bijapur; thirdly the imperial army will be relieved from the ardous task of campaigning in these two broken and jungly regions, as Shiva will himself undertake the task of expelling the Bijapuri garrisons from them." It was pregnant with political wisdom and was just the policy which would have contributed to the conquest of all Deccan. Shivaji had also agreed to help the Mughals in their war against Bijapur with 2000 cavalry under his son and 7000 infantry under him. Aurangzeb accepted these terms in June 1665, but had he carried them out in good faith later on, the annals of Mughals India would possibly have been different. That he was responsible for the reversion of this policy by imprisoning Shivaji at Agra, and that later in 1682 when he came to the Deccan he followed his own policy of fighting the Marathas and the Shah states at once, heighten the contrast between Aurangzeb and Jai Singh. In fact on the occasion of Jai Singh's appointment to the Deccan, he had been instructed by Aurangzeb to punish both Shivaji and the Bijapur king; but Jai Singh with his characteristic shrewdness and foresight had pleaded that "it would not be wise to attack both these fools at the same time," and so did he act, and won success. But in this single sentence lay the soultion of the Deccan problem of the Mughals. On that basis the Mughals should have framed their Deccan policy. That is why Jai Singh was successful and Aurangzeb failed.

In pursuance of his own policy, Jai Singh turned his arms against Bijapur after the treaty of Purandar. The king of Bijapur had not carried out the terms of his treaty with the Mughals, i.e. the payment of one crore of rupees, surrender of the fort of Parenda with the adjoining territories, and cession of the Nizam Shahi Konkan and actually avoided them during the war of succession. His assistance to Sayista Khan and Jai Singh against Shivaji was extremely indifferent. Hence a war was decided upon and with the assistance of Shivaji and after inducing Bijapur nobles to desert, Jai Singh started the campaign. For a month the march of the imperialists was uninterrupted and the forts surrendered without resistance. With high hopes Jai Singh pushed on, fought a pitched battle for the first time on 25th December 1665, and marching on halted within 12 miles of Bijapur (29th December 1665). But now he was threatened with a serious danger. All around the country had been laid waste; tanks had been emptied and wells filled up; "not a green branch or shade-giving wall was left standing." It was folly to advance and hence Jai Singh retreated on the 5th January 1666. Apart from the work of devastation by the enemy, the light bands of Bijapur cavalry had been raiding the imperial territory, which was also a cause of his retreat. The return of Jai Singh had forced the Bijapur troops to evacuate the imperial territory no doubt; but there occurred further misfortunes. Shivaji failed to take the fort of Panhala; his lieutenant Netaji deserted to the side of Bijapur, (though he was ultimately lured into Mughal service, captured and sent to Agra, where he was forced to embrace Islam), and lastly the Qutab Shah of Golconda sent an army of 52 thousand to the assistance of Bijapur, and the allies now converged on the Mughals. Then began a period of deadly warfare, for about six months (December 1665—May 1666) during which Jai Singh fought and won nine sanguinary battles, but was so hard-pressed and harassed that he ultimately decided to retreat. By this time the Bijapuris had also felt exhausted and the Golconda Sultan withdrew his divisions; and so both the parties were anxious for peace.

In the mean while Shivaji, who had been induced to go to Agra to pay court to the emperor (3rd week of March 1666) by the persuasion of Jai Singh and by his solemn assurance of safe return, had been insulted and imprisoned by Aurangzeb but had effected his escape (August 1666). This synchronised with the failure of Jai Singh in the Deccan, and so angered Aurangzeb that he openly censured him, forbade his son Ram Singh to attend the court and ultimately deprived the latter of his rank and pay. Jai Singh himself was superseded by Prince Muazzam in the Viceroyalty of the Deccan. All this was too much for the veteran fighter and loyal servant of the Mughal empire, and he died at Burhanpur on 2nd July 1667. His place in the Deccan was taken by Muazzam, assisted by Jaswant Singh (May 1667). But the incapacity of the one and the indifference of the other relieved Shivaji of all fear from the Mughal side. The unfortunate coincidence of the Yusufzai rebellion in March 1667 forced the emperor to ignore Shivaji. Shivaji on the other hand realized that he could not afford to quarrel with the Mughals, until he organised his resources. He therefore won over Jaswant Singh to intercede in his favour with the emperor for a peace, and the emperor equally eager for peace agreed to it. For three years subsequently, i.e. 1667, 1668, and 1669 Shivaji lived in peace with the Mughals, and it was then that he "laid the foundations of his government broad and deep." Early in January 1670, the rupture began and Shivaji started a vigorous offensive against the Mughals. The war could not be equally vigorously prosecuted by the Mughals, because the Mughal generals were quarrelling among themselves. Shivaji therefore found a splendid opportunity to raid the Mughal territories right and left, and extended his activities even into Berar. There continued a desultory and half-hearted fighting on part of the Mughals for some time, but after the transfer of Diler Khan to meet the situation at the Khybar pass in 1674 where the Afghans had rebelled, there was a lull in the Deccan war. Shivaji utilized this respite in celebrating his coronation.

It was a disgraceful show that the Mughals kept up in the Deccan, and one after another Aurangzeb invited a series of troubles on himself, by his reactionary measures. The frontier trouble continued for a long time, and relaxed the Mughal pressure on Shivaji. In July 1674 he plundered the Camp of the Mughal general Bahadur Khan; in August, September and October Maratha bands spread northwards into the Koli country and by the end of January 1675, another band of 3000 Maratha cavalry roved in the Kolhapur district levying Chauth from the towns. Shivaji next opened delusive peace negotiations with Bahadur Khan and for three months he cajoled him to remain quiet. Then he threw off the mask, made an alliance with Bijapur, and planned an attack on the Karnatak. By this time Bahadur Khan had grown weary of the roving bands of the Marathas, and was glad to make peace with Shivaji after receiving a bribe from him.

At peace with the Mughals he entered into a close friendship and co-operation with Golconda in order that his Karnatak campaign may be a success. "Madanna Pandit, the all powerful wazir of Abdul Hussain Qutab Shah, had already made a subsidiary alliance with Shiva, promising him annual tribute of one lakh of hun for the defence of the realm."[1] Shivaji wanted that the Qutab Shah should bear the expenses of the campaign and lend him an auxiliary force in return for a share of the conquest, and for that purpose, had an interview with him on his way into the Karnatak. It was agreed that the Sultan would pay four and a half lakhs of rupees a month and send an army of 5000 men to co-operate with Shivaji. It was an admirable plan of attack and resulted in the conquest cf of territories yielding 20 lakhs of hun a year, besides a very valuable loot, which replenished the empty treasury of Shivaji. By the middle of January 1678 he returned home and planned to capture Bijapur in which he failed. In his absence (1676-1678) owing to the Karnatak campaign his army left at home under More Trimbak in Desh and Annaji Datto in Konkan looked only to the defence of the realm without venturing to be aggressive against the Mughals.

But the last two years of Shivaji's life were not very glorious and happy even though after his return, he conquered the southern corner of the kingdom of Bijapur comprising Kopal, Dharwar and Belgaum districts, and thus combined his old possessions in Maharastra with the new ones in the Karnatak (central and eastern Mysore). Political and domestic troubles arose and poisoned the peace of his mind. A rupture took place between him and the Qutab Shah because he had not given him any share of the loot and conquest of the Karnatak, and had plotted to capture Bijapur. A war would have resulted had it not been for the hostile proceedings of the Mughal general Diler Khan against the Regent of Bijapur Sidi Masaud, who was an ally of the Qutab Shah in his designs against Shivaji. But if the war with Golconda and Bijapur was averted, another broke out with the Mughals, in which Shivaji and the regent of Bijapur were allies. At this juncture deserted his own son Sambhaji (November 1678) to the Mughals. In 1679 when Aurangzeb imposed the Jaziya Shivaji sent a letter of protest but to no effect. Towards the end of this year Shambhaji returned to his father (December 1679). Shivaji tried his best to convince him of his great heritage and exhorted him to

1. Sarkar's Aurangzeb, Vol. IV, p. 216.

be true to it, but was highly disappointed to perceive that all his sage counsel was lost upon him. A few months after this, Shivaji was taken ill and expired (5th April 1680).

At his death he left behind an independent kingdom that was the pivot of political achievements of the Marathas. His indomitable spirit that bade defiance to the five powers of the Deccan viz. the Mughals, Golconda, Bijapur, the Sidi and the Portuguese, continned to inspire the Marathas through all the phases of their existence—in sun and rain, in triumphs and tribulations. His system of government founded on very sound lines gave them the only symbol of unity of purpose and organization that the Marathas lacked so far. These were the achievements of the great hero of Maharastra.

After his death there occurred some trouble over the question of succession. At last Sambhaji succeeded to the throne (July 1860), and put his minor brother Raja Ram in the prison. Sambhaji gave promise of a capable and vigorous ruler at the start of his reign. But later on he degenerated and by that time there arose complications in the Mughal empire, which reacted adversely on his own life and kingdom. Before a year was out after he ascended the throne, there came to his court the fugitive Prince Akbar, flying from the wrath of his father Aurangzeb, whom he had betrayed in the Rajput war and had tried to depose with the help of the Rajputs. In an evil movement Sambhaji gave him shelter; for hardly had eight months passed when Aurangzeb with a vast army came and "took post at the strategic centre Aurangabad" (22nd March 1682). The concentrated strength of the Mughal empire in the Deccan gave rise to complications which Sambhaji was not capable of comprehending, far less of overcoming.

Aurangzeb's arrival with a vast army and his grim determination to destroy the Marathas stiffened the attitude of the Bijapur and Golconda Sultans, for they knew that if with their help Aurangzeb conquered the Marathas their own destruction would only be a question of time. Therefore when asked to render assistance to him in his task of conquering the Marathas, they refused and Aurangzeb became mightily annoyed, and made up his mind to destroy Bijapur and Golconda before he undertook to crush the Marathas. At this crisis of Bijapur and Golconda, Sambhaji should have made a common cause with them and should have tried his best to stay the work of destruction by the Mughals. But he did not; he perhaps did not realize that the destruction of Bijapur and Golconda would facilitate the task of Aurangzeb who would next turn on him. But nevertheless, the emperor accomplished nothing for more than a year after his arrival in the Deccan (March 1682—April 1683) owing to the desultory fighting and lack of able guidance. He himself had been shocked at the ungrateful behaviour of his son Prince Akbar whom he loved most, and this shock entirely upset the peace of his mind for a considerable time. He despatched an army into the south-Konkon under Prince Muazzam, but the expedition was a failure and ended in heavy losses to the imperialists (September 1683—May 1684). It was then that he became fully awake to the sense of danger threatening him in the Deccan, shook off the effects of his overpowering grief, and undertook the subjugation of the rest of the Deccan Sultanates. The reduction of the Marathas he thought was comparatively easy.

On the 1st April 1685 the siege of Bijapur was started by Prince Azam and Khan-i-Jahan Bahadur and on the 24th May the emperor advanced to Sholapur to be near the seat of war. Not satisfied with only directing the operations from a distance he arrived at Bijapur on the 3rd July 1686 and on the 12th September the king of Bijapur Sikandar Adil Shah surrendered. Aurangzeb ordered the annexation of the country and moved on to Golconda.

On the 28th June 1685 Muazzam was deputed against Golconda to prevent the Qutab Shah from joining the king of Bijapur. Haidarabad was captured in October 1685, but the king Abul Hassan shut himself up in the fort of Golconda. Hence Aurangzeb himself came to Golconda (January 1687) and pressed on the siege vigorously. When it was realized however that the reduction of the fortress was well-nigh impossible, Aurangzeb resorted to bribery. He won over the Afghan, Sardar Khan, one of the highest officials of the Qutab Shah and a "double-dyed traitor" and through him the fort was captured on the 21st September 1687. The king like his peer of Bijapur spent his days in the prison fortress of Daulatabad. Thus in two years Aurangzeb had conquered the two fairest kingdom of the Deccan and had wiped out the last Deccan

Sultanates, which removed all possibilities of a local rivalry for the Marathas. It was not wise for Aurangzeb, but he could not help it. With his deep-seated antagonism towards the Shia Sultanates, which he had evinced on a former occasion when he was the viceroy of the Deccan,he could not attract their willing co-operation. Unable to get their help against the Marathas, and unwilling to let them alone which was equally dangerous, for they might assist the Marathas against him, he determined upon the only alternative open for him—their total destruction.

But while Aurangzeb was directing the full strength of his empire against Golconda and Bijapur, Sambhaji had made no adequate efforts to avert the danger that threatened all the Deccan powers alike. His soldiers raided the Mughal provinces as usual no doubt, but Sambhaji was not wise enough to follow any well-concerted plan of action so that the Mughals might be diverted from the siege of Golconda and Bijapur. Further there were frequent rebellions, desertions and plots against him after 1684. He had gone from Raigarh to Khelna and from Khelna to Sangameshwar, where he spent several months in sensual pleasures and revelries. The usual Maratha vigilance was slackened, and apprized of it, a young and enterprising Mughal officer, Muqarrab Khan started with 2000 picked cavalry and 1000 infantry, and after a series of forced marches surprised and captured Sambhaji (3rd February 1689). Aurangzeb became very happy at his capture and ordered his execution at Koregaon on the 11th March 1689,after giving him the most barbarous treatment in a spirit of sheer revenge.

This incident closed the first phase of Aurangzeb's Deccan war. It was a period of triumph all around. The glorious achievements of these few years—the conquest of Bijapur and Golconda, the occupation of Sagar, Raichur, Adoni, Bangalore, Wandiwash, Conjiveram, Belgaum and Bankapur in the south and east, the conquest of many Maratha fortresses and crowning all the capture and execution of the Maratha king Sambhaji, created in Aurangzeb a spirit of robust optimism, about the accomplishment of the task he had undertaken. Prince Akbar had sailed for Persia, the year Bijapur fell, never to return to India again. Thus it appeared as if Aurangzeb had come to the end of his mission; that he had only to give a finishing touch to the newly conquered kingdoms by imposing imperial government on them; that he had to sweep off the "accursed Marathas" into the hell, devastate and annex their country; and then return home. But the seemingly easy accomplishment of his mission was highly illusive, and he had not reckoned the potentialities of the Marathas correctly. How vain were his hopes and wishes and how limited his pre-vision, was realized when he encountered a stubborn resistance actuated by a grim determination, on the part of the Marathas. The Deccan Sultanates had passed into extinction and could never rise to join hands with the Marathas in their national struggle for independence, because they had become totally bankrupt in energy, political power and capacity for initiative. The Marathas were on the other hand full of all these and they were a rising people.

"The capture and execution of Sambhaji stunned the Marathas. The prospect became still more gloomy at the end of the year (October 1689) when his sons and family were captured and Rajaram was driven south to take shelter in Jinji. In this terrible national crisis the genius of the Maratha people saved them. In that kingless state the people and their leaders took up the task of self-defence. It was no more a war between the Maratha king and the Mughal emperor, but a people's war against a foreign aggression." In these terse and telling sentences Prof. Sarkar analyses the situation in 1689 and visualises the sequel of Aurangzeb's war with the Marathas.

Only five days after the capture of Sambhaji i.e. 8th February 1689, Raja Ram was taken out of the prison in sullen resentment and set up on the throne in the fort of Raigarh. But the same month the Mughals beseiged the fortress. After holding out for a month he slipped out it (5th April) and passing through a series of adventures, he entered Jinji on the 1st November 1689 in the guise of a poor man. He had retired there with the intention of drawing the Mughals with him, and thus dividing their forces between Maharastra and the Karnatak, where he might be better able to make a stand against them with the help of Shahji II of Tanjore his first cousin. Accordingly the plan of campaign for the future was that Rajaram was to direct operation from Jinji in consultation with Prahlad Niraji, Dhanaji Jadhav, Santaji Ghorpade, and others while Ramchandra Pant Amatya was to take the supreme control of the affairs in Maharastra with the assistance of Shankaraji Malhar and others. Ramchandra Pant was bestowed the highest powers and the title of Hukumatpanah, which made him virtually the king in the absence of Rajaram. The wisdom of the course became apparent as the second phase of the struggle (1690-1698) well advanced.

Since by the year 1689 many important Maratha forts had fallen into the hands of the Mughals, along with their capital and the Siddi acting in the interest of Aurangzeb had compelled them to evacuate Chaul and Underi, Aurangzeb did not pay much attention to the conquest of the barren hill-forts of the west any further, and busied himself with the occupation of the rich dominions of the Adil Shahi and Qutab Shahi kings for three years from 1689 to 1691. That was the time when the Marathas made a supreme effort to recover from their first shock. On the 25th May 1690 Santaji surrounded Rustam Khan and won a decisive victory over the Mughals; the same year Ramchandra Pant and Shankaraji wrested the forts of Pratapgarh, Rohira and Torna from the Mughals and in 1692 Panhala was recovered. The fall of Panhala opened the eyes of Aurangzeb, and he deputed Prince Muizuddin to take it. The fort held out for a year till October 1693, when Dhanaji appeared with a vast army of the Marathas inflicted defeat on the besiegers and withdrew. Dis-satisfied at the incapacity of Prince Muizuddin the emperor sent Prince Bidar Bakht (1695) who did not fare any better. In the meanwhile severe reverses had been sustained by the Mughal arms in the south. By the end of the year 1695 Santaji Ghorpade defeated and killed Qasim Khan and Himmat Khan, two first-rate generals of the Mughal empire.

In the golden land of Karnatak, where Rajaram was directing activities, the year 1690 opened badly for the imperialists. It was heralded by the rebellion of the old Haidarabadi officers who had been taken over into imperial service. Zulfikar Khan suppressed the rebellion and was then ordered to besiege Jinji (September 1690). But to besiege it was not an easy affair. It consisted of a group of forts and Rajaram could conveniently manage to slip in and out. The imperialists could not achieve anything decisive in 1691 and 1692. In December 1692 Santaji looted Kanjiveram and arrested its governor.

Dhanaji in the meanwhile surrounded the trenches of Zulfikar Khan around Jinji and cut off his supplies. Prince Kambaksh opened treasonable negotiations with Rajaram, hampered the progress of the siege, and slighted Zulfikar Khan. These incidents forced the Mughals to abandon the siege, (January 1693) which was renewed towards the close of 1694. But again the appearance of Dhanaji and Santaji made the imperialists to decamp. In 1696 Rajaram pressed for money, opened negotiations for peace, but Aurangzeb rejected them and ordered Zulfikar Khan to capture Jinji without delay. Early in November 1697, the siege was renewed but two months later, Rajaram managed to escape with his chief officers first to Vellore and then to Vishalgarh, which was reached in February 1698. Thus inspite of the Mughal efforts for about seven years to capture Jinji and Rajaram along with it, they had failed. That was a standing disgrace to the name and fame of the Mughals. In September 1698 Rajaram sued for peace in vain, and early in 1699 he visited the Konkan country. In September 1699 he formed plans of raiding Khandesh and Berar, and was starting on his expedition when he was forced to give it up because of the opening of the campaign in October by Aurangzeb. This time the emperor conducted the campaign in person and pursued Rajaram from place to place, till at last Rajaram was tired out, and breathed his last on 2nd March 1700 at Sinhgarh. Another thorn had been removed from the path of Aurangzeb. But it did not matter if kings died or lived. The people had risen to its own defence and Aurangzeb had to fight against them. Aurangzeb, however, did not realize it. In his obsession for conquering the Maratha country, in his infatuation for the mission of crushing all opposition, he failed to scrutinise the real factors of the situation; and undertook at the age of nearly seventy-five the conquest of all the Maratha forts which he thought formed the back-bone of Maratha power. That it was extremely illusory he did not believe.

On the 19th October 1699, he started from Islampuri on that fateful campaign, which was to occupy the last six years of his life. One by one the important hill-forts of Satara, Parli, Panhala, Vishalgarh, Sinhgarh, Rajgarh, Torna and five others less important than these were captured. But all except Torana "capitulated after a time and for a price—none of these was taken by assault." This fact reveals the hard realities of the situation, that was not very hopeful for Aurangzeb. His last campaign was against Wagingera, which was obstinately defended from the 8th February to 27th April 1705. After this he felt strangely weak and withdrew to Devapur. In the rainy season of that year the Marathas recovered Sinhgarh and many other forts. As a matter of fact the Marathas had been recovering forts from the Mughals, the moment the emperor moved away from them. During the year 1706-1707 the roving bands of Marathas under Dhanaji, Nimaji, Sindhia, and others ruthlessly ravaged the imperial territories—Gujrat, Berar and Khandesh. Under the able guidance of Tara Bai, the widow of Rajaram, who had become the Regent for her son Sambhaji II, ever since 1700, the Marathas had followed this policy of carrying war into the enemy's country and it proved highly effective. Already the Mughal government in the provinces beyond the Narbada had been paralysed, owing to the lack of initiative and efficiency, as well as for the lack of Aurangzeb's personal supervision. Now the Maratha raids worsened their condition and all sorts of confusion began to reign there. Mughal prestige along with Mughal government had been wrecked.

In the midst of these, Aurangzeb lay sick to death at Ahmednagar whither he had removed in January 1706. Around him spread the distressing scenes of a sinking empire. But that was not all. His last days, in fact the last hours of his life, were poisoned by the mutual jealousies of Princes Azam a d Kam baksh, and hardly had a week passed after he could manage to separate them, by entrusting them the governments of Malwa and Hyderabad, when he died (20th February 1707). And it was a tragic death full of the painful consciousness that with the mightiest empire he had failed against the kith and kin of the "Mountain rat", that he had made more enemies than friends, and spent his resources for nothing. In short his efforts to conquer the Marathas Aurangzeb had failed and the failure had adversely affected the stability of his empire. It was now the turn of the Marathas to conquer the Mughal empire.

To sum up, Akbar began the Deccan conquest with the full support of the Rajputs, with the full sympathy of the Hindus, and with a strong and stable frontier line on the north-western border of the empire. His successors continued the work of conquest, but internal troubles of the Mughal empire, now the revolt of a royal prince, or of a noble, now the war on the north-western frontier or revolt of a people, came as great handicaps. In the time of Aurangzeb the situation became most deplorable. The whole of Hindustan was seething with disaffection; the frontier tribes were up in arms; and heedless of these Aurangzeb wanted to conquer the Marathas and the Deccan Sultanates. It was too heavy a task even for his abilities and resources. With the Rajputs alienated, the Hindus, the Sikhs and the Decanee Shiahs antagonised, and the government of the empire disintegrating, Aurangzeb wanted to conquer the Marathas. It was a vain hope. No wonder he failed.

CHAPTER VI

THE FRONTIER PROBLEM OF THE MUGHALS

The frontier problem of the Indian Mughals was no less complicated than that of the British. In fact the Mughals were more vitally concerned with the people and provinces of North-Western frontier, and to them, in a much greater degree, the frontier problem was the pivot of their political existence. Their home was beyond the frontier, and their ambition fondly cherished an empire in which the transfrontier provinces, once their ancestral dominions, should form a part. That was not all. The conquest of Hindustan had been achieved from a transfrontier kingdom, and throughout the existence of their empire they recruited their soldiers from those regions. Thus the love of motherland, the pride of possessing ancestral dominions, and the military needs of the empire had combined to make the frontier problem extremely consequential for the Mughals. As new tribes rose to power and endangered these interests, the Mughal empire grew nerveless and decayed. The satisfactory solution of the frontier problem in a way controlled the existence or extinction of the Mughal sway in Northern India, and hence it demands much more attention at the hands of the historian, trying to explain the downfall of the Mughal empire, than it has hitherto received.

The causes that were responsible for the flight of Babar from his ancestral dominions, for his unsuccessful attempts at their recovery, and for the foundation of the Mughal empire in India were also the deciding factors in the frontier policy of the Mughals. The steady rise of the Uzbegs under Shaibani Khan, and their gradual conquest of the whole Timurid kingdom compelled Babar to run away to Kabul, and to endeavour from there, to recover his lost dominions with the help of the Persians. Since he failed in his attempts, and his powerful allies, the Persians, occupied Khorasan and Bokhara he had to remain content with the poor principality of Kabul, and when opportunity arrived, turned eastward to India for fresh conquests. Thus the neighbourhood of two powerful nations, the Persians and the Uzbegs set Babar's foot on the road to India; for, Babar's relations with the former were none too friendly and the latter were his hereditary enemies. Kabul, hemmed in between the dominions of these two hostile nations, would have fallen an easy prey to either, had it not been for the fact that they were themselves mortal enemies of each other. In their mutual enmity they overlooked Babar, who thus had a quiet time for himself to consolidate his kingdom, and to prepare for the conquest of Hindustan. Babar handed down to his successors his transfrontier possessions, and therefore, ruling from India, they had to face the very same problems and had to come into conflict with the very same peoples—the Persians and the Uzbegs. The diplomatic relations subsisting between the Indian Mughals, and the Uzbegs and Persians, form the foundation of the Mughal frontier problem. The course, these relations took, depended, upon the comparative strength of the parties, and varied from time to time. Under Babar's successors, from Akbar to Shahjahan, the Persians were evenly matched, and the Uzbegs, overpowered; whil ebefore Akbar, both the Persians and the Uzbegs were overpowering. Hence the policy of the Mughals before Akbar was one of defensive vigilance towards the Persians and Uzbegs; while, after Akbar it assumed a pronounced form of aggression.

The nature of the problem was also determined by the geographical situations of these nations. The physical configuration of Central Asia necessitates the mastery of Badakshan, Balkh and Kandahar for the ruler of Kabul. Otherwise there is no scientific frontier and Kabul is exposed. In the north Kabul is bounded by the lofty walls of the Hindukush penetrated by several passes, the most famous of them being the Hindukush. "This has indeed been a veritable gateway of nations. This way came Alexander with his Greek following, and it would take a chapter to record the successive tides of human migration (Scythian and Mughal) which have swept through those frozen gateways to the north of Kabul".[1] To guard this gateway of the north, Balkh and Badakshan, situated between

1. *Imperial Gazetteer*, Vol. I, p. 19.

the mountains and the Oxus river flowing westwards, should be strongly held, and to hold these two provinces the line of the Oxus must be secured. In the south Kabul is equally exposed. The magnificent heights of the Hindukush as they run in a southwesterly direction sink into lower altitudes, and "the western borders of the country maintain a general average of about 3000 ft. from Herat to Kandahar".[1] From Kandahar to Herat, the country is also traversed by a number of rivers like the Helmand, the Harirud and the Khasurd, which make it fruitful. South-east of Kandahar is the desert, but north of it, as far as Ghazni and Kabul, the country is fertile, full of irrigated fields and green pastures. Once Kandahar is taken, Kabul is in a precarious position, for the distance between Herat and Kandahar is only 360 miles and takes ten days for the cavalry to cover it. "Herat was but the gateway to Kandahar and Kabul in the days when Kabul was India.".[2] Hence the two river lines, the Oxus in the north, and the Helmand in the south, were of supreme importance to the Indian Mughals, and so long as the Uzbegs were established on the former, and the Persians on the latter, they could not rest in peace at all.

But this was only a part of the problem. Behind this outer frontier there was another the inner frontier, and the Mughals were equally concerned to hold it in strength. It lay between Kabul and the Punjab formed by a rugged stretch of mountainous country from Baluchistan to Kashmere. This is inhabited by wild uncivilized tribes and through it run the chief passes to Afghanistan—the Gomal, the Tochi, the Kurram and the Khyber in succession from the south. To the north of the Khyber, there are the valleys of the Swat, Bajaur and Panjkora, affording facilities for human habitation. Still further north lies the Kashmere state, with its fascinating landscape and salubrious climate. The communication between the two parts of the Mughal empire—Kabul and Hindustan—was maintained through the passes, and their security was of as great a consequence to the internal peace of the empire, as that of the outer frontier. For, the perfect mastery of the inner frontier meant the security of Kabul and sure supply of recruits for the army of the Indian Mughals.

1. *Ibid.*, p. 11.
2. Holdich, *Gates of India*, p. 529.

Hence the Mughals had to tackle three problems in order to maintain their frontier defence intact. The first was to establish themselves in Balkh and Badakshan to the prejudice of the Uzbegs; the second was to establish themselves in Kandahar to the prejudice of the Persians; and the third was to keep the tribes on the North-western border of India under control, so as to keep the line of communication between Kabul and Hindustan open at all times.

With the expulsion of Bàbar from his ancestral dominions, and with his conquest of Kabul in 1504 began the frontier problem. Till he conquered Hindustan more than twenty years later, the line of Badakshan, Balkh, and Kandahar was of supreme importance. In 1505 Nasir Mirza took possession of Badakshan, only to be expelled by Shaibani Khan soon after. Shaibani not only conquered Badakshan, but Khorasan also. It was only after he was killed at the battle of Merv, that Shah Ismail occupied the latter province, and compelled, by his immense prestige, the Arghuns of Kandahar to recognize his suzerainty. If the death of Shaibani profited the Shah of Persia, it did Babar no less. With the help of the Shah he recovered almost all his ancestral dominions. But his truimph was short-lived, and he was once again expelled from those dominions, which were the glory of his youth, the dream of his life, and the mission of all Indian Mughals.

This expulsion, however, did not mean the loss of all. During those memorable days, when for the last time he ruled from the capital of Taimur, he had bestowed upon his cousin Wais Mirza, the provinces of Badakshan along with Shadman and Khutlan,[1] and these remained to the Mughals yet. Safe from the direction of Badkshan, which he acquired after the death of Wais Mirza in 1520 and fully aware of the futility of all attempts to recover Balkh, then under the Uzbegs, he turned his attention to Kandahar. In 1522, after much worry and vigilance he conquered it from the Arghuns, who retired into Sindh. Thus of the whole line one patch had slipped off his hands, and the rest remained under his control. But Babar was not satisfied. Six years later, when he had become the emperor of Hindustan he attempted to recover Balkh from the

1. *An Empire Builder of the 16th Century*, p. 104.

Uzbegs and used Badakshan as his base. Humayun had been placed in charge of the campaigns. His sudden departure for Agra, to counteract the conspiracy hatched by Khalifa and Mahdi Khwaja, to exclude him from the throne, spoiled the projects of Babar, and caused much annoyance to him. Babar asked his experienced minister Khalifa to take the place of Humayun in Badakshan, but he objected to go. Humayun also showed his reluctance to return to his post, and therefore, in the last resort, he deputed Suleiman Mirza, the heir-apparent, to take possession of his father's kingdom. Babar still considered that the retention of the province was of great importance for the recovery of his lost ancestral dominions.[1] But he did not live to realize his ambition, and he was laid in the grave before a year was out.

On Humayun fell the burden of maintaining the double line of defence—the inner and outer frontiers, besides a kingdom, whose stability was extremely precarious. He lost the empire of Hindustan by his own faults, and the most outstanding of them was his leniency towards his brothers. Out of that leniency he divided his dominions among his brothers, and Kamran received the whole of the transfrontier possessions of Babar. Hence so long as Humayun was ruling over Hindustan, as well as after his expulsion from India Kamran was concerned about the frontier defence. After 1540, he was required to maintain the outer frontier line alone. For five years more till 1545, he ruled Kabul, Kandahar and Badakshan, and successfully held his own against the Uzbegs and the Persians. He had deprived Suleiman Mirza of his hereditary principality of Badakshan, and had brought it under his direct control. When in 1544 Humayun came with Persian auxiliaries to wrest his kingdom from Kamran, he had made an agreement with the friendly Shah of Persia, that Kandahar, after its conquest, would be surrendered to him. Whether it was due to the offensive attitude of the Persians or to the strategic importance of Kandahar, whatever it be, Humayun took possession of it and broke faith with the friendly Shah. Shortly after, he recovered Kabul from Kamran, who fled away to Sindh. In the meanwhile Mirza Suleiman, who had been released by Kamran

1. *Ibid.*, p. 173.

at the time of Humayun's invasion in order that he might be of some help to him, had established his independence and taking advantage of the unsettled condition of Humayun's affairs, had annexed the districts of Qunduz, Khost and Anderab. These were the dependencies of Kabul under Kamran, and when Humayun demanded them Suleiman would not part with them. In 1547 Humayun led an army into Badakshan, and defeated Suleiman Mirza, who fled from his country. Though for some time the districts were annexed, Badakshan and Qunduz were bestowed upon Hindal, Khost upon Munim Beg, and Talikan upon Bapus, yet, political expediency dictated the restoration of the country to Mirza Suleiman, who thenceforth remained a failthful ally of Humayun.

But if secure from the side of Badakshan, he was not so from the side of Balkh. It was under the Uzbegs, and they had given offence to him by helping Kamran against him in 1548. In the spring of 1549, therefore, he marched into Balkh, and commanded Suleiman, and Kamran, who had in the meanwhile submitted to Humayun to join him with their forces. Suleiman did, and Kamran did not. In 1550 he "wandered about the country with bad intentions",[1] and because of these bad intentions Humayun achieved nothing. On the other hand he was severely wounded in a dastardly attack by Kamran, and thus ended the Balkh expedition never to be repeated till the time of Shahjahan.

Until Kamran was blinded and sent away to Mecca (1553), Humayun's position in Kabul was very unsafe. Hindal had been killed (1551) and Askari, taken prisoner, was also sent to Mecca, where he died in 1557. Kandahar and Badakshan did not give him any trouble. Suleiman remained loyal to Humayun, who sealed this goodwill by giving his daughter Bakshni Banu to Suleiman's son Ibrahim. Thus free from his brothers and all frontier troubles, he invaded Hindustan, and recovered it with comparative case. On 23rd July 1555 he sat on the throne of Delhi for the second time, and before six months were over he died by a fall from his library (27th January 1556).

Humayun left for Akbar the legacy of a contested succes-

1. Mrs. Beveridge, *Introduction to Humayun Nama*, p. 45.

sion in a nascent state. His minority and insecurity gave rise to all sorts of trouble on the frontier. Kandahar fell into the hands of the Persians in 1558, and Prince Suleiman assumed airs of independence. Taking advantage of the young age of Muhammad Hakim Mirza who was only five at the time, Prince Suleiman went so far as to invade Kabul, but he had to retire because his own kingdom was threatened by the Uzbegs on the north-west. In 1561 Munim Khan, the regent for Muhammad Hakim was called to the Court, and then began a really troublous time in Kabul. Munim Khan had been succeeded by his son Ghani Khan, but the government was seized by Mahachuchak Begum, Hakim's mother, with the help of three nobles, Shah Wali Afghan, Fazal Beg and Abul Fath Beg. When Akbar sent Munim Khan to set things right he was defeated by the Begum. In the meanwhile she had put to death the three nobles who had helped her in usurping power, and had taken one Haidar Kasim Kohbar as her adviser whom she had intended to marry. At this juncture arrived the fugitive, Abul Maali from India who wormed himself into her favour, married her daughter, and ultimately put her to death. Upon her lover also fell the same fate, and then Abul Maali seized power, and ruled like a tyrant over Kabul. Poor Muhammad Hakim fled away to the shelter of Prince Suleiman who took up his cause, defeated and captured Abul Maali, and handed him over to Muhammad Hakim who had him strangled to death in May 1564. This friendliness was cemented by the marriage of Prince Muhammad with the daughter of Prince Suleiman. On this occasion the ruler of Badakshan was given a part of Kabul in recognition of his services, but it offended the Kabulis, and there was an insurrection. Therefore, in 1566 the Badakshan prince invaded Kabul with the intention of seizing his son-in-law, but failed. Shortly after died his (Suleiman's) wife, the spirited Haram Begum, and her death landed him into all sorts of troubles. He fell out with his grandson and successor, Prince Shah Rukh, and was driven out of the kingdom. He wandered a good deal, seeking shelter first, with the Uzbeg ruler of Balkh and then, with the sovereign of Bokhara, Iskandar Khan, the father of Abdullah Khan Uzbeg.

But the unsettled condition of Badakshan and the loss of Kandahar did not stand alone. Kabul went its own way, and actually became instrumental in jeopardising the safety of Akbar's empire in Hindustan. Instead of being a bulwark of Hindustan, its ruler tried to imitate Mahmud of Ghazni and Muhammad Ghori in attacking Hindustan when Akbar was in a critical situation. Muhammad Hakim twice invaded the Punjab, once in 1567 when Akbar was exerting to crush the rebellion of the Uzbegs and the Mirza, and again in 1581, when Akbar by his religious speculations had raised a whirlwind in Hindustan. Be it said to the credit of Akbar, that he repulsed his brother both the times and in 1581, actually marched into Kabul. Muhammad Hakim had fled away before him and had retired into the hills leaving the capital to be occupied by Akbar. Though Akbar punished Muhammad Hakim by bestowing the kingdom on his sister, the wife of Khwaja Hassan, yet he realized quite well how very dangerous it was to be deprived of the control of the frontier; a less capable monarch than Akbar would have collapsed in the crisis of 1581. Its dreadful nature was due to the attack of Muhammad Hakim at a time when the Muslims of Northern India were seething with discontent. Whatever might have been the result of the triumphant return of Akbar from Kabul, he became painfully aware of the fact that as long as Kabul was not brought under his control, his empire of Hindustan would be threatened from behind the frontier, the moment there was some commotion in the tribal area.

Akbar's invasions of Kabul synchronised with a very dark period in Badakshan. Owing to the continuous strife between Suleiman and Shahrukh "the country was now in the most lamentable confusion; the soldiery was discontented, the rayats without justice, the garrisons dismantled, and the whole country desolate."[1] That was the opportunity of the Uzbegs. The days were long past when they were drifting along the current like atoms of sand. Now they were thoroughly organized under their powerful leader Abdullah Khan. Born in 1533, and the son of a petty chief Iskandar Khan, he had conquered Bokhara at twentyfour, and had proclaimed his father as the Khakan of the Uzbeg tribes at twenty-eight (1561). Then followed a series of victories, when Balkh, Samarkand, Taskand, Tur-

1. Von Noer, *Akbar*, Vol. II, p. 124.

kestan, Farghana and Andijan were conquered, and the glories of Shaibani again returned to the Uzbegs. In 1583 his father died, and he succeeded to the Khakanship. He had watched with a keen interest the civil war between the grandfather and grandson in Badakshan, and hardly a year was out (1584) when he invaded the kingdom and "without a blow struck seized the country." Fleeing for life Prince Shahrukh met his grandfather on his way to Kabul and the foes in prosperity became friends in adversity. They found a refuge, first at Kabul and then at the court of Akbar.

The fall of Badakshan completed the loss of the whole line of the outer frontier and it was fraught with grave consequences for the Mughals. Kabul immediately, and Hindustan remotely, were exposed. For a moment, therefore, it brought about a harmony of interests between Akbar and Muhammad Hakim. The latter applied for help to Akbar in 1584; and Akbar promised "in the first place, to despatch an embassy to Badakshan, manifestly hoping to set a bound to Abdullah's conquest by diplomacy, and if this should fail, to follow it by an army to Kabul fully equipped and with a sum of treasure under an able general."[1] Akbar, in fact, thought that he could for the time being treat Kabul as a buffer state. Therefore, he wanted to strengthen it, so that it may be used as an outwork for Hindustan. But before any definite steps could be taken in this direction came the news of Muhammad Hakim's death in July 1585. This changed the attitude of Akbar, and the relative importance of Kabul. It could no more be treated as a buffer; it had to be taken under direct control at once. "No question of formal annexation arose, because the territory ruled by the Mirza, although in practice long administered as an independent state, had always been regarded in theory as dependency on the crown of India."[2] Akbar, therefore, sent Man Singh with some troops so that he might maintain order till his arrival. Man Singh came not a moment too late, for "there was in Kabul a Turanian party amongst the nobles, which sought to subverse the ambitious designs by means of the young princes Kaiqubad and Afrasiab,"[3] at the instigation of Abdullah Khan, but Man Singh's arrival

1. *Ibid.*, pp. 128-29.
2. Smith, *Akbar*, pp. 230-31.
3. Von Noer, *Akbar*, Vol. II, p. 130.

frustrated their move. A general amnesty was proclaimed which created a favourable atmosphere for the Emperor's rule. Having thus pacified Kabul by politic clemency Akbar started northwards, and early in December, 1585 pitched his tents at Rawalpindi. There or in its neighbourhood he lived for full thirteen years, watching the affairs of the Uzbegs and of the Persians, and conquering the countries that formed the inner frontier of Hindustan. It is a glorious period in Akbar's career of conquest and empire-building. It reveals Akbar's insight into the importance of frontier defence, as also his consummate ability to plan extensive campaigns in one of the most difficult regions of the world, and to control each *minutiar* thereof. It is doubtful whether there is any other epoch in his life in which he showed in a more brilliant way that he had the head to plan and the hand to execute, that his originality of conception and boldness of design were on a par with his eye for strategy.

Hardly a week had passed when Akbar's ideas took definite shape. The whole of the frontier line formed by Kashmir, the tribal territory and Baluchistan had to be brought under his control. Kashmir was of great strategic importance for controlling all the hinterland between the last offshoots of the Himalayas and the Hindukush forming the south-eastern frontier of Badakshan. Inhabited by the most fierce and fickle Yusufzai tribes the tribal territory lay between the Khyber Pass and the Hindukush and between Chitral on the north of Kabul and Kashmir; and on its control depended the security of the pass which was the line of communication between Kabul and Northern India, and Baluchistan. It controlled the strategic passes and its conquest was necessary both as a precaution against the Persians at Kandahar, and as a preliminary for the subjugation of Kandahar. At a time when Abdullah Khan Uzbeg held the undisputed sway over Central Asia and threatened Kabul, it was certainly inexpedient to have the Yusufzais in open rebellion inspired by their religious zeal, and Yusuf Khan, the Sultan of Kashmir in a sulky mood at the demand of the emperor to submit and pay homage in person. Hence, from Rawalpindi Akbar moved to Attock and from there sent two expeditions into the Yusufzai country and Kashmir (1586). His motive in moving from Rawalpindi to Attock was to "occupy a position favourable for control of the operations against Kashmere and also against the Afghans of the Yusufzai and Mandar tribes."[1] The expedition against the Yusufzais tribesmen of the Bajaur country was led by Zain Khan Kokaltash, while other officers entered the Samah plateau, the home of the Mandar tribes. Zain Khan was reinforced later by Raja Birbal and Hakim Abul Fath, but the three commanders fell out, and could not decide upon a common plan of operation. While retreating in despair they were cut off by the tribesmen, and lost about half of their army. Raja Birbal was killed on this occasion. Then Raja Todar Mall was commissioned to proceed against the tribesmen, and he retrieved the lost prestige of the imperial arms. "Here and there he built forts and harried and plundered continually, so that he reduced the Afghans to great straits."[2] Man Singh subsequently won a great victory over their leader Jalal in the Khyber Pass. On the whole, the expeditions had a salutary effect on the disloyalty of the tribesmen, and they proved less troublesome, though they were never conquered. Jalal, their spiritual leader kept up the fight till 1600, when he captured Ghazni, but he was killed soon after.

As regards Kashmir Akbar had better success. Kasim Khan and Raja Bhagwan Das with some other officers had been entrusted with the task of conquering that state. Their first contact with the Kashmiris ended in a treaty that was not approved by Akbar. Soon after the Sultan and his son surrendered, but being ill-treated, the young prince Yakub Khan, the son of the Sultan, made his escape from the imperial camp and made warlike preparations in his state. Again, Kasim Khan was sent at the head of an army, and entered Srinagar after overcoming the resistance of Yakub Khan. Kashmir was then definitely annexed, and formed a Sarkar of the Subah of Kabul (1587-88). Thus Akbar became comparatively free from anxiety by the year 1581, and the next year he started to visit Kabul and Kashmir. Akbar must have derived immense satisfaction from the fact that Kabul and Kashmir could no more afford an opportunity for the ambition of the Uzbegs, and that they now formed integral parts of the empire.

So far only half the frontier line had been secured;

1. Smith, *Akbar*, p. 233.
2. Elliot and Dawson, Vol. V, p. 451.

there remained Sindh and Baluchistan. Akbar left Kabul in November 1589 in order to undertake the conquest of Sindh; and deputed in 1590, Abdur Rahim, Khan-i-Khanan for the purpose. Ever since 1574 the island fortress of Bakhar had remained under imperial control. Now the Khan-i-Khanan was appointed Subahdar of Multan and was directed to annex the kingdom of Thattah which was under Mirza Jani, the Tarkhan. The latter was defeated at two places, and surrendered in 1591. With his surrender the kingdom was annexed. Four years later in February 1595, the fort of Siwi, to the south-east of Quetta fell to the imperialists led by Mir Masum, the soldier and the historian. The Parni Afghans who stubbornly defended the fort were defeated and after their defeat, "all Baluchistan, as far as the frontiers of the Kandahar province, and including Makran, the region near the coast, passed under the imperial sceptre."[1] Akbar had considered the conquest of Sindh and Baluchistan as a necessary prelude to the recovery of Kandahar, and to an effectual warding off of any attack from there. Here he was more fortunate than his expectations, and without a blow struck he acquired Kandahar. In April 1505 its Persian Governor, Muzaffar Husain Mirza handed over the fortress to Akbar's officers, and thus, one of the vital problems of the frontier defence was solved for Akbar.

The conquest of Kashmir, Sindh and Baluchistan, the punishment of the tribesmen, and the surrender of Kandahar were great triumphs which revealed the mighty strength of Akbar. By 1595 the inner frontier as well as the south-western part of the outer frontier had been perfectly secured. These grand achievements highly impressed the contemporaries of Akbar, specially, Abdullah Khan. Now he could never entertain the idea of meddling in the affairs of Akbar's empire. He "must rather have felt relief that Akbar did not make a common cause against him with Shah Abbas."[2] But that was out of the question as long as Kandahar remained under Akbar. Abdullah Khan's apprehensions were rooted in his enmity with Shah Abbas to whom he had lost Mashad, Merv, Herat and most of Trans-oxiana before his death.[3] Therefore, he showed a good

1. Smith, *Akbar*, p. 258.
2. Von Noer, *Akbar*, Vol. II, p. 226.
3. Smith, *Akbar*, p. 271.

deal of concern to win the friendship of Akbar and actually proposed a matrimonial alliance between his son and a daughter of Akbar. Akbar treated his overtures with scant attention and wrote a diplomatic letter in 1596 emphasising his great power, enormous resources and vast dominions, perhaps, to convey that it was beneath his dignity to accept his proposal. Two years later the powerful Khakan died, and thus departed the greatest enemy of Akbar. Other affairs awaited his attention, and relieved from all anxiety in the north he returned to Agra the very same year. He had achieved much, but even with his great talents and vast resources he had not risked an invasion of Balkh and Badakshan. Perhaps, even after the death of Abdullah Khan, the Uzbegs were sufficiently strong in those two provinces, and Akbar felt that a campaign would have extremely indifferent results. For a long time to come the Uzbegs remained a decisive factor in the problem of the frontier defence of the Mughals.

Akbar left to his son, Jahangir (1605) a powerful and progressive empire with a strong frontier and organized system of defence. Kandahar had been strengthened, and the tribal trritories controlled by fortresses built at strategic points. The Uzbegs after the death of their leader had become disunited, and their chiefs were fighting among themselves for supremacy. Hence, Jahangir could afford to neglect them. But the case of the Persians was entirely different. Their king, Shah Abbas (1587-1629) was one of the greatest monarchs of the age. Shrewd and capable, he excelled in tortuous diplomacy no less than in the art of war. He had utterly humiliated Abdullah Khan, and had taken the easy Mughal acquisition of Kandahar very much to heart. He began to cast about for plans to recover it, shortly after Jahangir's accession, and did not cease until he had achieved it. Early in Jahangir's reign he secretly ordered his officers in the districts of Herat, Farra, Seistan, and Khorasan to make a surprise attack on Kandahar. But because the governor of Kandahar, constantly on the alert, had got timely information of his designs and was prepared to stand a siege, the Persians did not succeed (1607). The Shah, whose designs had thus been revealed, feigned indignation at the so-called unauthorised proceedings of his unruly officers, and sent an ambassador to Jahangir to explain and apologise.

Jahangir, of course, took it with good grace, but adequately reinforced the garrison at Kandahar, so that it might not be taken unawares again.

But the precautionary measures of Jahangir did not escape the eye of Shah Abbas, and he sedulously set to soothe his suspicions about Kandahar. His embassies to Jahangir came pretty frequently, and conveyed professions of friendship mingled with fulsome flattery. Costly and handsome presents were also not wanting. Between 1611 and 1620, there came four embassies, all of which assured the Emperor that the Shah bore sincerest regards and warmest affection for him. Deceived by these empty shows Jahangir slackened his vigilance and reduced the garrison at Kandahar. Nothing could be more welcome to Shah Abbas. He secretly prepared a strong army, besieged Kandahar in March 1622 and took it after a siege of forty days; Prince Shahjahan, who had been ordered to repulse the enemy revolted, and for the rest of Jahangir's reign the Mughal court had neither leisure nor the inclination to wrest Kandahar from the Persians. Thus, Jahangir lost what Akbar had gained on the outer frontier and Kabul became exposed again on the south-west.

But Kandahar was not lost for ever. In February 1638 it was again betrayed to Shahjahan by its Persian Governor, Ali Mardan Khan. Emboldened by this freak of fortune Shahjahan thought that he might undertake the recovery of Balkh and Badakshan. Nor were the circumstances unfavourable for such a project. Imam Kuli of the Astrakhanide dynasty died in 1642 after a prosperous rule of thirtytwo years, and his vast kingdom comprising Samarkand, Bokhara, Balkh and Badakshan plunged into confusion. His son, Nazar Muhammad had succeeded him, but he proved a failure, and owing to his high-handed proceedings the Uzbeg generals deposed him and set up his eldest son, Abdul Aziz in April, 1645. The deposed father was assigned only a portion of the kingdom comprising Balkh and Badakshan. This civil war resulting in the division of Uzbeg dominions was the opportunity of Shahjahan, and he planned an expedition promptly into Badakshan. In June 1645 the fort of Kahmard was occupied, but was abondoned soon after. In October another expedition was led by Raja Jagat Singh and it resulted in the occupation of the district.

After these two pioneering expeditions Prince Murad was sent at the head of an immense army, fifty-thousand strong in June 1646. Qunduz was occupied on 22nd June, and the city of Balkh entered on 2nd July; Nazar Muhammad fled away towards Persia leaving his treasures to the invaders, and it appeared as if the country had been subjugated.

But troubles started soon enough. Prince Murad hated the hilly country and its rustic inhabitants, and longed for Hindustan. Shahjahan failed to impress upon him the necessity of remaining there. He abandoned his charge without caring for his father's wishes, and came away. Terrible was the fate of the people of the country and of their new conquerors after his departure. The Uzbegs made their life miserable and the government of the Mughals fell into disorder. It was only when Aurangzeb came, defeated the Uzbegs and occupied the city of Balkh (May, 1647) that the situation was relieved. But the period of trouble had not come to an end for the Mughals. Hardly had Balkh been occupied when an army of Abdul Aziz appeared within forty miles of it. Aurangzeb repulsed it and advanced up to Timurabad amidst incessant fighting. The following week was a period of the most strenuous struggle, when the Mughal army covered itself with glory and the Mughal prince showed those sterling qualities of dogged resolution, cool courage and consummate generalship, for which he became famous later on. The king of Bokhara impressed by the bravery and skill of Aurangzeb, opened negotiation for peace. He proposed that Balkh should be bestowed upon his brother, though Shahjahan had already promised it to Nazar Muhammad. In the meanwhile the Mughals sick of the terrible warfare, the sterile country and the barbarous ways of the people, clamoured to return home. They constantly thwarted Aurangzeb's schemes for conquest because they thought if he was determined to conquer the whole of Transoxiana, of which he was not incapable, they would not return home for years. Circumstances, however, favoured their purpose, and by September a settlement was arranged with Nazar Muhammad who got back the province on his recognizing the suzerainty of Shahjahan. Aurangzeb returned to Kabul by October and was followed by the whole army. The latter suffered untold hardships because of the severe winter, and lost five-thousand men. Besides these losses, the Indian treasury had spent four crores of rupees for no gains whatever. "Not an inch of territory was annexed, no dynasty changed, and no enemy replaced by an ally on the throne of Balkh."[1] The frontier line formed by Balkh and Badakshan was not recovered, and never afterwards did the Mughal emperors indulge in the vain attempt of recovering these provinces.

Equally unfortunate was Shahjahan with regard to Kandahar. After Ali Mardan Khan had betrayed it into the hands of the Mughals, Shahjahan had spared no pains to strengthen it. Nevertheless, Shah Abbas II was determined to take it and made vigorous preparations secretly. The news, however, leaked out and Shahjahan began to show some concern. It had been intimated that the Shah wanted to besiege the fortress in the winter. This unnerved the carpet-knights of the Mughal court, for they disliked a campaign in the bitter cold of the frontier regions. They, therefore, advised the Emperor that it was not likely that the Shah would choose the cold weather for a siege, and Shahjahan listened to them. He did nothing beyond sending a reinforcement, but the Shah was not deterred from his task by the cold weather. He attacked Kandahar about the middle of December, 1648, and took it on 11th February, 1649.

The news of the commencement of the siege received at the court on 16th January, 1649 served as an eye-opener, and Shahjahan issued immediate orders to Aurangzeb and Sadullah Khan to proceed to Kandahar with a relieving force. Before the commanders reached Kabul, Kandahar had capitulated, and there they were detained owing to a heavy snow-fall. Consequently, they reached Kandahar on the 14th of May. The relieving force was employed as a besieging army, and the lack of siege-guns seriously hampered their operations. After months of futile work, they were ordered to give up the attempt and to retire (5th September, 1649), and thus the first Mughal effort to recover Kandahar ended in cloud and smoke.

Shahjahan could not rest in peace, but neither could he rush to recover Kandahar from a foe whose strength he knew only too well. He took two years to prepare, and ordered Aurangzeb with an army of fifty to sixty thousand men and a

1. Sarkar, *Aurangzeb*, Vol. I, p. 113.

fine park of artillery to take it. With great vigour the siege began on May 2, 1652, but by the end of June it was realized that the Mughal guns were incapable of breaching the walls. Once again Shahjahan had to eat the humble pie, and was forced to beat a retreat.

A year later, Dara was directed to undertake the task. With a vast army, seventy thousand strong, and huge field-pieces, as also with a good deal of conceit, he commenced the siege on 28th April, and continued it till 27th September. In spite of his equipments and unflagging zeal he failed to make an impression on the Persians, and was, therefore, ordered to retire. That was the third time that Shahjahan, and the last time that any Mughal Emperor attempted to recover Kandahar from the Persians.

Thus, in the heyday of Mughal rule, in the regime of the glorious Shahjahan, the outer frontier of the empire could not be recovered. It betokened ill for the future safety of the Mughal rule both in Kabul and Hindustan. It was specially so when the empire was expanding southwards, and new knigdoms were being brought under the Mughal sway. It was, in fact, getting unwieldy, and the effects were felt during the reign of Aurangzeb. The unwieldy size undermined the efficiency of frontier defence, and soon after Aurangzeb's succession there arose troubles on the inner frontier.

In 1667 the Yusufzais started trouble. At a time they were rapidly expanding they found a leader in Bhagu, who organized them, and sent them to attack the Mughal territory. They crossed the Indus, invaded the plain of Pakhali, and captured several Mughal outposts. The Emperor, therefore, planned a grand campaign, and ordered three divisions to attack the enemy, one from Attock, another from Kabul and the third from the court. The last two divisions took time to arrive on the scene and, therefore, the Foujdar of Attock led his own division against the Yusufzais. A battle was fought on the south bank of the Indus in which the rebels were defeated, and then they evacuated the imperial territory on the right side of the river. Not venturing to enter the enemy's country all alone, the Foujdar awaited reinforcements, and when they came, Shamshir Khan of Kabul took over the supreme command. He won many victories, and made a fair headway into their country. In the meanwhile came Muhammad Amin Khan from the court with nine thousand troops, and joining Shamshir Khan, took over the supreme command from him. Under his able leadership the Mughals entered the Swat Valley, and forced the inhabitants to keep peace for some time. Strong Mughal garrisons were stationed at different points, and they kept the country under control.

"In 1672, however, began a formidable danger. The tactless action of the Foujdar of Jalalabad bred discontent among the Khyber clans. The Afridis rose under their chieftain Acmal Khan........."[1] To supress them Muhammad Amin Khan was sent in the spring of 1672, but he suffered a severe defeat and heavy losses at Ali Masjid in April. It is said that forty thousand Mughals were cut to pieces, and many, including the commander, had to leave their families as prisoners in the hands of the barbarians. The disaster was aggravated at the news that Khushhal Khan of the Khatak clan had also taken up arms against the Emperor. It was a national rising and the whole Pathan land from Kandahar to Attock was seething in rebellion. The Emperor deputed Mahabat Khan but he proved a failure. Then Shujā'at Khan was ordered to punish the Afghans (14th November, 1673), in co-operation with Jaswant Singh. He failed even more ignominously than Mahabat Khan, and was severely defeated and killed at the Karapa pass (21st February, 1674).

The repetition of these disasters compelled Aurangzeb to come to the spot and direct the operations himself. In June, 1674 he arrived at Hasan Abdal, and remained there for a year and a half. With his arrival "imperial diplomacy, no less than imperial arms began to have effect. Many clans.........were won over by the grant of presents, pensions, jagirs and posts in the Mughal army to their headmen. As for the irreconcilables, whom neither the concentration of imperial force could overawe, nor the treasures of India could buy, their valleys were penetrated by detachments from Peshawar. Thus in a short time the Gholai, Ghalzai, Shirrani and Yusufzai clans were defeated and ousted from their villages. A Mughal outpost held Bazarak, the Shirrani capital. At this the Daudzai, Tarakzai and Tirahi tribes made their submission. Muhammad Asharf, the son of Khush-hal......entered the imperial service......Similarly the son of Bhagu, the Yusufzai ringleader, offered to wait on the

1. Sarkar's *Aurangzeb*, Vol. III, p. 260.

Emperor on receiving an assurance of safety. Darya Khan's Afridi followers promised to bring the head of Acmal, the Afridi pretender, if their past misdeeds were forgotten, (end of August)."[1]

In the meanwhile the imperial armies were closing round the Mohmand tribe and their allies. They were defeated with heavy slaughter at Ali Masjid and Gandamak, but were not crushed. Early in 1675 they recovered their lost ground by inflicting two defeats on the imperialists. Towards the end of the year 1675, however, the situation had considerably improved, and the Mughal outposts had been pushed forward. The Emperor returned to Delhi (March, 1676) with an easy heart. Throughout the year 1677 peace reigned, because the Mughals and the Afghans suffered from a seven months' drought and famine. In 1678 Amir Khan, a very able man, was appointed Governor of Kabul and retained the office for twenty years till 1698. He excelled in diplomacy no less than in the art of war, and he followed a policy of "divide and rule." "Under his astute management they ceased to trouble the Imperial Government, and spent their energies in internecine quarrels."[3] The Yusufzais submitted, though the Afridis remained in arms longer.

On the whole, the frontier became quiet for some time. The war had cost much to the empire. Apart from the financial loss, the political effect was grievous. "It made the employment of the Afghans in the ensuing Rajput war impossible, though the Afghans were just the class of soldiers who could have won victory for the imperialists in that rugged and barren country. Moreover, it relieved the pressure on Shivaji by draining the Deccan of of the best Mughal troops for service on the N .W. frontier."[3] Thus, the frontier trouble adversely reacted upon the stability of the empire. Already the outer frontier had been lost, and now the inner frontier became the source of all sorts of trouble for the Mughals. The cumulative effect began to be felt after the death of Aurangzeb. Hardly thirty years had passed after the frontier defence had collapsed, when taking advantage of it came Nadir Shah like a whirlwind, and swept off the last

1. Sarkar's *Aurangzeb*, Vol. III, pp. 271-72.

2. Sarkar's *Aurangzeb*, Vol. III, p. 278.

3. *Ibid.*, Vol. III, pp. 281-82.

vestiges of the imperial prestige. His invasion resulted in the annexation of the whole country to the west of the Sutlej. The inner and outer lines of frontier were thus lost, and that sounded the death-knell of the Mughal empire. Loss of the Rajput adherence would have meant nothing had the frontier provinces, the prolific land of soldiers, remained under the Mughals. The loss of the frontiers was a double danger : it exposed the kingdom of Hindustan to external attack, and it weakened the military resources of the Mughal empire. The rapid expansion of the empire southwards, made it unwieldy, and also weakened the frontier defence to a degree unknown before.

CHAPTER VII

THE NEW FOUNDATIONS OF MARATHA POWER

The period extending from the death of Shivaji to the death of Aurangzeb is a remarkable epoch in the history of the Marathas. The Marathas, fighting in defence of their country and for the honour of their nation, at last succeeded in rolling back the tide of the Mughal onslaught. But, when the war of defence or 'the war of independence' as it is called, was over, their internal dissensions broke out with greater fury, and all semblance of unity of authority and of common interest that had characterized their activities of that period receded into the background. Sovereignty was divided between Shahu and Shambhaji; and the country broke up into numerous fiefs under different sardars. When Balaji Vishwanath failed to mediate these differences Maharastra was drawn into the vortex of the Imperial politics. The attention of the Marathas was diverted from their domestic troubles to politics beyond their own country which held out promises of a glorious future for them.

It is hardly true to say that just after the death of Aurangzeb the Marathas planned an aggressive warfare against the Mughals with the deliberate determination of founding an empire. For a few years after the arrival of Shahu in Maharastra they were absorbed in their domestic troubles, and Shahu himself was strongly opposed to the very idea of making war on the Mughals. They certainly never thought of building up their power over the ruins of the Mughal empire until Balaji Vishwanath and his Marathas returned from Delhi in 1719 with first-hand knowledge of the Imperial politics. They could not have gained this knowledge but for the violent currents and cross currents convulsing the very core of the empire. It was by a mere chance that the Marathas befriended the Sayyids and were ushered into Delhi, where they had a glimpse of the ghastly rottenness of the empire and the crumbling condition of the 'prop of the universe' (Mughal Empire). Here we have to trace the outlines of Delhi politics, the activities of the chief wire-pullers there, and the circumstances in which the Marathas were drawn into their intrigues. It will be clear at the end of the narrative how the Marathas were amazed to witness the degrading condition of the successors of the Great Mughals and got the idea of building up their own power at the cost of the Mughals.

By the time of Aurangzeb's death the Mughal Empire was on its downward course, and his weak successors only accelerated the process. The Deccan, like all other imperial subahs, was in a welter of anarchy. When Shahu was released by Azam Shah he had been granted the right of realizing the Chauth and Sardeshmukhi from the six subahs of the Deccan. Azam Shah, however, was killed in the battle of Jajau, and when Bahadur Shah came into the Deccan to suppress the rising of Kambakhsh, Shahu rendered military service to him in return for which he pressed for the confirmation of the rights granted by Azam Shah. But on account of the rivalry of Tara Bai, who also advanced the claim of her son to the throne of the Maharastra and to the right of realizing the Chauth and Sardeshmukhi, the prayers of Shahu could not be granted. After the overthrow of Tara Bai, Shahu commissioned his Maratha Sardars to ravage the territory of the Mughals. The Deccan was again harried by roving bands of the Marathas. At this time the Imperial Court was in a deplorable condition and was the seed-bed of all intrigues. There was no knowing as to what would happen to the Deputy Governor of the Deccan.[1] Daud Khan Punni who had been left as the Deputy Governor of the Deccan, pestered by the Marathas on the one hand, and bandoned by the emperor on the other, made the best of a bad situation, and promised to pay the Chauth and Sardeshmukhi to Shahu for the six Subahs of the Deccan according to the agreement of the Emperor Bahadur Shah. But Daud Khan made it a condition that these taxes were to be collected and paid by his officer, Hiraman; the Maratha generals or Shahu's officers were not to rove in the country and collect these taxes.[2] Thus, though Shahu had received the Farman for the collection of the Chauth and Sardeshmukhi as far back as 1707, he did not succeed in realizing these till about the year 1712.

1. Iradat Khan, Scott's *Deccan*, Pt. IV, p. 57.
2. Khafi Khan, Elliot, Vol. VII, p. 466.

In 1713 Daud Khan Punni was transferred to Gujrat and his place in the Deccan was taken by Nizam-ul-Mulk. Nizam-ul-Mulk plays an important part in the history of the Marathas, and in fact, the Deccan politics till the year 1748 centre round the personality of this remarkable man. Hence, it will not be out of place here to add a few words about him.

Ever since the foundation of the Mughal Empire a steady stream of Muslim immigrants had kept on flowing into India from beyond the passes. They often migrated to India with the prospects of trade or service. But, besides mere traders and service-seekers, there came many a devout pilgrim into India to sail for Mecca from the Indian ports. One of such pilgrims was Khwaja Abid Shaikh-ul-Islam of Bukhara. He was the grand father of Nizam-ul-Mulk. About the year 1655-56 he passed through India on his way to Mecca, and on his return took service with Aurangzeb. He rose to distinction in the Imperial service and after him, his eldest son, Ghaziuddin, the father of Nizam-ul-Mulk, filled several important offices of the Empire.

'Mir Qamar-ud-din, son of Ghaziuddin Khan by the daughter of Shah Jahan's Wazir, Sadullah Khan, was born on August 11, 1671. In 1683-84, when in his thirteenth year, he received as his first appointment in the services of the state the rank of four hundred Zat, one hundred horse. In the following year the title of Khan was added to his name. In 1690-91 he received the title of Chin Qilich Khan, and at Alamgir's death in 1707 he was Governor of Bijapur. His father and he took no part in the contest for the throne between the sons of Alamgir; and when Bahadur Shah had succeeded in defeating his rival, he removed the Turanis from the Dakhin.' Accordingly Ghaziuddin Khan Firoz Jang was sent to Ahmadabad in Gujrat, and Qilich Khan was appointed Subahdar of Oudh and Faujdar of Gorakhpur (December 9, 1707). At the same time the title of Chin Qilich Khan was changed to that of Khan Dauran Bahadur and he was raised to 6,000 Zat, 6,000 horse. 'A few weeks afterwards (January 27,1708) he resigned all his titles and appointments; but at the desire of Munim Khan, the Wazir, he withdrew his resignation and was promoted to 7,000 Zat, 7,000 horse. When his father died and the deceased's property was confiscated, Chin Qilich Khan (Khan

Dauran as he then was) sent in his resignation afresh, February 6, 1711; this time it was accepted and 4,000 rupees a year were granted for his support. Quite at the end of Bahadur Shah's reign he returned to the active list with the titles of Ghaziuddin Khan Bahadur Firoz Jang. On Bahadur Shah's death, he attempted to espouse the cause of Azim-ush-Shan, who long before had promised him high office, and he had made one march from Delhi at the head of 3,000 or 4,000 men, when he heard of the Prince's death. Thereupon he discharged his men and retired into private life. Towards the end of Jahandar Shah's short reign, he was appointed to the defence of Agra. Then he and his cousin were brought over to Farrukhsiyar's interest, through Shariyat-Ullah Khan (Mir Jumla) and as a reward for his neutrality he was made Governor of the whole Dakhin, with the new titles first of Khan Khanan, and then of Nizam-ul-Mulk, Bahadur, Fateh Jang.'[1]

In 1713 he was appointed as the viceroy of the six subahs of the Deccan each of which was under an Amaldar. Ambitious and unscrupulous, he wanted to rule over it independently of Delhi, and he turned the troubles prevailing at the court to his own advantage. But he had to reckon with enemies nearer home. There were the Marathas who claimed the blackmail on his subahs, and until he was rid of them, he could not get a free hand in his affairs. Hence, from the very start of his career in the Deccan he determined to check the growing rapacity of the Marathas. The first step was to stop the payment of the blackmail as agreed to by Daud Khan Punni, and then to rally round him all the disaffected chiefs of Maharastra.[2] After the overthrow of Shivaji II, Chandra Sen Jadhav had fled from Kolhapur to seek shelter with the Nizam-ul-Mulk who gave him a sumptuous jagir at Bhalki, to the north of Bidar. Another Sardar, Sarje Rao Ghatge left the service of Shahu and joined his standard. There was, already on his side Rambhaji Nimbalkar, the Thanadar of the important Mughal outpost of Baramati, near Poona who became famous later on under the style of Rao Rambha Nimbalkar.[3] Besides these chieftains, he artfully won over

1. Irvine, Vol. I, pp. 168-72.
2. Khafi Khan, Elliot, Vol. VII, p. 450.
3. Rajwade, Vol. XX, p. 72.

Shambhaji to his side, on the understanding that he would support him against Shahu. Thus an imposing array of adversaries with Nizam-ul-Mulk as its leader was formed against Shahu. When the ground plan was complete, he told the Marathas with a show of reason that he could not pay the fixed contribution, because he did not know who the real king of Maharastra was, whether Shahu or Shambhaji. His next move was to foil the attempts from Poona and its neighbourhood. But the Peshwa had yet much to do and Nizam-ul-Mulk had not yet achieved any appreciable success, when owing to the court intrigues at Delhi he was suddenly called back after a reign of only a year and five months, and Sayyid Husain Ali was appointed in his place. This occurred by the end of 1714 and upset all the plans of the Nizam.[1] He had hardly formed his ambitious schemes when they came to naught. It was, therefore, with great resentment and disgust that he left the Deccan, and on April 4, 1715 the new Viceroy started from Delhi to assume his charge. This incident, the transfer of Nizam-ul-Mulk and the appointment of Sayyid Husain Ali, was fraught with significant consequences for Maharastra. For the present, it relieved Shahu and Balaji Vishwanath from great calamities, and left the country free from a determined enemy and his bloodthirsty proceedings. The regime of the new Viceroy, as we shall presently see, forms a landmark in the history of the Marathas.

In the meantime events were taking place at Delhi that betokened ill for the empire. It was the scene of petty jealousies and mean faction fights. The Emperor, Farrukhsiyar, had become a mere tool in the hands of unscrupulous nobles. His incompetence and worthlessness had made him contemptible to all. The court had become a hot bed of sedition. There were two parties, one of the Emperor, the other of the Sayyid brothers. The Emperor's party conspired to destroy the power of the Sayyids, and the kingmakers' party plotted to counteract their designs. Many a time it seemed that matters would be pushed to the extreme and the Sayyid brothers would be thrown overboard. But clever and cautious as the Sayyids were, they successfully thwarted all the attempts of the Emperor and still retained their position intact. At last it was arranged that one of the kingmakers should be transferred to the Deccan.

1. Iradat Khan, Scott's *Deccan*, Pt. IV, p. 152.

Accordingly the younger and the more capable Sayyid, Husain Ali Khan was appointed to assume the charge of the Deccan as the viceroy in 1715.[1] On 4th April 1715, Husain Ali reported his departure from Delhi. On the eve of his departure he had definitely told the Emperor, 'that in case of designs against his brother Koottub-al-Moolk, he would return to Dhely in twenty days'.[2]

Thus administering a threat to the Emperor and armed with all the authority necessary for independent action he left for the Deccan. Hardly had he turned his back when new plots were formed, and Daud Khan, then, Governor of Ahemadabad, Gujrat, was secretly instructed to resist the Sayyid to the best of his ability and if possible to kill him.[3] The reward promised was the viceroyalty of the six subahs of the Deccan.[4] When Husain Ali marched into the Deccan, Nizam-ul-Mulk passed him on the way, but burning with resentment he did not even pay a visit to him. Then came the alarming news that Daud Khan was preparing to resist him in alliance with the Marathas led by Nemaji Sindhia.[5] In great trepidation Husain Ali awaited the encounter with Daud Khan and fortunately defeated and killed him in the battle near Burhanpur on the 6th September, 1715.[6] The defeat was due to the inaction of the Marathas who withdrew to a distance, and actually joined Husain Ali when the day was won.[7] On the defeat and death of Daud Khan his belongings fell into the hands of the Sayyid and among these were found the letters sent from the court incriminating the Emperor in the intrigue against him.

Master of the situation, Husain Ali now resolved to put down the Marathas. Khande Rao Dabhade, a chief of great power, had set up a number of outposts and realized the Chauth between Surat and Burhanpur, and further claimed it from Gujrat and the Deccan on behalf of Shahu. Husain Ali, at first, deputed his commander Zulfikar Beg against Dabhade, but the

1. Irvine, Vol. I, pp. 293-300.
2. Iradat Khan, Scott's *Deccan*, Part IV. p. 140.
3. Khafi Khan, Elliot, Vol. VII, p. 452.
4. *Ibid*., p. 451.
5. Iradat Khan, Scott's *Deccan*, Part IV, p. 140.
6. Khafi Khan, Elliot, Vol. VII, p. 453; Iradat Khan, Scott's *Deccan*, Part IV, p. 141.
7. Khafi Khan, Elliot, Vol. VII, pp. 453-4.

latter tired out the Mughal soldiers by a series of rapid marches and at length surrounded them in the mountainous regions, and cut off Zulfikar Beg from the main Mughal army.[1] It came as a shock to the Sayyid. He was not aware of the power of the Marathas and this humiliation rankled in his heart. He made more vigorous preparation for their reduction. But Dabhade who seemed to take no notice of it went to Satara and paid his court to Shahu, who in recognition of his services appointed him the Senapati in the place of Man Singh More.[2] This elevation of Dabhade made the Sayyid more cautious and this time he deputed his Diwan, Muhakkam Singh, and his own brother, Saif-ud-din, Subahdar of Burhanpur, against him. As Khafi Khan writes "These two famous chiefs pursued Khandu in the hope of retaliating upon him, or of removing his posts so that they might no longer trouble the country and people of Khandesh. But they accomplished nothing."[3] A contested battle was fought near Ahmadnagar with indecisive results. The Mughals were harassed everywhere and it appeared as if their sway would be stamped out from the Deccan in spite of the presence of the ablest man of the empire. Shahu was not slow to take advantage of these victories. He commissioned Dabhade to levy contributions on Gujrat and Kathiawad. The news of these discomfitures suffered by the Sayyid at the hands of the Marathas elated the emperor and he wrote urging them to make war on his viceroy without respite.[4] This was just the thing the Marathas wanted, and encouraged by the emperor they harassed the Viceroy incessantly. But when Husain Ali was apprised of the underhand dealings of the emperor, he completely changed his attitude towards the Marathas and recalled Muhakkam Singh to the head-quarters.[5] He knew there was only one way out of it, and in utter disgust, he proceeded to make the best of a bad situation. On the advice of Shaikhzada Anwar Khan of Burhanpur, he opened overtures for an alliance with the Marathas and sent as his envoy Shan-

1. *Ibid.*, p. 463.
2. Rajwade, Vol. II, p. 28.
3. Khafi K Vol. VII, p 464.
4. *Ibid.*, p. 464.
5. Iradat Khan, Scott's *Deccan*, Part IV, p. 151.

karaji Malhar, who had been the Sachiv in the reign of Raja Ram.[1] In his old age Shankaraji had retired to Benares and from there he had gone to Delhi.[2] At this time he was in the Mughal camp as the Karbhari of Sayyid Husain Ali. Shankaraji met Balaji Vishwanath, and after a good deal of deliberation on both sides, it was decided that the following conditions should constitute the treaty :—

(i) All the territory comprising the Swarajya of Shivaji, including all the forts therein, should be handed over to Shahu,

(ii) The portions of Khandesh, Gondwana, Berar, Haidarabad and Karnatak conquered by the Marathas, should also be resigned to Shahu to be added to Swarajya.

(iii) The Chauth and Sardeshmukhi over the six subahs of the Deccan should be assigned to Shahu, who in return for the Chauth should maintain a contingent of fifteen thousand Maratha troops for the service of the Emperor, and in return for the Sardeshmukhi should maintain peace and order in the six subahs of the Deccan.

(iv) Shahu should not molest Shambhaji of Kolhapur.

(v) Shahu should pay an annual tribute of ten lacs of rupees.

(vi) The mother and family of Shahu, and Madan Singh (the son of Shambhaji by a concubine) who were at Delhi in the custody of the Emperor should be sent back home.[3]

These terms were accepted on the whole, with slight changes here and there, in February 1718. Shahu proceeded to act upon the treaty as soon as it was ratified by the Sayyid. But when the emperor got it, and was requested to ratify it, he simply rejected it with indignation. Nothing was further from his intentions than that Sayyid Husain Ali should make 'peace and bind the Marathas to his interest.'[4]

Whatever the emperor might do, Sayyid Husain Ali had accepted it; and his acceptance was a matter of necessity rather than of choice. The peculiar circumstances of his situation had forced his hands, and it was with great hesitation that he

1. Khafi Khan, Elliot, Vol. VII, p. 466.
2. Rajwade, Vol. II, pp. 29-30; Khafi Khan, Elliot, Vol. VII, p. 466.
3. Khafi Khan, Elliot, Vol. VII, p. 467; Iradat Khan, Scott's *Deccan*, Part IV, p. 152; Rajwade, Vol. VIII, Doc. 78, pp. 102-8; Rajwade, Vol. II, pp. 30-31.
4. Iradat Khan, Scott's *Deccan*, Part IV, p. 152.

had concluded the treaty. It proved advantageous to him, and the country got a short respite from 'the calamities of war and its attendant famine which had vexed the Deccan for a long series of years no doubt, but the governors of districts and farmers of revenue were more distressed than ever as they had now three collectors, one for the presence, one for the Choute, and a third for the Deesmukee.' Nevertheless the treaty raised the prestige and helped the rise of the Marathas. Vast privileges and important demands were conceded to them. They were recognized as more or less supreme in their own country, and on account of their being entrusted with the maintenance of peace and order they automatically acquired semi-sovereign rights. They maintained fifteen thousand troops for the service of the emperor but at the cost of the Deccan viceroy. This was a sort of subsidiary alliance formed by the Marathas. In short, the treaty made the viceroy dependent on the Marathas for military help and for the maintenance of peace and order. It is, therefore, a landmark in Maratha history.

But amidst all his activities Husain Ali kept a close eye on the affairs at the imperial court. In the meantime his brother's position at Delhi had become extremely perilous. Not only had the emperor's wrath dogged him into the Deccan, Husain Ali's own perfidious conduct had thrown his brother into a critical situation. Dark webs of intrigue were closing round him, and there was no knowing when he might be overthrown.

Between 1715-17, the emperor started on a series of hunting expeditions, of which the principal object was to form plans and find opportunities to get rid of Abdullah Khan. New favourites were created. Nizam-ul-Mulk who had reason to be hostile towards the Sayyids threw in his lot with the Emperor's party, and Khan Dauran and Mir Amin Khan, hitherto the chief advisors of the emperor, were removed to make room for a Kashmiri favourite, Muhammad Murad. Unprecedented honours were bestowed on him in almost bewildering succession, and his rapid rise disgusted many of the sober and right thinking men. Everyone's claims and everyone's abilities were subordinated to his and hence they left the emperor in disgust to side with the Sayyids. On August 27, 1718 the emperor attempted to seize Abdullah Khan but failed. On September 29, 1718 becoming aware of further designs against his life, Abdullah Khan wrote to his brother asking him to return to Delhi as quickly as possible.[1]

Soon after his brother's letter reached him Husain Ali made preparations to leave the Deccan. About November 1718 he started from Aurangabad at the head of 8,000 or 9,000 of his own troops and about sixteen thousand Marathas under the command of Khanderao Dabhade accompanied by Balaji Vishwanath and Santaji Bhonsle.[2] The Maratha leaders "received horses and elephants, robes of honour, and money for expenses, with many promises of future reward in addition to the release of Rajah Sambha's wife and son. These promises included ratification of the treaty for a grant of the Chauth; grant of the Sardeshmukhi,.........and a confirmation of the hereditary Maratha territory or Swaraj. Each Maratha trooper was to receive from the viceroy's treasure chest half a rupee, or, as some say, a rupee a day."[3] Thus reinforced by the Marathas, and his heart easy with regard to his government of the Deccan on account of the recent treaty with them, he reported to the court that the Deccan climate did not agree with him, and that he wanted to present to the emperor a son of the rebel prince Akbar (Aurangzeb's son) by name Muinuddin who had been captured by Rajah Shahu. Farrukhsiyar ordered him to Ahmedabad for a change and to send Muinuddin to Delhi. Without paying any heed to these orders Husain Ali started for Delhi, left Burhanpur on December 14, and Ujjain on December 26, 1718.

As he advanced towards Delhi consternation seized the imperial court and all Farrukhsiyar's schemes one by one fell through. The emperor sent his messenger Ikhlas Khan, who was supposed to have great influence with the Sayyid, to persuade him to return.[4] By the end of December 1718 he met the Sayyid at Mandu, and instead of persuading him to return filled his ears with all sorts of alarming news. His way was made clear by the withdrawal of Muhammad Amin Khan Chin from Malwa without orders. He had been posted there

1. Iradat Khan, Scott's *Deccan*, Part IV, pp. 152-54; Khafi Khan, Elliot, Vol. VII, pp. 469-71; Irvine, Vol. I, pp. 339-53.
2. Khafi Khan, Elliot, Vol. VII, p. 472.
3. Irvine, Vol. I, pp. 359-60.
4. Iradat Khan, Scott's *Deccan*, Part IV, p. 155.

to prevent the Viceroy from coming to Delhi. His withdrawal enraged the emperor, but there was no help.[1]

At length Delhi was entered on February 16, 1719 "with sovereign state, kettle-drums beating and clarions sounding" in entire disregard of the prevalent custom. Fear seized all men great and small, and there were wild rumours afloat throughout the city. Raja Jai Singh advised Farrukhsiyar at this crisis "to take the field and fall upon the Sayyids" and promised his whole-hearted support to him. But "the infatuated emperor persisted in his attempt to buy off the Sayyids by concession after concession; and a few days afterwards, yielding to the insistence of Qutab-ul-Mulk, he, by a note written with his own hand, ordered Rajah Jai Singh and Rao Budh Singh to march from Delhi to their own country."[2] Thus, he sent away his staunch adherents from his side, and now his fall was inevitable. On February 27, hot words were exchanged between the emperor and the Sayyids, in consequence of which the latter posted a strong guard round the palace, and thus had the emperor in their custody.

"At last the fateful morning dawned on February 28, 1719. Shortly after daybreak, a great disturbance arose in the city." A few hours later the Sayyids entered the palace, declared Farrukhsiyar deposed and set up Prince Rafi-ud-Darajat on the throne. Then followed a scene the like of which had never been enacted in the palace of the Imperial Mughals. It came as a rude shock to the sense of loyalty of the people of Delhi, and to the Marathas who though not loyal, yet retained a great respect for the power and prestige of the House of Taimur. Poor Farrukhsiyar a prisoner in his palace was "dragged out with great indignity" to the presence of Kutab-ul-Mulk Abdullah Khan and was ordered to be blinded in that Diwan-i-Khas where he used to sit in state, and at whose entrance Shah Jahan has inscribed these memorable lines :—

"*Agar Firdaus Bar Ruye Zamin Ast,*
Hamin Ast O, Hamin Ast O, Hamin Ast."

i.e. if there is a paradise on earth, it is this, it is this, it is this. But even worse fate awaited the occupant of the Peacock throne.

1. Irvine, Vol. I, p. 373.
2. *Ibid.*, p. 376.

After he was blinded he was confined in a room above the Tirpoliya gate, "a bare, dark, unfurnished hole containing nothing but a bowl for food, a pot of water for ablutions, and a vessel with some drinking water." Fitting paraphernalia for the descendant of the Grand Mughals indeed! He lived there in that lonely cell for a few weeks till at last he was strangled to death on April 28. Thus ended one of the saddest episodes of the Delhi Court.

A few days after the accession of the new Sovereign, Rafi-ud-Darajat, Balaji Vishwanath received in confirmation of each of the main provisions of the treaty, a Farman from the emperor. One, dated March 13, granted the Marathas the Chauth of the six Subahs of the Deccan including the tributary states of Tanjore, Trichinopoly and Mysore. Another, dated March 24, granted them the Sardeshmukhi over the Deccan; and the third, confirmed Shahu in the possession of the Swarajya of Shivaji at the time of his death in 1681.[1] Besides these grants, the mother and family of Shahu along with Madan Singh were released and were given over to Balaji Vishwanath.

This journey of the Marathas to Delhi produced far-reaching consequences in their history. Besides its immediate advantages, it deeply coloured the later policy of the Marathas, and served as an eye-opener to them in many respects. The Marathas who had looked upon the imperial power and prestige with awe, witnessed at Delhi what that power actually meant. The halo of glory that surrounded the name of the descendants of Babar and Akbar, to whom the President of Fort William addressed as "the Absolute Monarch and Prop of the Universe," vanished into the lurid light of utter contempt when the Marathas found them reduced to mere tools at the hands of unscrupulous courtiers, and dragged to dishonour and ignominous death. Delhi reeking with blood, courtiers thriving in machination, the Emperor an instrument of the ambitious nobles, the central authority reduced to impotence —all these exposed the weakness of the Mughal empire. Long before their great king Shivaji had proved to his people that the Mughal army was not invincible and the Mughal territory not inviolable. Further,

1. Irvine, Vol. I. p. 407.

the real strength of the Mughals had been disclosed to the Marathas during their war of independence (1690-1707). Now they realized fully that the Mughal Empire was rotten to the core, that it could never sustain its pristine glory and perhaps, who knows, it might fall to the powerful blows of the Marathas. Balaji Vishwanath a shrewd man of affairs as he was, must have seen with the eyes of a statesman that now the splendid structure of the Mughal Empire was tottering to its fall, and was a prize worth attempting, and worth fighting for. His other Maratha leaders must have thought similarly. They must have conjured in their minds a glorious picture of Hindusthan, the home-land of Hinduism and the treasure-house of Asia—a land consecrated by a thousand memories of Ram and Krishna so dear to the Hindu heart. This holy land, this rich country they must have thought, would be theirs, if they could but overthrow the Mughals. And then what a difference it would make to Maharastra ! Maharastra, sterile and rugged, where "nature enforces a spartan simplicity", would flow in riches, milk and honey ! And the way to achieve this had been shown by the courtiers at Delhi, by the Sayyid brothers themselves.

The prestige of their presence at the imperial capital, not as mercenaries, but as the allies and supporters of the King-makers, held out to them a promise that they might some day make and un-make Emperors. Indeed, it was the surest foundation on which Balaji Vishwanath could confidently build up the Maratha power. Actuated perhaps by this ambition, he took the preliminary steps when he passed through the Rajput states in order to form friendship with them. He knew that the Mughals and the Rajputs were gradually drifting apart. Ten years back the premier chiefs of Rajputana—of Jaipur, Jodhpur and Udaipur—had "openly shewed their designs to fight for independence in close alliance with each other."[1] They had failed to co-operate, and therefore they had suffered in their struggles with the Mughals. But now the disorderly condition of the empire was very favourable to their designs. And Balaji deliberately marched through their country, in order to 'help in their designs' thus paving the way for the work of Baji Rao. Jai Singh of Jaipur, as is well known, was a great friend of Baji

1. Iradat Khan, Scott's *Deccan*, Part IV, p. 58.

Rao. In 1719, Baji Rao was about twenty and Jai Singh, thirty. It is possible that Baji Rao who accompanied his father might have met Jai Singh at this time, and might have won his friendship. Whatever it might be, it is important to bear in mind that the Peshwa rightly foresaw the utility of Rajput friendship for the foundation of Maratha power and, therefore, made a move in that direction.

Building-up of the Maratha power on new foundations, as indicated above, first of all, required the adjustment of a number of interests and the creation of internal peace. The second requisite was the continuous creation of a sphere of influence. Balaji Vishwanath tried to fulfil the first requirement in his own way. After his return from Delhi he took up the organization of the Maratha affairs. He brought the quarrelling and ravaging Maratha chiefs into a system of interdependence which came to be known as the Maratha feudatory system. Thus, he secured peace in the country and adjusted the interests of the king and his chieftains. His next concern was to secure a sphere of influence. This he had achieved by the treaty of 1718-19 which granted the Marathas their Swarajya, and the right of collection of the Chauth and Sardeshmukhi. Within Swarajya they exercised semi-sovereign rights and they realized the Chauth and Sardeshmukhi from the six subahs of the Deccan on the condition of preserving peace and order. The collection of the blackmail defined their sphere of influence, and tightened their grip on the country subjected to the payment of the taxes. Thus, the Emperor by granting these rights assigned to them a part of sovereign rights, i.e. preservation of peace and order. Vast territories round about the Swarajya paid tribute to the Marathas, and were considered as half-subjugated by them. Thus was created a sphere of influence which went on increasing with every Peshwa and with the decay of the Mughal Empire.

These arrangements combined with the conviction that the Marathas could now think of making and unmaking emperors, which was the results of their journey to Delhi, and which found aptest expression in those memorable words of Baji Rao "strike, strike at the trunk and the branches will fall off themselves", formed the new foundations of Maratha power as built by Balaji Vishwanath.

SELECT BIBLIOGRAPHY

ORIGINAL SOURCES

Beveridge, H., (Tr.) Akbarnama by Abu'l Fazl, Shaikh, Calcutta, 1907, 1912, 1939.

——, (Tr.) Babur-nama, London, 1921.

——, (Tr.) Humayun-nama by Gulbadan Begum, London, 1902.

——, (ed.) Tuzuk-i-Jahangiri, 2 Vols., Delhi, 1968.

Blockmann, H., (Tr.) Ain-i-Akbari by Abu'l Fazl, Shaikh, Calcutta, 1873.

Briggs, J. History of the Rise of the Mohammedan Power in India, 4 Vols., Calcutta, 1908, Ferista, II.

Elliot, H.M., & Dowson, J. History of India as Told by Its Own Historians, 8 Vols., London. 1867

——, Tarikh-i-Daudi by Abdullah, Vol. IV.

——, Khafi Khan, Vol. VII.

——, Waqiat-i-Mushtaqi by Shaikh Rizqullah, Vol. IV.

Edwards, Michael, (Ed.), Memoirs of the Moghul Court by Manucci, N.

Irvine, W., (Tr.) London, 1957.

Ranking, G.S.A., (Tr.) Muntakhab-ut-Tawarikh by Badauni, Abdul Qadir, Asiatic Society, Calcutta, 1898.

Smith, V.A., (Tr.) Travels in the Moghul Empire, 1656-58 by Bernier, Francois, London, 1916.

SECONDARY SOURCES

Abd-ur-Rahim, Mughal Relations with Persia and Central India. Aligarh Muslim University, n.d.

Beni Prasad, History of Jahangir, London, 1922.

Bhandarkar, R.G. Vaishnavism, Saivism and Minor Religious Systems. Poona, 1938.

Bhargava, V. S. Marwar and the Mughal Emperors, 1526-1748. Delhi, 1966.

Burn, Richard, Cambridge History of India, IV, Cambridge, 1937.

Carpenter, J. E. Theism in medieval India. London, 1926.
Crooke, W. Islam in India. n.d.
Dasgupta, S. N. Hindu Mysticism.
De, U. N. Some Aspects of Medieval Indian History. New Delhi, 1971.
Duff, Grant. A History of the Marathas. 3 Vols., London, 1826.
Erskine, W. A History of India Under Baber and Humayun. Vol. I & II, London, 1854.
Hopkins, E. W. The Religions of India, Boston, 1895. Imperial Gazetteer of India, Vol. I.
Iqbal, Muhammad, The Reconstruction of Religious Thought in Islam. Oxford, 1937.
Irdat Khan, Scott's Deccan, IV.
Irvine, William, The Army of the Indian Moghuls. London, 1903.
Kennedy, Pringle, History of the Great Moghuls. Calcutta, 1968, (Reprint).
Lane Poole, S. Aurangzeb and the Decay of the Mughul Empire, Delhi.
Lane Poole, S. Babar, London, 1899.
Lane Poole, S. Medieval India under the Mohammedan Rule. Delhi, 1963 (Reprint).
Moldich, Gates of India.
Moreland, W. H. From Akbar to Aurangzeb, London, 1923.
Nicholson, R. A. The Mystics of Islam. London, 1914.
Noer, Graf von, Kaisar, Akbar, 2 Vols., Leipzig, 1880, 1885. Tr. A. S. Beveridge, Calcutta, 1890.
Prasad, Ishwari, History of Medieval India. 3rd edition, Allahabad, 1940.
Qanungo, K. R. Dara Shukoh, Calcutta, 1952.
Qanungo, K. R. Sher Shah and His Times. Bombay, 1965.
Rahim, M. A. History of the Afghans in India, 1545-1631, With Special Reference to Their Relations with Mughals. Karachi, 1961.
Rajawade, V. K. *Marathyanchya Itihasachi Sadhanen*, 4 Vols.
Saran, P. Studies in Medieval Indian History. Delhi, 1952.
Sardesai, G. S. Shivaji and His Times. Calcutta, 1929.
Sardesai G. S. Studies in Mughal India, Calcutta, 1919.
Sarkar, J. N. Fall of the Mughal Empire. 4 Vols., Calcutta, 1949.

Sarkar, J. N. History of Aurangzeb. 5 Vols., Calcutta, 1912-25.
Sen, K. M. Medieval Mysticism in India. Tr. M. Ghosh, London, 1936.
Sharma, S. R. Mughal Empire in India. Agra, 1966.
Sharma, S. R. Studies in Medieval Indian History. Sholapur, 1956.
Smith, V. A. Akbar the Great Mughal. Oxford, 1919.
Srivastava, A. L. The Mughal Empire. Agra, 1964.
Srivastava, A. L. Akbar the Great, Vols. I & II. Agra, 1962-67.
Stewart, C. History of Bengal. London, 1813.
Thomas, E. Chronicles of the Pathan Kings of Delhi. London, 1871.
Tod, James, Annals and Antiquities of Rajasthan. 2 Vols., Delhi, (Reprint).
Tripathi, R. P. Rise and Fall of the Mughal Empire. Allahabad, 1956.
Varma, R. C. Foreign Policy of the Great Mughals. Agra, 1967.
Williams, L. F. An Empire Builder of the Sixteenth Century. Rushbrook, London, 1918.

ERRATA

Page	*Read*	*For*
2	21st April	26th April
4	Chausa	Chaunsa
6	1605	1603
6	(delete)	eldest
9	Muhammad Hakim	Mahmud Hakim
9	Baluchistan	Beluchistan
10	patronage of men	Patronage to men
10	all walks of life	all the walks of life
10	Muslims	muslims
10	magnificent	magnificant
10	1627	1628
10	Khusrau	Khusrou
11	Nurjahān	Nur-jāhān
11	conjunction	conjuction
12	(1628-58)	(1628-59)
12	disastrous	disatrous
12	did not mind it much	did not much mind it
13	Samugarh	Shamugarh
13	1658	1659
14	Diwan-i-Khas	Diwani Khas
14	Diwan-i-Aam	Diwani Aam
14	Peacock Throne	peacock throne
15	at about	about at
16	Yadavas	Jadhavs
16	Yadava	Jadhav
16	guardian	gauardian
16	and aimed	and early aimed
17	1665	166
17	Carnatic	Karnatic
18	Belgaum	Belgam
18	beginning	beginnings
18	enemy's	enermy's
19	Narnaul and Mewat	Patiala state

Page	*Read*	*For*
19	Khusrau	Khusrou
20	19th century	9th century
20	joined	joinned
21	come	came
21	3rd March	21st February
21	built by	built up by
23	Hyderabad	Haidarabad
23	around	round about
23	Panipat	Panipath
24	fall off	fall of
25	Bhonsale	Bonsle
25	Hyderabad	Haidarabad
25	Carnatic	Karnatic
26	dared to do	dared do
26	Hyderabad	Haidarabad
26	Carnatic	Karnatic
26	Thaneswar	Thanewswar
28	phase	phases
29	chief	chiefs
30	powerful	poweful
32	hesitation	hasitation
34	Bahlol Lodi	Buhlul Lodi
35	the tribal	The tribal
36	himself	himslef
40	about imperceptibly	about impeceptibly
42	insuperable	inasuperable
44	Gaur	Gour
45	rising	raising
45	his father	this father
46	fort	ford
47	possible	possilbe
48	Nasir Khan	Nazir Khan
49	Azami Humayun	Azam Humayun
49	Etawa	Etawah
52	ordinary enemies	ordinarynemies
53	1526 and 1630	1526 abd 1630
53	Bayana	Biana

Page	*Read*	*For*
53	Qutb Khan	Kutb Khan
54	Qutb Khan	Kutb Khan
55	create	creat
56	Lodis	Lodies
57	Kabuliats	kabuliats
58	Buxar	Baxar
58	Jalal Khan	Jelal Khan
60	fled away. Khan	fled away Khan
63	Bharkunda	Bahrkunda
63	Humayun	Humaun
64	Chausa	Chaunsa
64	Buxar	Baxar
64	Shaikh Khalil	Shaik Kalil
64	the capital. Humayun	thecapital. Humayun
64	except	expcept
64	Chausa	Chaunsa
64	Jahangir Beg	Jahagir Beg
65	Qutb Khan	Kutb Khan
66	Khizr Khan	Khizir Khan
67	Kosi	Koshi
67	Raisin	Raiseen
68	Raisin	Raiseen
68	families	family
68	Narnaul	Narnol
69	of false	offalse
69	Chitor	Chittor
69	Kalinjer	Kalinger
70	Sujat Khan	Sujjat Khan
73	Bayana	Biana
73	Badakshan	Badkshan
74	Rewari	Rawari
75	indulged	uindulged
75	Chitor	Chittor
76	Todar Mal	Todar Mall
76	defeated him in a	defeated him at a
78	Kalinjer	Kalinger
80	Afghans forged	Afghan forged
81	Aurangzeb	Aurangeb

Page	*Read*	*For*
82	Bayana	Biana
83	Bayana	Biana
84	Hussain Khan Lohani	Hasan Khan Lohani
84	Qutb Khan	Kutub Khan
84	Quran	Quaran
84	Bayana	Biana
85	Bayana	Biana
86	Chitor	Chitore
87	full of generous	full, of generous
87	custom Humayun	custom. Humayun
88	through	throug
88	Amarkot	Umarkot
89	enable	enabled
89	Sher Shah, Akbar	Shershah Akbar,
90	Amarkot	Umarkot
90	Rai Singh	Ray Singh
90	earlier	early
91	Akbar	Akabar
92	Asirgarh	garh, Asir
93	Kachhwaha	Kachhwa
94	wanting in	wantingin
94	Bihari Mal	Bihari Mall
94	Sharaf-ud-din	Sharf-ud-din
94	Puran Mal's	Pooran Mal's
95	Kaçhhwaha	Kachhwa
95	Bihari Mal	Bihari Mall
97	Kalyan Mal	Kalyan Mall
99	Kota	Kotah
100	Kota	Kotah
100	Muazzam	Mauzzam
101	Jai Mal	Jai Mall
103	Sind	Sindh
107	Chitor	Chitore
107	Rajputs	Rajpus
113	India, China	India China
116	Hirat	Herat
117	viz.	voz.
118	fourth century B. C.	fourth B. C.

Page	*Read*	*For*
118	Vishnu Purana	Vishnu Puran
118	Bhagwad	Bhagwat
120	Brindaban	Brindavan
122	Abdullah Niazi	Abdulla Niazi
122	Shaikh Abdullah	Shaikh Abdulla
122	Bayana	Biana
124	Pushtus	Pustus
126	religions	religious
132	Sadr-us-sadur	Sadr-i-sadr
133	Sadr-us-sadur	Sadr-i-sadr
133	gospel	Gospel
135	Herat	Hirat
137	Trans Oxiana	Transoxiana
137	Aziz Koka	Aziz Kokah
137	Khan-i-Azam	Khani Azam
139	Deccanese	Deccaness
141	Purna	Purta
141	kos	koss
144	kos	Coss
147	Kalinjer	Kalinger
149	Sultans	sultans
149	Junar	Junnar
150	Golconda	Golconds
150	Khan-i-Duran	Khan-i-Douran
151	Todar Mal	Todar Mall
152	Godavari	Godavary
152	Mir Jumla	Meer Jumla
153	Hyderabad	Haidarabad
153	unaware	unawares
155	Maharashtra	Maharastra
156	Mores	Moreys
156	Ghatges	Ghatgeys
156	Gharpures	Gharpureys
156	Maharashtra	Maharastra
157	Kond Dev	Konddeo
158	Shayista Khan	Sayista Khan
158	Hun	hun
159	Shivaji	Shiva

Page	*Read*	*For*
159	Mughal India	Mughals India
159	Shayista Khan	Sayista Khan
162	Shivaji	Shiva
162	Hun	hun
162	Maharashtra	Maharastra
164	Hyderabad	Haidarabad
165	Khulna	Khelna
166	slipped off	slipped out it
167	Conjiveram	Kanjiveram
168	five other	five others
169	and	a d
174	Sind	Sindh
176	ease	case
177	regent of	regent for
177	Abul Fateh Beg	Abul Fath Beg
181	Abul Fateh	Abul Fath
181	Todar Mal	Todar Mall
182	Sind	Sindh
182	Thatta	Thattah
185	Beside these	Besides these
187	Faujdar	Foujdar
188	Faujdar	Foujdar
194	Azim-us-Shan	Azim-ush-Shan
194	Thanedar	Thanadar
194	Rambhaji	Rambha
198	Hyderabad	Haidarabad
201	Raja	Rajah
203	Rama	Ram

INDEX

T

U